MW01690412

GIFT OF INJURY: THE STRENGTH ATHLETE'S GUIDE TO RECOVERING FROM BACK INJURY AND WINNING AGAIN

STUART MCGILL PhD AND BRIAN CARROLL

GIFT OF INJURY:

THE STRENGTH ATHLETE'S GUIDE TO RECOVERING FROM BACK INJURY AND WINNING AGAIN

STUART MCGILL PhD AND BRIAN CARROLL

© 2018 Dr. Stuart McGill and Brian Carroll

All Rights Reserved

No part of this publication may be reproduced, stored in a retrieval system, or transmitted, in any form or by any means, electronic, mechanical, photocopying, recording, or otherwise, without the written permission of the author.

Please do not participate in or encourage piracy of copyrighted materials in violation of the authors rights. Purchase only authorised editions.

First published by Backfitpro Inc.

ISBN: 978-0-9735018-6-5

This book is printed on acid-free paper

Printed in Canada

TABLE OF CONTENTS

FOREWORD BY WORLD'S STRONGEST MAN BILL KAZMAIER

Injury. To most athletes, this event is a tragedy, a career ender. However, there are some who weather the physical trauma to share remarkable stories of how injury became their greatest tutor. Adversity makes the man. The crucible of such a setback, comprised of the incident, diagnosis, and subsequent rehabilitation taught these athletes more than they expected. Some even consider their injury a blessing, one that showed them what is truly valuable, which practices should be left in the past, and ways to perfect their methodology for even higher levels of performance.

Despite the apparent benefits of wisdom and mental toughness, this knowledge comes with a price. The initial period post-injury can be devastating for the athlete. Lowered self sufficiency, physical weakness, and the inevitable loss of confidence robs some of their drive to compete.

Climbing this hill demands discipline, power of will, and above all else - access to credible information. This book is about one such athlete, and how his relationship with an expert in back injury allowed him to rise from a state of utter defeat, to setting records once again. Brian's injury was massive, to say the least. A split sacrum coupled with a crushed vertebra may as well be a death sentence to the career of any professional powerlifter. This was a man who possessed titanic powerlifting numbers flanking his world record squat, now reduced to struggled walking accompanied by blinding pain.

These pages tell the story of a carefully-designed, step by step process to eliminate pain and restore one's athleticism to its full potential. They describe the journey of an athlete who refused to accept the notion that he could not heal, and the guidance of a professor who used scientific methodology and his unique approach to beat the odds.

The proof of their mutual success is undeniable. Brian's record-shattering numbers speak for themselves as he continues to amass lifting titles, train and compete at an elite level, and most importantly, remain pain-free. His quality of life is a testament to Dr. McGill's expertise, insight, and coaching.

Brian's story is truly inspiring as it demonstrates the power of sound rehabilitation. When applied correctly, such programming can allow one to overcome physical setbacks, and mental blocks to dominate once again. As every athlete's journey is different, this book provides a clear guide to finding one's personally tailored path to rehabilitation and continued success.

I implore any strength athlete, whether they are injured and at their wit's end, or healthy and striving to achieve their best with longevity, to read this book. I have preached the phrase "I can, I will" to foster the attitude required of champions. The attitude which perfectly encapsulates the ideas in these pages. The wisdom in these pages has helped me and Brian Carroll, and it will help you. Professor McGill brings science to the forefront while Brian musters the real world validity. There is no faking this. This is the real deal.

Bill Kazmaier, 3 time World's Strongest Man

ACKNOWLEDGMENTS: STUART

In 2013 I received a phone call from an athlete desperate to find a way to recover his back. As often happens in life, many gifts come from difficult circumstances. In this case the extensive injury was the gift - it made the players in the story better people, they became good friends, and as you will have guessed resulted in this book. Thank you Brian. You have taught me and I suspect you will teach many more through our collaboration.

The "World's Strongest Man," Bill Kazmaier, wrote the foreword. The older readers among you will have enjoyed his strength feats from WSM seen on TV. You will have seen his personality shine through as he cajoled and encouraged his competitors. He won "World's Strongest Man" for the first several years and then they changed the rules to give other competitors a chance! The younger readers will know him as the color commentator on the current "WSM." His grace and kindness always apparent. "Kaz's" training techniques, and cerebral approach to all things strength has taught me much over the years.

I called on several friends to assist with technique photos – powerlifters Ken and Sheri Whetham, "The Vanilla Gorilla" Blaine Sumner, Kevin Chapman and friends at Mark Fitzgerald's Elite Fitness Systems, thank you for your good grace.

Many others have become friends and influenced my work from the clinical world and the high performance sport realm: the late Mel Siff and Charlie Francis, my first high school coach Ralph Colucci who spent too many hours with a very mediocre athlete, and contemporaries Juan Carlos Santana, Al Vermeil, Jerzy Gregorek, Pavel Tsatsouline, Mark McCoy, Art McDermott, John Chaimberg, Chris Duffin, Mark Verstagen, Dan John, and Dr. Clayton Skaggs, to acknowledge just a few.

The many patients and athletes referred to me for consultation – I know I have been able to help a number of you but in our experimental work to prevent, rehabilitate and train, you have taught me immensely.

Once again my son John McGill, based in New York City, did his usual editing to remove my medical jargon improving readability (he did not edit that sentence!). Trey Volmer and Michael Andreas were the cover photographers, Tim Dallinger did the cover layout while Warren Mason did the layout for the book pages - thank you all.

And finally my wife Kathryn, who I have known for 55 years! She supports all of what I do. She hasn't figured out yet that she could do so much better. Please don't tell her!

Stuart McGill

ACKNOWLEDGMENTS: BRIAN

In 1999, my high school senior year, I competed in my first bench press competition. I had no real direction or path. I knew I enjoyed lifting weights, but so does most every jock at that age. As my passion grew for strength training, eventually my path became clear: I wanted to be involved in the strength training industry and make an impact. My hope is this book created by the professor and the athlete will have this impact.

The process of writing was not easy. I had to admit, document, relive, and deal with the challenges throughout the injury-recovery journey. But, to preserve integrity, I had to be an 'open book' and hold nothing back. I believe that events in life, by accident and/or self-inflicted, can act as a teacher for myself and others to learn, overcome and in the best case scenario – avoid them.

I am not only a better lifter/coach for meeting Stu, but absolutely a better man, friend and husband. I have learned so much from Stu not only during our work together in the lab, time in the gym, but also from collaborating on this book. He has become a very important part of my life as a mentor. Thank you so much, Stu for being such a friend. I'm forever changed.

I am extremely honored to have the great "Kaz" write our foreword. I grew up not only in awe of Kaz's power, strength and stamina from "World's Strongest Man," but his massive feats on the powerlifting platform as well. He was the first man I ever got to see squat over 800lbs, bench over 600lbs and deadlift over 800lbs. I remember looking at him and saying, "he looks as strong as he is, incredible." Kaz, thank you for leading the way in so many ways. You are a pioneer for us all.

I have been fortunate and learned so much from the many athletes I've coached and had the pleasure to work with. Their feedback, progress, victories and defeats have taught me so much about programming, coaching, performance and injury resilience. An additional thank you to ALL of my team at PowerRackStrength.com for your assistance with photos, proofing and feedback during this awesome project. Thank you also to John McGill for editing reinforcement, Ken Richardson, Ken Hicks, Tim Dallinger, Michael Andreas, and Trey Vollmer for the photo and book cover help. And to Warren Mason for the beautiful layout of this book!

I owe a great deal of my powerlifting success to Inzer Advance Designs for the amount of support they've shown me during my powerlifting career, going back to 1999. Thank you! Inzernet.com.

A very special thank you to the early mentors in my lifting career: Skip Sylvester, Adam Driggers, Jake Blanton and all of my current and former training partners at Team Samson. Jonathan Byrd, Paul Key, Clint Smith, Shane Ford, Channing Doyle, Filipe Gusmao, Jason Kowalewski, Keith Price, Wayne Pullum and Cranford.

A special thank you to my wife, Ria. Those that know Ria, know how much she means to all of us, how much her support and always being in my corner throughout all this means to me. It won't ever be forgotten.

Brian Carroll

HOW TO READ THIS BOOK:

Gift of Injury is ultimately a collaboration between the athlete and the professor, bringing you the true account of a champion's massive injury and his subsequent recovery with the help of one of the world's leading experts. It is also somewhat of a self-help guide for strength athletes who wish to recover from the physical traumas associated with the sport, and return to competing at their optimal level.

Between the two of us, there was much back and forth on the best way to format a book that was part narrative and part instructional guide. We are hopeful that its current layout presents the material in its most comprehensive and digestible configuration. Although different parts of the book highlight different aspects of training, recovery and personal insights, we recommend reading it cover to cover first, in order to see the "big picture" and understand the message in its entirety. Then, as you begin to apply the guidance found within to your own training and/or rehabilitation, refer back to the pertinent sections as you go, rereading and making notes as necessary. We've even provided a personal diagnosis and training log in the back pages of the book for you to easily track your progress.

The first section of the book takes you through Brian's early career and outlines how he turned himself from scrawny kid in the outfield to a globally respected powerlifter and strength authority. You'll read about his perceived fall from grace as his worsening back condition began to cripple his performance and challenge other areas of his life as well (we don't hold back with some very dark and trying times). And you'll read about the lead up to a meeting with Dr. McGill that would change the way he sees his sport and himself.

Next, we'll guide you through the assessment performed by Dr. McGill and show you how to understand your own potential injury in relation to your movements and your strength sport of choice. As you begin to piece together a regimen that best suits you, you'll learn how Brian took Dr. McGill's words of advice and incorporated them into his daily lifestyle, leading him out of a vicious cycle of pain.

Lastly, as you begin to recover strength and feel the power returning to your body, the professor and the athlete will lead you through tips and cues to optimize your athletic performance. They will share insights they've discovered over the years that contribute to successful lifts and a sustainable career that doesn't tear the body apart as you strive towards future goals.

The most important thing to remember as you read, is that Brian's story offers some excellent insight into overcoming pain, injury and getting back on track. But, the specifics of his program and regimen were fine-tuned to him, as each athlete is unique. As you progress through the book, you will learn how to assess your own personal strengths and weaknesses and design a path to recovery and success that is best suited to your situation. Brian is an excellent example of someone who knew his body well, but was interested in rediscovering components of his unique athleticism, some of which could be viewed as hindrances and many which were great assets. He learned how to strike an internal balance of eliminating painful movements, while creating and engraining new spine-sparing movement patterns that rejuvenated his career and ultimately his life. This is possible for you too! As you read, be sure to listen to your body as you make your own assessments on what soothes versus exacerbates pain. Again, every athlete is different. Not only will the types of exercises you add and eliminate from your training program differ based on what you learn about your own spine, but the rate at which you recover and develop will be unique to you as well. Take comfort in the fact that your body will repair at its own rate and that you may experience some setbacks along the way, but as long as you are disciplined in your approach to training, better days are truly achievable!

We are excited to share our joint expertise and expect there to be something for everyone in this book, no matter whether you are a seasoned champion, or someone in the early stages of learning how to apply their body to achieve remarkable feats of strength and lifting. A goal of all strength athletes, brothers and sisters in power, is to increase strength, while maintaining resilience to injury. We're going to show you how. As you follow the guidelines laid out in the following pages and begin to achieve personal victories, whether it be the ability to finally reach down and tie your own shoes again, or that feeling of standing at the top of a podium at an event, know that you are on a proven road to recovery that brought an international champion out from the gutter of frustration and self-doubt, to realizing the "Gift of Injury."

MEET STUART AND BRIAN

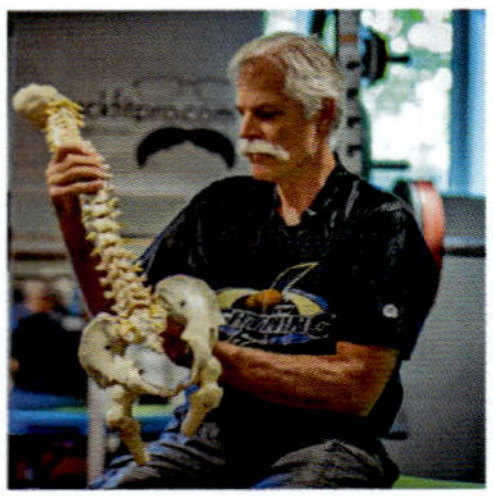

Dr. Stuart McGill: McGill has been a Professor of Spine Biomechanics at the University of Waterloo since 1986. He developed a reputation for creating an understanding of how the back works, becomes injured and exhibits pain. Using this foundation, he has created rehabilitation approaches and performance enhancement programs that have restored numerous injured top athletes to success in a wide variety of sports. He acts as a consultant in difficult back injury cases and provides performance-enhancement programs for individuals and teams alike, working with Olympians from around the world, as well as athletes in the NBA, NFL, PGA, NHL, and UFC, among others.

He has written one book to guide clinicians who treat back pain (*Low Back Disorders: Evidence based prevention and rehabilitation*), another to guide coaches, athletes and trainers enhancing back performance (*Ultimate Back Fitness and Performance*), and his recent book to guide the lay public out of their back pain misery (*Back Mechanic: The step by step McGill method to fix back pain*). www.backfitpro.com

It will come as a surprise to many that he went to University for sports, not academics at the University of Toronto. While there, some key professors lit the fire of science under him and redirected his energies into developing an understanding of the articulated linkage of the body, how they cooperate to meet the demands of sports, and how the system sometimes fails. He has had many mentors in both academics and sport. One of the great joys has been to train and do a little sparring with the great ones. Now living in Gravenhurst, Ontario, he still trains and enjoys time with his wife Kathryn, an athlete herself who followed her early career as a national team rower in the 80s and is a current masters level champion in Canada and the U.S. Stepping away from his usual habitat in the research lab, clinic and lecture hall, Dr. McGill now enjoys spending more time as Kathryn's boat mechanic and water boy.

Brian Carroll: Carroll is a world class powerlifter with over a decade of elite lifting under his belt. Coming back from a devastating back injury in 2009 that broke multiple bones and compiled with years of destructive mistreatment to his body, most experts said he would never recover. Nonetheless, Brian returned to the pinnacle of world class lifting, while successfully becoming 100% pain and symptom free. He is now dedicated to helping others avoid the same mistakes that he made through private and group coaching.

A competitive powerlifter since 1999, Brian Carroll is one of the most accomplished lifters in the history of the sport. Brian was recently named as having two of the "top 20 greatest powerlifting performances of All-Time" with 2651lbs total at 242lbs and 2730lbs total at 275lbs, respectively. Having lifted at the elite world-class level since 2005, he has totaled more than ten times his bodyweight in three different classes, and both bench pressed and deadlifted over 800lbs in two different weight classes. In his career, he's totaled 2500lbs over 20 times in two different weight classes. Since 2005, and even during his years of being injured, Brian has not fallen out of the top two American rankings in both the squat and total, as well as been ranked number one in both categories, multiple times at 220lbs, 242lbs, and 275lbs weight classes. With over 50 official competition squats over 1000lbs, spread over three different weight classes, he's indisputably one of the best lifters and in particular - best squatters of all time. Most recently, post-recovery, he achieved a 2615lbs total at the 2017 Arnold Sports Festival, claiming the 242lbs class open and the overall titles for the 3rd time.

Brian's impressive recovery has given him the opportunity to teach and present talks to physical therapists, chiropractors, medical doctors, professional strength and conditioning coaches and experts from all facets of sport, on how to avoid injury, while building anti-fragile strength and resilience in athletes. Brian is also an accomplished author, having written the best-selling strength training book 10/20/Life – The Professional's Guide to Building Strength. He runs PowerRackStrength.com where he shares the articles and training logs of a host of athletes of all domains who utilize his 10/20/Life methodology. His personal articles have been published in multiple magazine publications, including Men's Health, Power, Powerlifting USA, Ironman, Muscle & Fitness, and Flex, as well as Medical Journals such Journal of Body Work and Movement Therapies.

Brian is happily married to Ria and currently resides in Jacksonville, Florida with their two pitbulls, Bruiser and Steel.

Working on the book using gym time, clinic time and computer time

LIFTING CAREER HIGHLIGHTS:

Holds, or has held, multiple All-Time World, national, and state records in the 220, 242, and 275lbs weight classes.

—

One of few lifters to attain a professional powerlifting total in three different weight classes at the same time.

—

One of even fewer lifters to be ranked in the top ten on the all-time ranking list in three different weight classes at the same time.

—

Ranked second in the world in the 275lbs weight class with a total of 2730lbs and a historic 1185lbs squat.

—

Ranked first in the world currently in the 242lbs weight class with a total of 2651lbs with an 1102lbs squat.

—

800lb bench press in three different weight classes: 242lbs, 275lbs and 308lbs.

—

WPC World Champion

—

WPO Semi Finals Champion

—

3x Arnold Sports Festival Overall champion - 2012, 2015, 2017 (2 of these wins being post back rehab)

—

2016 US Open Overall champion

—

220 Class:
1030lbs squat (at the time, the biggest squat ever done at 220lbs circa 2006), 633lbs bench, 755lbs deadlift

2376lbs TOTAL (tenth best of all time).

—

242 Class:
1102lbs squat, 788lbs bench press, 780lbs deadlift

2651lbs TOTAL (second best of all-time and currently ranked number one in the world).

—

275 Class:
1185lbs squat (at the time, the biggest squat ever done in that class circa 2011), 825lbs bench press, 800lbs deadlift

2730lbs TOTAL (third best of all-time).

—

SECTION ONE

A STRENGTH ATHLETE'S STORY

SECTION ONE

CHAPTER 1
BREAKING POINT – THE FORK IN THE ROAD

They say that life must be lived in a forward progression, but can only really be understood looking backward and seeing the events that led you to where you are in reverse. Sitting in that parking lot, wracked in pain, and contemplating taking my own life is one such instance for which time has provided clarity. That moment is still branded into my mind, and although I never wish to go down that dark hole again, I take some comfort in knowing that the lessons learned in the years that would follow have better prepared me for a career in one of the most taxing and rewarding pursuits: strength sports. As I reflect back on that period of my life, and that horrible day in my car, I see how the years of misinformation and mistakes led me to my lowest of lows. If only I knew then what I know now.

I could not have rushed the surgical process any more. I remember exactly how desperate I was becoming like it was yesterday. The pain was becoming more severe by the day and this day in particular was worse than ever - immediate excruciating pain as I arose out of bed and limped to the coffee pot. It was April 3rd, 2013 and luckily for me, I was finally seeing the neurosurgeon after waiting four long weeks and I had been looking forward to this appointment with a glimmer of hope. I just knew he was going to see my issue, develop a plan, schedule my surgery, and I would become pain free. IT'S JUST THAT EASY, RIGHT?

Unfortunately, many people fall into this trap – the notion that surgery is the only fix for chronic and debilitating back pain, and I was no different.

Much to my chagrin (but really my benefit looking back), the MRI taken a month prior was not 'clear' enough for this surgeon to "determine the exact cause of the pain" and I was instructed to have another MRI taken and was turned away, zero discussion, or progress made. I was rescheduled for another scan and a follow-up with him on another day, a seemingly common first response for many other sufferers of back pain around the world. I had come into this meeting prepared to finally reach a solution. I had gone into great detail both orally and through my "intake" paperwork describing my symptoms and my pain patterns, including what I felt was causing the issue. However, once we reached the MRI and it was determined not legible, the consult was concluded. I was given no suggestions in the interim to relieve pain, not even a bit of friendly advice.

As I stormed out of the surgeon's office that morning, after a month of stagnation, worsening pain, so many dead ends and so much time wasted, I'll admit I totally lost it. I stomped through the parking garage at Baptist Hospital in a blind rage of anger. I was yelling and cursing and out of pure frustration chucked the "useless" MRI disk across the concrete. After somehow locating my Hyundai Sonata (there are a million in Jacksonville where I have lived all my life) I found myself sitting in the driver's seat in sheer panic mode - wondering what I was going to do. So many thoughts and questions raced through my head: How did it come to this point? What is it like to feel pain-free? Did I even remember? Would I ever be able to lift again, to LIVE again, to not think about my back 24 hours a day - 7 days a week. In my current predicament, I woke up each day, knowing what was waiting for me: a giant dagger of pain twisting through my hips and up my back while simply trying to rise from the mattress. I could count on sensations of fire ants running down and biting my left leg relentlessly throughout the morning and afternoon. This was officially rock bottom, such a frustrating, helpless and low feeling, so useless, so weak, so used and washed up.

Was this really my life?

Those that have suffered disabling back pain over the years can relate to the feeling of high hopes for a miraculous breakthrough, so thoroughly dashed when another medical consult feels more like a scam than a solution. I had been so dead-set on finding a cure and enacting a plan into place on this day that the thought of waiting any longer seemed intolerable.

Sitting in my Hyundai Sonata, perplexed, in shock and in a frenzy, I started to become a little nostalgic, although my reflection was less warm and fuzzy, rather more resentful and bitter. I thought - the all-time world records, the championships, the head to head match-ups, the top 1- 2 overall rankings every single year and accolades for a decade, the notoriety, all for what? All for this polar-opposite, empty feeling? What happened, how am I here now, unable to walk without a limp, hobbling around my house day-to-day, cautious to have sex with my wife, or even sit, or stand with the looming severe pain that I am faced with?

Powerlifting was not only my passion, but it had become my livelihood. Taking that away and replacing it with the brutal pain that accompanied even the most menial tasks left me feeling I had little left to live for. I looked over at my dashboard console and thought about my Glock 22 40 cal. that was sitting inside, just an arm's length away. In that moment, I seriously and thoroughly considered pulling it out and eating a bullet to put me out of my misery. I weighed my options and thought of my wife Ria, who would be forever impacted and I thankfully and rightfully decided that that course of action was a bit extreme and excessive. One thing was certain: something had to change, and fast.

Leading up to this appointment with the surgeon, I had become increasingly obsessed with finding a cure for my back, some might even say crazed. But, like many people I talk to who suffer back pain, I had been barking up the wrong tree. In an effort to push myself through the painful zone and reemerge triumphant, I had only been doing further damage to my body. I would constantly "test" and seek out my back pain in a convoluted effort to "track my progress" and say, "yep, still there, still hurts", as I bent over awkwardly, putting my spine into flexion. To contribute to my underlying extreme frustration, the month prior, I had seen two other well-renown orthopedic surgeons. The first refused to work on me and told me I was going to need a lumbar spinal fusion no matter what. The second, wouldn't work with me unless I promised to quit any sort of lifting for good, and affirmed that a fusion was imminent. This was not acceptable to me, but admittedly, I was starting to succumb to the fact this may be a life sentence.

Little did I know that the days that would follow my rock-bottom experience in the car would be a major turning point for me. Just a week later, thanks to my client Richard Brown's suggestion, I contacted Dr. Stuart McGill and my whole world changed. This would be where I learned how mighty and powerful the **Gift of Injury** truly is.

True to the cliché that hindsight is 20/20, looking back it's as clear as day: I simply was not meant to have that surgery. I saw multiple different surgeons. One in particular was going to do a micro-discectomy, which likely wouldn't have helped me recover as the disc damage was the least of my worries. The procedure would only be addressing a minor part of the symptoms, not the **cause** of pain.

SECTION ONE

The back problems I faced leading up to that day had to happen in order to set me back just enough time to get another MRI, send it to professor McGill and set up an in-person assessment to get the real 411 on back pain. I still followed up with my neurosurgeon a couple of weeks later with a consult (out of obligation), but I already knew my path. I remember Dr. McGill saying during our first consultation "I'm looking at your imaging now – I recommend 100% that you avoid surgery. You have a lot of issues going on and these surgeries aren't likely to remove your pain." I believed him. He had shown me on the spot that by controlling my movements and postures, I could find immediate relief and I was confident that the plan we were building together was the answer I had been looking for all along. At the time of our first consultation, although he felt good about the prospects of me eliminating pain from my day-to-day life and of the return of some of my former athleticism, the professor was doubtful on my return to lifting record-setting loads. Ever the stubborn child, I was determined that if I could become pain-free, I could build on that progress and once again return to my status as an elite athlete. It wouldn't be an easy road, but I was willing to do whatever it took to reclaim my life and my career; one step at a time. I was ready to commit to Dr. McGill's approach. I cancelled my next procedure through the surgeon's office, which was a myelogram, and never went back to see another doctor again. The rest is history.

As I left Dr. McGill's clinic after our first meeting, I shook his hand and told him I'd be back, to which he smiled and said "who knows? Maybe we end up writing a book on it to share your story"...

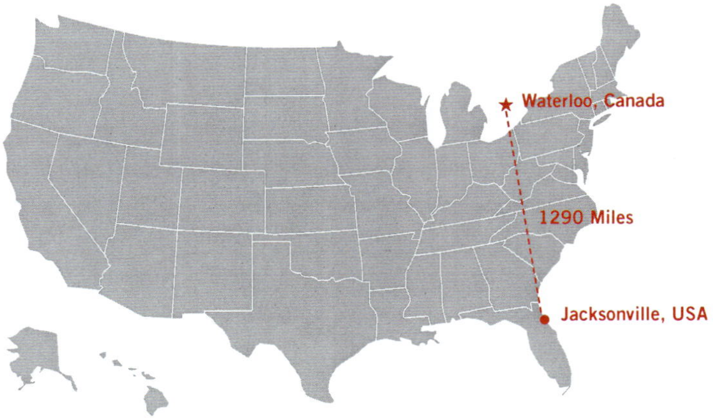

CHAPTER 2
THE EARLY YEARS

I have never been one to settle. Although I was known as a pretty athletic kid around the schoolyard, my build was on the shorter, "stockier" side and the truth is, I wasn't carrying very much muscle. This became especially apparent for me in 7th and 8th grade when the bases, infield and homerun fences all went big-boy size. I could tell that I was falling behind the curve and this was a problem for me. I was not explosive, strong, or powerful enough to compete at the other kids' levels. I knew something needed to change.

Left: 7th grade, quite undersized

Right: 9th grade, just started lifting weights and the mold was cast

So, I did something about it. In 1995 when I was in 9th grade, I started lifting weights. To be totally honest, it was for a couple different reasons. 1. I wanted to be better at baseball and 2. As the other kids were hitting puberty, not only were they sprouting taller than me, but seemed to be "filling out" much more as well. I was just over 5ft tall and 100lbs. Although I couldn't force myself to gain a few vertical inches, I felt that my build was something that was in my control. So, I grabbed a weight set and never turned back. To me, I had no choice. I was far too small, was considered a weakling and was starting to become a target for bullies. This was not the high school trajectory I had envisioned for myself, so I made the change. My smaller stature fueled my drive and became motivation to better myself and was a very good thing looking back, even though initially it caused me a lot of frustration.

At 15, starting to fill out

The rapid progress was undeniable. In no time, my increased power, strength and speed transferred onto the baseball diamond. Watching my body begin to transform and my game simultaneously improve was thrilling! Keep in mind, this was the 90's and our school didn't really have a strength coach, or any educator properly informed on weight training. I would just do my own thing in the gym while the coach would yell at us to lift more and lift hard. There were charts on the wall with pyramids and such, and although they helped me shape my regimen when I was just getting started, I quickly learned that they became less helpful and relevant as I continued to grow and amass strength. My coach wanted me benching three to four times a week and even back then I knew that this was too much. It was just my instinct. I suppose I could earmark this moment as the start of my *10/20/Life* philosophy, I just didn't know to call it that at the time. Listening to your body is one of the biggest things I learned early on and a huge key for anyone who wants to attain longevity in the strength game.

This concept of benching four times a week didn't sit right and I couldn't understand what I would gain by pushing and training again before I had completely recovered and was still dealing with residual soreness. I was chastised by the coaches at the school for not wanting to bench Monday, Wednesday, Thursday AND FRIDAY, but I didn't care. As athletes, we are our own best advocates, and it is to our advantage to learn this sooner rather than later.

The foundation was forming as a 16-year old kid

As I continued to lift and advance through high school, the strength I was building in the weight room carried over into being able to go toe to toe with the best football players in school on the sandlot, as well as being able to grapple with the best wrestlers. I was holding my own in sports in which I didn't have a whole lot of experience in. As my friend Jonathan Byrd says, "strength is a great equalizer," and I agree one hundred percent. Through 10th and 11th grade is where I hit my first 300lbs bench and in 12th grade, where I started to squat and actually train more than my bench press, I could feel myself becoming hooked. I just loved getting stronger, being more powerful and looking good.

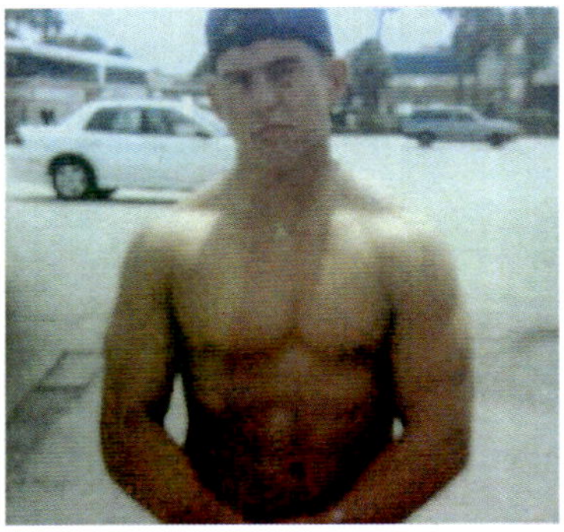

17 years old in 1999 – senior year. 190lbs 350 bench press

I started to become the leader in the gym (a true gym rat) and began designing comprehensive training sessions for myself when I joined the local Powerhouse at age sixteen. I got a few of my friends to come and join the gym, but most of the time I trained alone. I was falling in love, but I never knew exactly what I was in love with. Was it the process, the weight room, or the girls noticing me more on the field? Instead of going out to parties on Friday and Saturday night, I would go to the gym right before it 'closed' and stay until 1am at times. It's what I wanted to do.

Towards the end of high school, strength training began consuming more and more of my time, to the point where I was turning my focus away from baseball, something which was alarming at the time. After I graduated high school in 1999, instead of pursuing any other baseball opportunities locally, I played my last game on July 17, 1999 and never looked back. Even though I loved the sport, I had made the decision that I was finished with baseball and I have yet to step on a diamond again, even recreationally.

THE PATH

I buried myself into lifting weights and it was becoming my

life. When I think about it, it was no accident that this happened. This was the progression I was meant to take. The more time I committed to the gym, the more my gym "crew" became an integral part of my life. Several of my training partners would ask for help with their lifting programs and technique and I began to find a natural affinity for coaching and guiding others. At this point, I was instructing based mostly on my instinct, which in retrospect was sometimes flawed, but this type of instruction became as much a learning process for me as it was a teaching opportunity.

My training, which was imperfect, but well-intentioned and thoroughly planned (it just needed to be mastered and tweaked), had many parallels with my career trajectory. It was full of highs and lows, but always focused on growth and development. Like just about everything, it certainly has not been as direct of a route to success as you will read in this book. Experience, to me, is the best teacher.

After I graduated High School in 1999, I didn't know what I wanted to do with my life and it was time to man-up. As stated, I innately knew that baseball had run its course, so it was time to look ahead to a sustainable career. With some luck, I landed a merchandising/sales job at Coca-Cola starting at 18 years old and it lasted the next seven years. I quickly worked my way up while attending community college part-time, but struggled to find anything that seriously interested me. My coaching was my most enjoyable source of income, working as a personal trainer to a variety of clientele - including moms, grandmas, dads and grandpas.

Meanwhile, I stayed with Coca-Cola, all the while beating my body to bits, pulling pallets, filling shelves, building displays and working in sales and merchandising. For the young buck, this was a great gig. I made good money and was given lots of opportunity. I was the fastest route runner that existed, at least in my mind. On some days I would even start my work route, take a break to go to the other side of town to squat and deadlift, then go finish working! The downside of this type of work is that it's awfully rough on your body. After a few years of 'humping it' out in the grocery market, I made a decision – I needed to go to school. I needed a formal education, but knew it had to be in a hands-on setting to provide training that would directly benefit my future work. A trade school of some sort was the ticket. In 2002, I pulled the trigger and applied to a big, private massage therapy school. As a part-time student, I was able to continue my day job with Coca-Cola until I finished my degree in 2004. I graduated with a license in massage therapy, both state and nation-wide. For whatever reason, I knew this would somehow come in handy down the road.

I didn't know this yet, but the extremely thorough anatomy and physiology I was studying, along with the overall general understanding of the human body we learned in school, would not only greatly help my powerlifting, but also teach me a lot about my recovery from the brutal training I was going to endure for years to come.

By 2006, I had had enough of the hustle and physical labor demanded with Coca-Cola. As I was making this decision, I'd been busy working on building a clientele and gaining experience in massage therapy in my spare time (in preparation to leave Coca-Cola when the time was right). It was May 2006, and time to take the leap of faith with a brand new, multi-million- dollar spa that was just opening up - to work as a licensed massage therapist (LMT).

Leaving Coca-Cola and what I knew was hard for me. Sales, hustling and throwing Coke cases was all familiar, but I also wanted to utilize my skills and be better to my body (this was another instinct kicking in). This was always apparent to me, and especially as I would see some of the older "20 year vets" at Coca-Cola hobble around, I knew that I couldn't do that to my body; at least not from slinging cases.

There was more to the story of leaving, I'll admit. I had the desire to have more energy, a more predictable schedule and less overall physical stress to be able to dedicate more of myself to.... wait for it... my ever-increasing love of powerlifting!

Don't get me wrong. Working my way up at Coca-Cola hadn't come without reward: I got the chance to buy a brand new hotrod truck in cash; a 2001 Ford Lightning. I had also learned by 20 years of age, how to manage accounts and how to speak to people in positions of power. With Coca-Cola, I was speaking with district managers, regional managers and plant managers. I was also dealing with the customers. These were managers of grocery chains, from local level to region and nationwide. Some were quite difficult and some were even impossible to deal with. I learned quickly in the industry that not everything works smoothly, no matter how well you plan it out, even with trial runs and jotting ideas down on paper. I learned to improvise and bust my ass to make things happen. The crap-load of money wasn't too bad either for a kid right out of high school who still lived with his parents. This allowed me to pay for my massage therapy school in cash and start my life off debt-free.

This new career path in massage therapy, much like my lifting trajectory that you will read about in this book, was not paved in gold. It has brought its share of trying and difficult times. I had years where I didn't make much money and battled demons of self-sabotage, but one thing is for certain – taking this path, and in particular being on staff at the spa, was meant to be.

Brian apparently has GREAT hands: Ria and Brian married in 2010 after having met in early 2008

As a strength athlete working over 10 hour days, at times doing very extensive and deep therapy on clients of all shapes, sizes and demands (some major athletes), my appetite increased to meet my body's caloric demands. Finding proper and adequate fuel became an important part of my daily life. There was a great little BBQ joint across the street that I would frequent during and after work to fuel up my training sessions. A certain good-looking waitress had caught my attention after a few visits. After several failed attempts to be seated in her section with the hopes of talking to her, one day she was FINALLY my server and I had the chance to introduce myself. Her name was Ria, and I am thrilled to report that she is now my wife. Ria has been the most important part of this process and a crucial catalyst to my personal and professional growth. Having her by my side has been a gift to me, more than anyone will ever truly know. I know that this fateful path was ordered by a higher power.

While working at the spa in July of 2009, the idea of becoming a police officer began to seriously intrigue me. This was something I'd always been interested in when I was younger, but never seriously enough to take any action. Massage therapy had provided a useful skillset and was something I knew I could always fall back on for extra money, but I knew that a bigger calling existed out there for me: a calling that would allow me to make a difference. As you will see in the coming chapters, the police gig was not meant to be, and was part of setting my life's GPS directly toward this very day that I'm sitting here writing this book.

I didn't even realize this until the last couple of years, as I've gotten into public speaking more - I'm never socially uncomfortable. Why? I don't think it was just the experience of dealing with managers with accounts at Coca-Cola. Think about this: Learning to deal with clients on a massage table taught me a lot about how to speak with clients of all walks of life in a professional way. I got all of the awkwardness out of me about 1 year in!

Let's face it, it takes skill to casually, but appropriately talk to/entertain/humor a client, and believe it or not, give advice in some cases. These discussions of situations and even business took place while rubbing their feet or their head. If you can do this and not be awkward, you can speak to anyone about anything. Boy, if only I could tell you some stories about some of these experiences, but legally, I cannot. This has taught me a whole lot about etiquette in general that comes in handy while teaching/instructing/speaking at seminars and summits. This has also given me a perspective that many could never know without having done it. Much like the case with my back, having been through the steps in writing this book has given me yet another experience that I can say has shaped me into who I am today.

Looking back, I'm quite glad I didn't go to college and instead went down this path. I'm grateful I went straight to work in the real world. Honestly, at times, I've wrestled with this because I do know an education is important, but I didn't feel it was for me. I'm glad I went to massage therapy school and took a job at a spa. It's how I met my wife, it's how I learned "small talk" and to get people to open up to you without having to say much of anything. This has been a huge part of being an effective coach.

I'm glad I had the opportunity to learn how to interact with high ranking individuals while working with Coca-Cola and doing business with them. I'm actually thankful that I didn't become a police officer and for what happened the day I was moving in that direction – although it sure didn't seem like "a gift" at the time. But, this all lead me to this path of learning the body, making mistakes, having success, failing, winning, losing, getting hurt, struggling, and ultimately focusing my efforts on training myself and others professionally.

EVERYONE NEEDS A MENTOR

While training at the local gym in 1997, I met a guy named Skip Sylvester who taught me a lot about lifting. I remember seeing this guy around the facility who everyone called "Skip." Skip, constantly with a smile on his face, training multiple clients and always on the move. Those that know Skip, know exactly what I mean. Keep in mind, this was a small box gym, so everyone was pretty familiar with each other as we all had our routines. I would listen in to Skip giving his clients advice, that smile beaming and warming them up to his advice and knowledge. It was a pleasant smile nonetheless and definitely contributed to his approachability. Skip was your typical bodybuilder in the mid 90's – the big flare pants, the cut off shirts, and the Otomix shoes. Every chance he seemed to get, he said something nice to me, or gave me a tip.

Skip was someone that everyone admired. He was a former Mr. Jacksonville, a powerlifter (which came into play later) and generally, someone who everyone liked and wanted to be around. The life of the party everywhere he was, and naturally, not having a clue as to what I was doing, I gravitated toward Skip. At the time, I had no idea how this would impact my future, I just knew I needed direction and I was like a dry sponge willing to soak up any information I was offered.

I also met a fireman (through my Father, who is also a fireman) named Jake Blanton who competed in bench press mostly and occasionally full meets. Jake was another gracious gym buddy who let me train with him and come to his competitions. One day, toward the end of my senior year, as I was at a bench competition (in Tampa) helping Jake warm-up in the back, I eyeballed the competition roster and had the sudden urge to jump into the bench press competition on the spot. I became a last-minute entry and pressed a PR (Personal Record – my best yet) of 325lbs raw even though I had trained heavily the day before on bench! I finished in second place and loved every second of it. I went on to do a few more bench competitions in '99 and 2000 and then kind of lost interest since there weren't a whole lot of teenagers in this bench-only category. At this point, I didn't think I would ever want to compete in the men's open. Boy, I was wrong.

1999, my second bench only competition hoisting a massive 320lbs with my training partner Jake Blanton coaching and spotting me

MENTORSHIP – ANOTHER STOP: BODYBUILDING

As I lost interest in the bench only meets, Skip and I decided to have me try a bodybuilding show in 2001. I remember I thought it would be cool to get on stage, be ripped, and have the girls give you a nice trophy. I was training hard (I thought), even though in retrospect, my focus on my upper body caused me to neglect my back and legs.

Skip was intent on proper form and he was the first to give me the solid corrections I needed. Although I didn't do them very often, one day I decided to join Skip as he was doing squats and ended up pleasantly surprising him! "Your squat looks good," I remember him saying. "You are doing 225lbs for 20 repetitions for your glycogen depletion? I didn't know you could squat like this. Who taught you how to squat, Brian?" "I just squat – it feels natural," I responded honestly. As my technique developed, I picked up on certain cues inherently, and others had to be deeply grooved into my body before they felt natural.

I ended up doing two shows that year and to be honest, I didn't enjoy myself. There was nothing appealing to me about eating super small amounts, sucking myself down, then prancing around the stage feeling like death. My foray into bodybuilding left me more than a little bit bitter actually, because I didn't place very well. I didn't like the subjectivity of the sport and the judging. The silver lining is that I was exposed to the type of high level preparedness and event-specific training that are a part of the competition world. At the time, this was an aspect I was not great at, but that I would learn to embrace later as a part of the journey.

THE PATH TO POWERLIFTING

I went back to the gym with a tenacity that I had never had before. The chip on my shoulder coupled with a slight embarrassment from my humbling bodybuilding experience, turned to motivation to dig in harder and focus in on my strengths while attacking my weaknesses. I had no plans of competing in powerlifting, but I did plan on mastering proper rowing, chinning, and squatting. Shortly into my harder, more complete training, I was taught how to deadlift by Skip and quickly added this to my repertoire as well. Skip taught me proper form and would even comment to me when some of the bigger guys were pulling in the gym with bad form, "they will regret that soon, I've tried to tell them." And sure enough, he was right, as I saw several of those guys crippled with lifting injuries. In these days, following this advice from Skip became my only focus: eat a lot and train heavy. I was essentially testing and developing my training philosophy and principles, while building the foundation for full meets to come. I just didn't know it yet. I was instructed by those who came before me to stick to the basics, and do what was necessary to make progress. This was key for me. I would get chastised for doing 'dumbbell front raises' instead of, or before standing over-head press and rightfully so! "Save those for the end, or how about never," I remember some of the more savvy veterans telling me. "Between bench press and overhead press, you're getting plenty of work in that area, right now you're wasting your time," they would say. I came to realize they were right. Which one is going to bring a 16-year-old kid more benefit? Clearly the compound movement - the overhead press!

After about a year heavy benching, overhead pressing, squatting and subsequently deadlifting, I was starting to move some serious weight. I was benching over 425lbs with a pause, squatting 500lbs for reps and singles over 600lbs. For the deadlift, I was pulling over 500lbs for reps. Although I was experiencing notable progress, I still hadn't reached that prime level of strength required for powerlifting.

In 2002, during a seemingly normal day at the gym, Skip walked by quickly with a smile on his face and a client not far behind, as he always did. In once sentence, Skip said, "There's a full powerlifting meet in March of next year here in town, you're doing it," and kept walking. I jumped up and hollered "OK!" somewhat blindly agreeing to another opportunity to add purpose to my training. I agreed, but told him I didn't know what was expected of me. He replied with, "Just promise you'll do it and I'll take care of the rest." And so, I did. Skip helped me set up my training, and with a clear objective in front of me I was able to focus my program. Even back then, certain things just made sense and came naturally to me. For instance, the idea of easing off and giving yourself permission not to pull and squat heavy all the time, having light weeks, just seemed right. The concept of 'peaking' to ensure I was in my prime at the time of an event also made a lot of sense to me even though I'd never really done it before. I would need to incorporate this mentality into my training if I wanted to be competitive, and with my first meet coming up I had to learn fast.

Before I knew it, three months flew by and it was March 15, 2003 and I was set to lift in my first full meet. I was as green as baby shit, but strong. I didn't know what to expect, but I was blessed with that "beginner's luck" naivety that can work in your favor especially when partnered with smart training and natural skill. I ended up surprising myself, beating out some experienced veterans on my first day. Come the end of the meet, I had placed in the top 3 overall, something many lifters work years to achieve!

I had somehow managed my way through the meet only missing 2 lifts. I squatted 705lbs, benched 424lbs and pulled 622lbs. I only missed a 435lbs bench and a 644lbs dead -1752lbs total. This was good enough for a current top 25 total in the country! Something clicked internally, during that first meet. I came away feeling like I had found the closest thing to a "calling" I've ever experienced. I had found a sport that I could finally use to channel my many hours in the gym and that I happened to also enjoy and be good at!

CREATING THE MONSTER

I had my first taste of success and returned to training with newfound vigor. I quickly realized that if I could focus my work ethic and natural intuition, over time I could transform myself from a novice powerlifter to an accomplished one. How accomplished? I had no idea. All I thought about was powerlifting. Nothing else. I simply wore out anyone and everyone who would listen to me going on about lifting, namely powerlifting. "Obsessed" would be a massive understatement. Ask my girlfriend at the time, as well as my friends. Did I mention she dumped me because I was in love with something else? That love spills over into everything that individual touches. It's truly one of the most intoxicating drugs, and it makes focusing on anything else a challenge. This was me to a "T." I was the annoying CrossFit guy before annoying CrossFit guys were around.

2003 at my first ever meet with one of my first powerlifting mentors, Adam Driggers

I never had that moment that some of the powerlifting greats talk about, where they knew they would squat x, bench x and pull x and have x ranking someday. My quest for achievable numbers grew slowly. I knew that I liked being seen as a strong guy. I thought that when I was 'strong', squatting 800lbs would be a great goal one day... but, I didn't think I would ever squat 1000 (and manage to do so over fifty times – the most by any lifter in competition history as far as I'm aware), much less 1200lbs, bench over 825lbs and pull 850lbs. Early on, these higher numbers weren't even on my radar. With a couple more meets under my belt, I had created an email address that had the numbers 2100 in it for a '2100lbs' total that I wanted to hit one day. Well, this total came less than two years after doing my first full meet (squat/bench/dead). As I continued to meet and exceed my early goals, I learned I needed to raise the proverbial bar for myself. By the end of 2005, I was at a 925lbs squat, 600lbs bench and a 733lbs dead, all within two years of my first full powerlifting meet. I was ranked in the top 5 in the country, and was closing in on a top 10 All-Time World Record squat and total ranking very quickly. The All-Time World Record list is compiled by a guy named Michael Soong, a former lifter who has taken interest in documenting powerlifting records for as long as I can remember. This, in my humble opinion, is the ONLY list that matters. Not the small federation records, the tiny division, or state records that people set that were just vacant and set arbitrarily – this is the best of the best list regardless of affiliation, testing, or rules. Seeing my own name added to that prestigious list was a thrill and it only fueled my drive to want to watch my name progress higher and higher into the ranked lifters. There are also yearly, overall rankings as well, regardless of federation or division. But, the All-Time World Record list is what everyone strives to be included on. Though competitive at every meet I went to, totaling more each meet and always placing in the top 3, I still had a long way to go before I was a real contender in the international arena.

TUNNEL VISION

What followed, was a period totally engulfed in a tunnel-vision like focus from 2005 to 2011 in which life, training, and competing was all a blur. I was only focused on the next meet, the next training session, the next meal, and getting stronger was my only driving force. During this time, I was able to take my competitive edge to the next level, but it came with a price. The piper always comes for payment.

With training partners and friends in 2011

I experienced some minor injuries here and there, mostly soft tissue, a pec and a hamstring here, a labrum there, but nothing I couldn't sort out and fix by taking a little down time. What I started to notice was that even as I continued to find success at meets, I had some serious holes in my 'game.' In other words, I felt my body and my training were missing a few things and I was starting to feel it. I could feel that I was starting to slow down a little bit, and that I was taking much longer to recover after heavy days. I was experiencing some back pain from time to time, but I would just shake it off and push through. My back was strong, right? I'd be fine.

The problem was that I didn't know about proactive stabilizing core work, rehab and taking prolonged breaks to settle my pain. I was bullheaded and dumb. I was under the impression that a strong back was bulletproof, and that any sort of fine-tuning of this crucial part of my body was just peripheral material. Getting as strong as possible was my only focus. To be frank, it's amazing that I didn't beat myself up more than I actually did. Looking back, it's hard to believe that my background in massage therapy hadn't better prepared me to understand the type of deterioration my unbalanced form and poorly crafted training program was causing my body. I had ceased my learning and become pretty closed-minded about things. To be blunt, the way I used to treat my body was downright abusive. Although I wasn't training using an absurd amount of weight, or frequency (I trained basically the same program then as I do now), it was what I did not do that was FAR more damaging. I wasn't behaving like an athlete 24/7. I was way too casual in my approach to handling light weights. But, what does it mean to be an athlete 24/7? What does it mean to be "casual" in training? I'm talking about the need to be constantly aware of your body and the positions you put it in. It means being just as aware of your posture, form and movement, not only in the gym, but during off-days.

Yanking on barbells, getting loose under giant loads, bending over to change the weights on a deadlift bar, and not bracing the spine and core when weights were light, were all cumulatively contributing to my grief. Overall, I was being far too casual because, frankly, I felt as though I could be. I thought I was superman – unstoppable and careless. Over time, the constant bending over, both in and out of the gym, as well as utilizing poor form under big loads, ignoring my lifting cues during the squat, bench and dead in the gym, and overall poor posture and body mechanics were catching up to me.

My poor form and lackadaisical approach to lifting, carrying the trash out, or picking up and pouring a 50lbs bag of dog food may have seemed inconsequential at the time, but I was paying for it when I would get up on the platform to squat 1200lbs the next day. The bottom line was that I had lost touch with how to listen to my body, and that early instinct and intuition that had served me so well as a beginner had run its course. I was failing to build a capacity for higher level training. I was going to have to relearn a thing or two.

EARLY SUCCESS

Although I was experiencing some occasional pain and discomfort, I continued to plow through. Surely this was just part of the sport, I had thought to myself. At this point, I couldn't fathom that my own movement was actually to blame, and I probably wouldn't have listened to someone even if they had pointed this out. I had to truly reach rock bottom and have my ego recalibrated before I was ready to see my own flaws. More on that later. For now, I was way too focused on increasing my strength and enjoying my early success to listen to any "background noise."

In 2006, I set the biggest squat ever (All-Time World Record) after only three years of powerlifting full time with a 1030lbs squat at 220lbs. I was 25 years old, and you couldn't tell me anything. Early success is a double-edged sword. To a gifted kid, who is stronger than anyone else in the world in the weight class, it's hard to get ANYTHING through to his young brain and body full of testosterone. My younger self was the epitome of this. I ran on high octane gas (in every way) VERY hard each year as I climbed weight classes from 2005 to 2011, collecting wins, resetting world records and winning battles, all the while oblivious to what I was doing to my body. Correction – not caring. I wanted more and nothing was going to stop me. I was all in, one hundred percent, with no regard for consequences.

SECTION ONE

My progression was as follows:

2005 – 220lbs weight class: 2222lbs total, 925lbs squat - #5 in the country, #10 total in the country, creeping up on the All-Time World Record list.

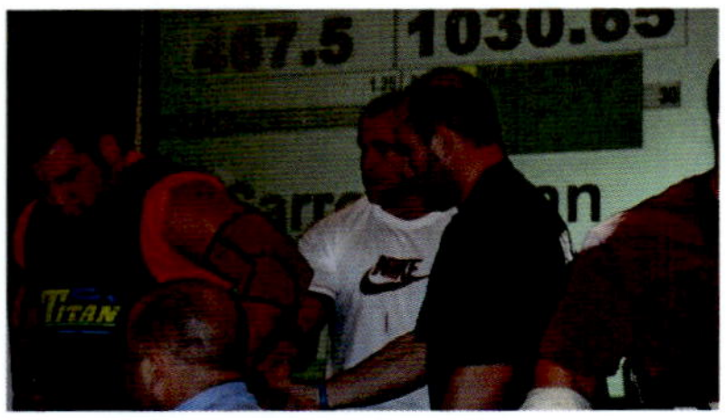

2006 – 220lbs weight class: 2376lbs total, 1030lbs squat - #1 in the country, #1 on the All-Time World Record list. #1 total in the country, #2 on the All-Time World Record list.

2007 – 242lbs class: (went up a weight class) 1040lbs squat - #2 in the country, 2442lbs total - #2 in the country. Total #4 on the All-Time World Record list.

2008 – 242lbs class: 2570lbs total #2 in the country and #2 biggest All-Time total ever, 1052lbs squat - #1 in the country. Total #2 on All-Time World Record list.

2009 – 275lbs weight class: 2660lbs total, 1100lbs squat - #1 in the country, #1 total in the country, #2 on the All-Time World Record list.

2010 – 275lbs weight class: 2700lbs total, 1145lbs squat - #1 in the country, #2 total in the country, #2 on the All-Time World Record list.

2011 – 242lbs weight class: #1 squat in the country with 1063lbs, and total of 2503lbs, as well as #1 squat in the country with 1185lbs All-Time World Record squat, and #2 total current on the All-Time World Record list with 2730lbs at 275lbs.

As you can see in this time span, I moved up 2 weight classes and had top 2 minimum rankings in 3 different classes. By this time, I was already considered one of the best and most consistent lifters of my generation.

CHAPTER 3
CHARTING MY SPINE'S DEMISE

To fully understand the history of back trouble that led me to that dark day sitting in the parking lot at Baptist Hospital, it's important to look at the more minor episodes that I may have dismissed at the time, or took no comprehensive steps to correct. Let's take a pass through my timeline:

FIRST ENCOUNTER WITH BACK PAIN

1996 - My first encounter with lower back pain – real pain. I was playing baseball for the high school and after weeks and weeks of plyometric and dot drills, running and sprinting stadiums and useless stretches, my lower back started giving me fits of debilitating pain. After a couple of months of blindly trying the horribly counterproductive knee to chest low back stretches (which are unfortunately still recommended to many pained athletes twenty years later), I found that it wasn't until I took time away from the conditioning drills over Christmas break that my back was able to settle on its own and heal.

SECOND ENCOUNTER WITH BACK PAIN

2003 - This was my first FULL year of a powerlifting season. I was deadlifting at a brand-new gym. I rushed a set-up and let the deadlift slip out of my grip. Being the aggressive young man that I was, I went right back to the bar and tried again. POP! I was fatigued under-load and had suffered what I had thought was a strained facet joint in my lumbar spine. I was incorrect in my self-diagnosis. I gave it about five weeks of rest and once again, things seemed to heal on their own.

THIRD ENCOUNTER WITH BACK PAIN – FOR REAL THIS TIME

2009 - During this time, while competing for a police academy scholarship, I finally did it– I really hurt my back. One hot July morning, while running full speed on the obstacle course, I fell while hurdling a wall wet with morning dew. I slipped and landed directly on my butt/sacrum like something from a highlight video of epic falls, as my feet went over my head. I somehow finished the course, even though my legs simply stopped working toward the end. I had to literally fling, or throw them each step to move forward. I figured it was just from an adrenaline dump, a bit of fatigue and exhaustion. But, looking back – I had dismissed the damage once again. I managed to get a ride back to my truck, then collapsed and writhed in pain as I made a temporary home in the parking lot for the next thirty minutes. Once I got myself together enough to move, I cranked the A/C to max, and sped home as fast as I could with the seat reclined back as far as it would go because I couldn't bear to sit upright. This was the 'big one,' and I am sure was the root of my problems to come.

My back bothered me on and off in the months that followed. I felt a lack of stability and stiffness – as if my back were suddenly weaker. I pushed on and went to a competition just three months later and deadlifted my first 800lbs deadlift and first of many, 1100lbs squats. Miraculously, through another short period of rest, I had healed enough to compete and bounced back yet again.

My back seemed to calm down for about a year following the wall injury, and I didn't feel much pain, or have many issues. It seemed to have fully recovered, so I proceeded forward – hammering my body into top shape for the year of competitions to come. Although I was continuing to train heavily, I had a series of months to focus purely on strength as opposed to the rigorous event-specific training and schedule that proceeds a meet. Looking back, this down time probably let my back desensitize and heal up to an extent, but unfortunately my poor spine hygiene and overall movement patterns probably undid all the good that downtime may have done.

MY LUCK WAS STARTING TO RUN OUT

All-Time World Record 1185lbs squat

2011 - During my second All-Time World Record squat of 1185lbs, I felt my back give mid-way through the sticking point: a massive lift of 1185lbs (the most anyone had ever had on their back in competition in the history of powerlifting while weighing under 275lbs). What came next was a monsoon of pain, followed by an odd sensation of weakness radiating down my left leg, to a point where it flat-out stopped working during the lift. I willed the leg to work as hard as I could and ultimately barely came up with the lift. But, it came with a cost, part of which was immediate, I basically had to drag my left leg off the lifting platform. I kept quiet about this, I had a meet to finish and money to compete for and win. This day marked the official turning point from which I could not recover.

Looking back, one massive mistake I made was not taking sufficient down time between meets to let my body recover and adapt. I jumped from cycle to cycle, without properly addressing my mounting cumulative back issues. I was blindly letting my pain issues snowball and compound. My recommendation for younger lifters now is to only compete twice a year. I learned this one the hard way.

BAD BACK TO WORSE – BROKEN BACK

2013 - Fast forward about 18months. I'd just finished the XPC Arnold Classic in March, where I finished second overall and didn't retain my title from 2012. This was now the second year in a row at the Arnold where I literally could barely walk to, set-up and grip the deadlift bar at the end of the day. Something had to give.

Competition day had initially started off perfectly, my body felt solid and was moving well – snappy and fast. I was locked in mentally (thankfully), but my back pain reared its ugly head when taking my last warm-up in the practice room, right before the meet was about to start. As I exploded up out of the hole with 975lbs, I felt my back 'pop,' then shot mind-numbing pain locally in my lumbar spine and through to my left glute, extending all the way down that same left leg, right to my foot.

I did what any meat-head, oblivious to basic spine biomechanics knowledge would do – I laid on my stomach and had everyone I could find walk on my back to try to 'pop it back in.' This, of course, made it much worse, severely irritating and sensitizing the area, making the pain almost unbearable.

I limped through the meet, with nothing but mental toughness, stupidity, heart, and the will to win. Actually, limping through the meet would be an understatement. Setting up and reaching down to the deadlift bar were all I could summon the will to do, I could hardly get to the bar and pull 315lbs (something I could do when I was 15). Somehow, despite my obvious struggles, I was willed by a competitor into pulling well into the 700's and just missed an 804lbs dead for the win. As it turned out, this last-minute burst of over-ambition would come at a dear, dear price.

Keep in mind, even getting me to the meet was daunting, reckless and nearly impossible. At these meets, it isn't until after 3 grueling and heavy squat and bench attempts, that the bar hits the floor and then, time to deadlift, which decides the outcome of the meet with the aggregate of all 3 lifts. "The meet doesn't start until the bar hits the floor," is a phrase commonly used by every great puller.

During this time, I was already filled with copious amounts of pain-masking and anti-inflammatory medication, nerve root blockers, facet injections, epidurals and good-old-hard-headed-stupidity and stubbornness. Looking back, there is NO WAY, I should have been competing! Not a chance.

I left that meet at a crossroads. I was very disappointed that my body, and in particular my back, was failing me and that I came up short due to an injury, which not only hindered my lifting, but rendered me unable to properly prepare like I had in the past. I had done everything I could within my capability and knowledge base and was still hurt, not to mention the fact that my deadlift was rapidly regressing. I had done literally everything I knew to do. EVERYTHING. But, even with all of the things I did along the way, (including a potent combination of medication, caffeine and energy drinks which sent me to the hospital for kidney stones), it still wasn't enough, and I was approaching the 'danger zone' of desperation.

Over 10 years of 1000lbs – 1200lbs squats, 50+ official squats over 1000lbs, 800lbs deadlifts, all with a body weight under 275lbs, had taken its toll on my body and in particular, my spine. Years of poor movement patterns, allowing my form to be loose under load and having energy leakages without proper stiffness, improper strength progressions and lack of "down" weeks had finally caught up to me. And, with my body down and out, my psyche was the next thing to give. I was washed up not only physically, but emotionally and mentally as well, depressed, down and out. I felt like a fool. Not only was my back broken, but so was my heart. I had lost myself along the way and let so many things fall to the wayside. The tunnel vision that had driven me forward and kept me focused on success, had cost me many of the "peripheral" aspects of my life. My injury was drastically decreasing the amount of exercise I could manage in a day, and the more inactive I became, the deeper the pain sunk in, ensuring I stayed crippled. I was unhealthy, overweight (regardless of how much I justified it to myself for 'power') and I was sick and tired of daily pain.

I had such tunnel vision while searching for a solution to my pain that I was becoming a horrible husband and friend to those close to me. I was driving 3 days a week, 1 hour each way to train. Add in the 2-4 hours of training, traffic and going to eat afterward and this could sometimes mean being gone for 6 hours. The lack of my physical presence at home, coupled with my miserable attitude when I was around, makes for a bad combination.

Of course, now I see exactly how unavailable I was for just about anything. I can remember in 2012, not wanting to go to parties because I would have to stand around and this caused pain. I remember being depressed and not wanting to have sex because of my constant back and leg pain and feeling that I was becoming the epitome of fat and lazy. It snowballed into my life where I secluded myself, mentally and physically and in my wife Ria's words, "You weren't happy and overall difficult to be around since you were in pain."

SEARCHING FOR RELIEF

I tried going all types of routes with really no relief. I took time off and tried to loosen up my quads and hamstrings – tons of stretching and foam rolling. I even tried a core work regimen that consisted of weighted sit-ups and reverse hypers, but I found the pain too great. What I did find was that by bracing my core at all times (duh) and by shedding a few pounds, I could find some minor relief, but even this would prove temporary. Congruently, I was still on anti-inflammatory meds like prednisone that were designed to take the edge off. We all know the side effects of these types of drugs and how hard they can be on the body and besides, even this type of solution is merely a short-term band-aid.

A word from McGill on Reverse Hypers: Reverse hypers have been part of many athlete's programs, but also have formed injury mechanisms for others. Thus, they are revered by some and hated by others. Many variables influence whether they are helpful, or detrimental for a lifting individual. This includes lifting technique, training volume, programming, anatomy, previous injury, etc.

Out of desperation, I went to a pain management specialist. Dr. Claudio Vincenty who was well known in his field and treated all sorts of back issues. He listened to my story and looked over my images and decided to start me on epidurals and facet injections. He didn't force-feed me any pain medication, or even offer any. Most people know that these injections are only temporary and that the more you do of these type of treatment, the less they work. This was exactly what happened. I got temporary relief and nothing more. The first and longest lasting corticosteroid injection provided about three weeks of relief then simply wore off. The next round eased my pain for only one week, and the subsequent rounds of injections had no effect at all. I was pushing for a meet, and I'm grateful he took the time to talk to me and see what I was about, then did his best to work with me.

Addressing the cause of pain: The issues lay in the fact that I wasn't addressing the structural problem and I allowed my movement patterns to continue to exacerbate the pain.

Not only would the medication wear off faster if I was moving poorly, but the numbing provided by the medication would only encourage me to further stress the "trouble-spots" in my spine. No wonder I felt worse when the medication wore off; I **was** worse!

Dr. Vincenty was very professional and I have to say, had my best interest in mind. As the series of injections began to provide less and less relief, I came to him about getting a surgery referral in 2013. At this point, I believed it to be one of my last remaining options. To my surprise, he actually suggested that I avoid surgery if possible. He explained that the spine, the layers of musculature and nerves are never the same once tampered with and that surgery never had a promised outcome. In other words, it is essentially a crapshoot. I distinctly remember him telling me not to "open up what God intended to stay closed." I listened and took some time to think about it, but all signs pointed to surgery. As I progressed ahead and found no other available options, I figured this was my only solution. It was decided. I would get surgery, and the pain would be eliminated and all would be well with the world.

After the series of appointments with various surgeons that led nowhere, culminating with the appointment that left me physically and mentally broken in the parking lot, fate intervened. I had been open about my back issues with various clients I had been training at the time and one day a client by the name of Richard Brown suggested I reach out to a spine specialist from Canada, who often worked with elite athletes. At this point, I figured I couldn't possibly get any worse, and, having nothing to lose, I decided to reach out.

As I discussed earlier, this was one of the hardest times I've had to deal with in my entire life. Life had been a blur. I was completely obsessed with lifting and my life revolved around the sport in every way. When I started to realize something was very wrong with my back, I had hoped that it was one of those things that I could easily address with a simple appointment, heal, and get back to training and competing.

At this point, my condition had progressed from occasional back pain during lifting, to unavoidable pain during training that continued to plague me throughout my daily activities outside of the gym. I was not in a good place, and was praying my turning point would come sooner rather than later.

Smiles never truly tell the tale of what you have to do and go through to get on the podium. This picture in 2012 was after the overall win, but I had to pay dearly to accomplish that. I was in incredible pain but the win helped subside it. For that brief instant.

Thank God my client Richard Brown made that suggestion that I reach out to Dr. McGill. After looking into him online and asking some of my contacts in the medical field, I was seeing a faint light at the end of the tunnel, maybe this could be my guy. My research suggested he was known as THE back specialist in the athletic world. Others agreed that this expert was the real deal. I remember Canadian powerlifter Shane Church even telling me point blank "He will fix you." So, I phoned his University office hoping he would at least be able to provide me with some insights. Little did I know all that would come of this initial contact.

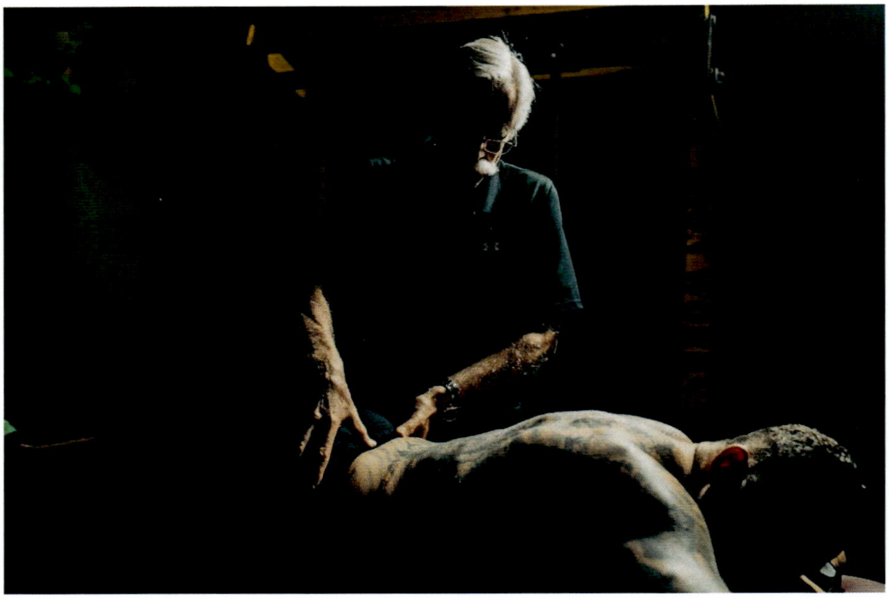

CHAPTER 4
RECOVERY: THE ATHLETE AND THE PROFESSOR

STU:

The phone rang in my University of Waterloo office. It was Brian calling from Florida. I get many more requests each day to see back-pained people than I can grant, but Brian was respectful, smart and genuine, so I agreed to meet with him. I will often Google my "big name" patients before I meet them to get some background and framing of how I can make a difference. My assessment of a patient starts the second I lay eyes on them. I notice how they walk, sit, stand up, shake my hand, and speak. I try to quickly "read" the athlete: What is their mental state, personality type, learning style, and their movement patterns? Then, we start an interview to formally characterize their pain, and for me to gauge their current daily routines and training programs. I let the patient just talk so I really get to know them and glean clues as to why their back pain has eluded the other clinicians. Following this office session, we head to the lab-clinic where I conduct a thorough session of pain provocation testing to precisely define their pain triggers. We begin finding the motions, postures, and loads that trigger pain and then deliberately stress specific tissues in order to identify the pain mechanisms. Using this method, we are able to isolate specific vertebrae, nerves, facet joints, sacroiliac joints, ligaments, muscles etc. as to which are the pain culprits. Next, we experiment with different postures and muscle activation patterns in an effort to find ones that immediately reduce pain. This allows me as a clinician, to pinpoint both the causes and the symptoms of pain that are unique to each of my patients. For example, if we have determined that the pain is due to a disc bulge that changes as a function of hydraulic pressure under certain loads, we will deliberately create a different type of loading to reverse the pressure and neutralize the pain. If the symptoms resolve immediately, we have confirmation of the pain mechanism. I am a huge advocate for physical assessment, stress testing and deliberate pain-provocation as part of a patient exam. Some doctors and surgeons rely solely on MRI, CT, and X-Ray imaging to determine the source of back pain, which is a huge mistake. This equates to treating a bunch of lab tests. This type of malpractice is akin to a car mechanic reviewing a picture of the under-hood of your car and trying to determine why it wasn't running, without ever examining it himself, or turning the ignition. Of course, we also spend great effort reviewing the medical images, but only after the patient assessment. MRIs, for example, show both the wound and the scar. This means that the interpretation of the image needs the context of the patient's assessment to interpret whether the feature is a painful feature, or simply an old injury that has gristled and scarred over. For the reader interested in reading the full description of this procedure, we refer them to my clinical textbook, "*Low back disorders: Evidence based prevention and rehabilitation.*"

As I took Brian through these initial pain-provoking assessments, he seemed blinded by his frustration into not realizing that his daily activities were further irritating his injury. The movement patterns (or lack of patterns), he both described and exhibited right in front of me, were clearly loading his spine into constant pain. Frankly, he was disgusted with himself and seemed to almost be deliberately punishing his body with awkward and excessive loading. Through the interview process, as well as during our provocative testing, and review of his medical images (MRI scans) etc., we were able to determine that he was intolerant of any spine bending and compression loading. The tissue damage was substantial, one of the nastiest fractures I have seen in my career. How he had been continuing to compete and train like this was beyond me.

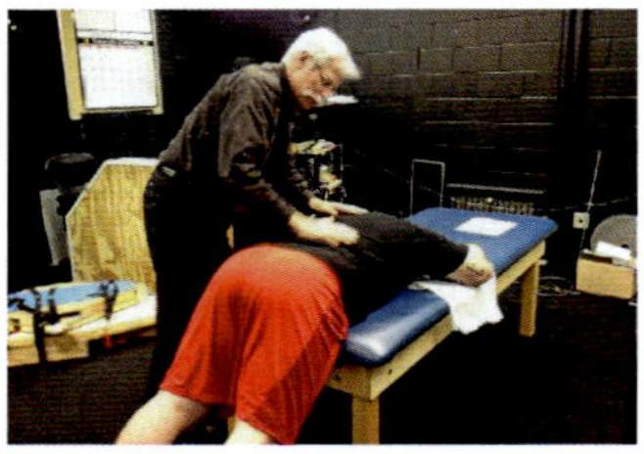

Following the pain mechanism assessment, we moved onto assessing some athletic patterns. Observing his lifting form with an unloaded bare bar revealed many flaws. For starters, he failed to establish the essential "lifter's wedge." This is the locked in and stiffened set-up required for the body to pull load. I wondered if maybe he considered the bar too light to merit respect and by extension - proper form, so I asked Brian to try again, but this time with more seriousness setting up the wedge. It simply wasn't there. It was hard to think that this was the athlete I had read about. Pain is a terrible robber. Here was a superb athlete with an obvious talent, whose lifting form had been corrupted by his effort to compensate for his injury.

Although he was tender and I didn't want to push him too hard, I continued the session and decided to focus the rest of our time on coaching him to lock in stiffness in the torso, cue bending the bar, gripping the ground etc. to stabilize his spine.

Summary of clinical notes (greatly abbreviated): Brian Carroll assessment 1 May, 2013

Reported pain triggers: Spine movement, catches of pain with daily movement.

Symptoms: Back pain and left foot drop.

Documented pain triggers found: Shear load induced pain at L3, L4, L5 levels, Pain reduced with extensor muscle stiffening; LBP with leg raise, but not with neutral lumbar curve.

No pain generated from the hips, or sacro-iliac joint.

Pain reduced with disc bulge vacuum posture (prone traction in extension).

Hip mechanics – femur collides with acetabulum pushing pelvis to flex spine in deep squat. Back and radiating pain. Pain reduced flossing hip and cervical spine.

Standing left rotation with extension created referred left ant. Hip pain, but reduced with standing stork stance.

Visible spinal hinges at T12-L1 and L5-S1.

Iliac manual compression reduces symptoms.

Sciatic nerve tension both sides, but worse on right – worse with cervical flexion. Symptom lessen following sciatic flossing. Nerve is flossing, but has viscous drag.

Medical image findings: Massive sacrum superior end plate fracture, crushed L5 vertebral body, flattened L4/L5 and L5/S1 discs with broad based posterior bulges. Edema in vertebral bodies adjacent these discs. Rest of the spine appears quite unremarkable.

BRIAN:

Needless to say, going into this appointment with Dr. McGill I was fairly fed up with doctors and disappointments, but something felt different about this one. I decided before our meeting that I had to let go of a lot of pent up anger and open myself up to change. I had gotten fat, sloppy, moody, and lost my zest for life. It was time to check my ego at the door and soak up any credible advice I was given and for the inner control freak to relinquish control. I wasn't going to fix myself and knew it. It just wasn't going to happen on its own. Although I was anxious, I was desperate for change and ready to one hundred percent commit to a program and reclaim my life. Could this be the breakthrough I had been praying for? We boarded the plane in Jacksonville and flew to Canada full of hope.

On the morning of my appointment, I reiterated my cautious optimism to Ria as we waited on a beautiful Canadian day in May, for Dr. McGill to come to the Applied Health Sciences facility of the University of Waterloo. While I had a good feeling about this trip, I was still uncertain of my future. By now, I had done my background research and was very familiar with Stu's work, but was of course, still unsure of what to expect once I set foot in his office.

As fate would have it, I felt an almost instant connection and mutual understanding with Stu. He actually listened to me and quickly incorporated everything I was telling him about my body and my injury into his decisions in building an optimal personalized recovery program. No one had ever listened to me like this before. As a former jock himself, he understood the athletic demands I was under. My only source of frustration during our first meeting was my realization that there were many flaws in my training and lifestyle that were perfectly avoidable! I had caught myself in a vicious cycle of pain and my own actions were responsible for my inability to break out. This was an angering epiphany, but I quickly got over it and ingrained in my brain that I'd never let myself go down that road again. From this day forward, I vowed I would be a changed man!

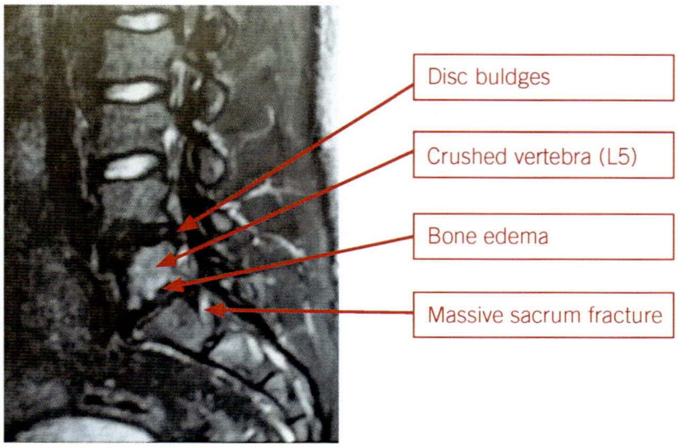

As we chatted and reviewed my scans, Dr. McGill pointed to a dark shadowy area running between two vertebrae. He asked if anything seemed odd to me. "It almost looks like my sacrum is cracked," I responded. According to Dr. McGill, that's exactly what had happened, but worse – it was a massive fracture cleaving the sacrum into front and back halves. Oddly enough, this is something that the two neurosurgeons, orthopedic surgeons, and various radiologists had all either never noticed, or never pointed out to me, with the exception of my Chiro Dr. Amy Bernstein telling me it didn't look right. (Note: I don't think she has the computer capabilities I witnessed in Stu's office computer to zoom in, clarify and highlight certain areas other than her typical board you see in most offices.)

It appeared the damage I had done to my spine was even more significant than I had originally understood. I have seen plenty of bad MRI's before, as I had been researching injuries on my own, but the clues hidden in the shadows of my own, I had overlooked. I suppose it's much easier to make conclusions and suggestions about other people's issues rather than your own. I knew that my back was bad, but to be honest, I was oblivious to the extent of the structural damage until Dr. McGill pointed out the trouble spots in my own images.

I knew that jagged edges, flat discs and black cloudy marks weren't normal, but beyond that it wasn't until a quick and brilliant tutorial from Dr. McGill that I understood the severity of what I was dealing with. It was a very grim moment for me. I can remember looking at my wife through a fog as I was processing the realization that I had been forcing myself to function with multiple broken bones. This was a moment that I'll never forget. My sacrum was nearly split in half. I knew my discs had issues, but this took things to a whole new level. The first thing I thought about was the fall from 2009, how I fell, where it hurt and how it's hurt since.

As we continued chatting, I began to realize that the fall and competition strain alone weren't the cause of my issues. They were major contributors sure, but they wouldn't have progressed to such a debilitating level had I taken more care in my day to day approach to my physicality. Just as I was starting to piece all of this together, Dr. McGill told me to look over my shoulder at the mirror. Sure enough, the image looking back at me was slouched over in the chair, exhibiting horrible posture, and only further exacerbating my pained discs. Embarrassed, I quickly sat up and tried to adapt the natural curve in my low back we had been discussing, only minutes before. Awareness is the first step in correcting your habits and someone was finally forcing me to see my flaws for what they were. All of these great realizations, and we hadn't even moved to the lab-clinic yet!

During the coaching session that followed, movements and physical cues were brought to my attention that I had just flat out quit doing, ignored, or had never done in the first place. I was taking everything in as fast as I could, recording, and making mental and physical notes. Everything he was saying was very calculated, accurate, and insightful. I was very humbled by the fact that this guy who is considered the best in the world at what he does, was willing to take the time for me and was living up to his reputation. I was honestly on a HIGH the whole time, it was surreal. Learning, discussing and having so much in common with this professor I had never met was exactly what I needed. Seeing my athletic ability and injury through an academic lens, and learning how science could lead to my recovery and benefit my training was not only interesting, but essential to me getting myself back on track. My good feeling that I had outside of the university clinic waiting for Dr. McGill was confirmed as we quickly went from strangers, to two guys who clicked and genuinely liked and respected each other. Although we were coming at the issue from different backgrounds, we quickly found common ground and found we were speaking the same language. We simply flowed together.

Clearly no lifter's wedge established

The first thing Dr. McGill noticed when he had me deadlift an unweighted bar, was that I was not setting my lifter's wedge. I had become far too lax and casual for my own good – and it showed even with a 45lbs bar which I could lift with my pinky finger. This was a serious problem. I wasn't gathering my back, doing an anti-shrug preparation and squeezing my rhomboids, nor pulling my lats down. As a powerlifter, this is what you should be doing on every squat, deadlift and any other lift that involves these types of movements. I was lacking one of the most elementary lifting cues known to man: my core and back were not nearly as stiff as they needed to be. In my head, I knew that this type of bracing should be a given, but my back pain had, over the years, removed this crucial element from my prep. I had been subconsciously teaching myself poor lifting form and in the process, was only further damaging my spine on squats and deadlifts as I tried to fight my pain. I had kicked my body into survival mode without realizing. Each time I lifted this way, things got worse, and the more my form suffered, the more I tricked my body into forming a habit that felt right.

Slowing things down and starting over as a beginner

Once Dr. McGill slowed me down and brought all of this to my attention, I almost laughed at how simple he made it seem. How could I have missed these seemingly obvious fixes? I guess sometimes high-level athletes get so used to their own ingrained movements that they forget about the basics of form necessary to the sport. The old adage that we need to practice the way we plan to compete, is so true. If I wasn't putting in the proper prep and set-up for lighter loads, how did I expect my form to magically appear when I stepped up to the platform to break a record? I vowed I would never let anything be casual, loose, or lax again. I would approach every lift with intent and meaning, no matter what the weight, whether I was in the gym, competing for a title, or taking out the trash. This adjustment was as much mental as it was physical and it would involve a total 180 degree turn in my approach. Dr. McGill worked with me and even tricked me (would have me grab something from the floor while distracting me to see how I'd move) into re-learning how to move, sit and stand without irritating my spine. Reflecting back, learning to move correctly and avoid my pain triggers was mindlessly simple once I was instructed by a true professional.

One of the most shocking discoveries was that my back already felt distinctly better leaving Dr. McGill's office than it had when I arrived. By recalibrating my movements and mindfully adjusting my physicality for a mere four hours, I had already noticeably reduced my pain! I couldn't wait to apply this to my everyday life and was confident that things would only continue to improve from here. With Stu's help, I had finally set myself on the road to recovery I had been so desperately searching for! I just felt so liberated and empowered! There was no turning back now.

SECTION ONE

CHAPTER 5
THE INJURY EXPLAINED

STU: The tipping point

Powerlifting and strongman events take an athlete to the physical precipice of ability unlike nearly any other sport. The natural safeguards for self-preservation to avoid injury must be subdued to achieve the maximum exertion required to compete. These sports demand that the athlete command their bodies to defy their better judgments and coax more loading ability than any other time in their lives. Approaching this physical tipping point produces peak performance. Cross that tipping point, and the supporting tissues will crush under compression, or tear under excess strain.

These crushes and tears range from the massively debilitating, to the less noticeable micro-fractures. Building a spine to bear more load actually requires forcing some micro-fracturing by training with heavy weights. I have never seen an elite powerlifter who did not have evidence of a history of micro-fractures in their spines – they are inevitable and part of the adaptation process. Most lifters who see me for back pain have larger endplate fractures, which have caused significant enough damage to compromise their ability to bear load. Overloading during training is a common practice that will either cause an adaptation that increases spine strength or, when pushed too far beyond the tipping point, micro-fractures accumulate into macro-damage and pain. Knowing when to stop adding weight and recognize how much is too much is not an insight every lifter intuitively possesses, but it is one that can be trained.

I will explain the process and mechanism of spine load adaptation and how this relates to rest during training cycles in subsequent chapters.

GENERIC INJURY PROCESSES AND PATTERNS:

The injury-causing variables of greatest concern for the strength athlete are compressive stresses and spine bending loads. The majority of the compression load on the low back actually comes from the back and torso muscles as they contract to support load. It's the function of leverage. The load on the bar is in front of the lumbar spine. The muscles in the back must contract to counter and support this bending moment. Because they are closer to the spine than the load force vector, they must create higher forces than the load on the bar. These muscle forces, together with the bar load, and the upper body mass are imposed on the spine, and can be enough to cause serious damage. With all of these added factors, the loads carried through the spine are often 10 times the actual load on the bar. For example, in the lab we have measured over 2000 kg of compressive spine load from lifting 200kg on the bar!

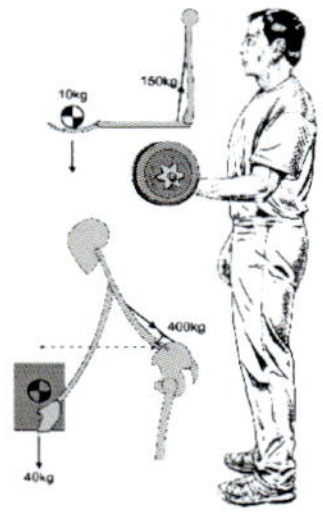

Consider holding 10kg in the hand. This torque is supported by the flexor muscles at the elbow. The hand load has a lever distance 15 times greater than the supporting muscle – this means the muscles contract with 15 times the force. This muscle force crosses the joint and imposes 150 kilograms of load to the elbow joint (15 times the hand load). Now, apply the same leverage principle to the back: 40 kg in the hands that has 10 times the distance in front of the low back compared to the supporting back muscles means the muscles must contract with 400 kg of force (10 times the load). This is why the majority of spine compressive load comes from the back and torso muscles contracting to support the bar load. This is largely influenced by lifting form. These loads will produce damage when they exceed the tolerance, or load bearing strength, of the spine.

End-plate fracture with the disc nucleus squirting into the vertebral body.

Excessive compressive load will initiate micro-fracturing of the disc end-plate and underlying bone. Brian's micro-fracturing had accumulated over time, resulting in a major fracture and split to the end-plate at the top of the sacrum.

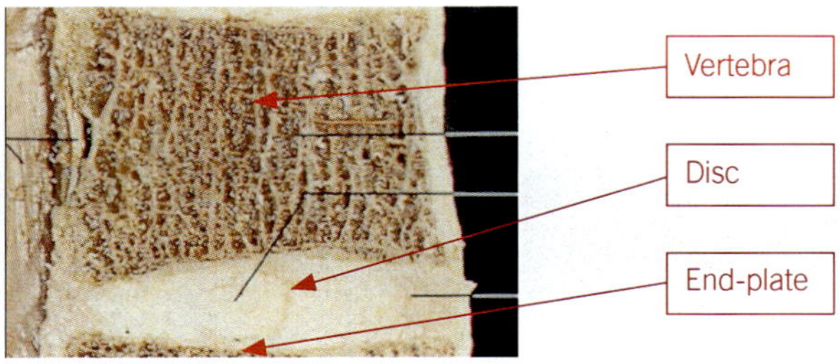

The inside of each vertebra has many struts of bone, which support loads and allow the transmission of weight throughout the structure. It is essential that the struts run both vertically and horizontally to prevent the vertebrae from buckling and breaking. These struts are what determine the vertebra's ability to bear heavy loads successfully. Strength training that causes progressive overload thickens these struts, but this process takes years. Being too aggressive with load increments causes the athlete to cross the tipping point. Being patient, and properly structuring loading cycles that include sufficient rest periods. stimulates bone growth and encourages a sport-specific adaptation.

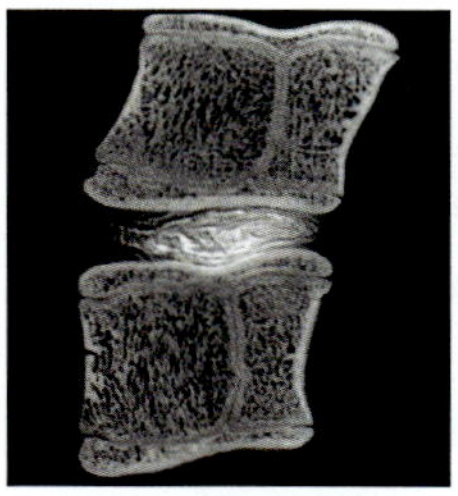

This is what a normal vertebra looks like (high resolution CT scan image). It is neither damaged nor adapted with thicker and stronger bone. For obvious reasons, I have used a young animal specimen here to demonstrate the injury pattern.

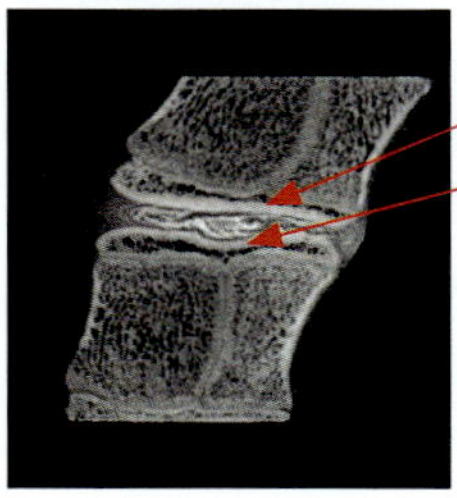

End-plate with fractured bone scaffolding after excessive compressive load – compare to the previous figure.

This is a high resolution CT scan image of a virgin uninjured spine (top image) taken from a cadaver. Then, we applied a load mimicking a heavy deadlift to a level deemed beyond the tipping point, or beyond the spine's physical tolerance level. The first signs of micro-fracturing became evident underneath the cartilage end-plate. When damaged in this way, the cartilage no longer serves its supportive purpose, which is similar to that of scaffolding, or an anchor. With adequate rest, and through properly periodically designed training cycles, the endplate will slowly gristle and callous, giving the spine the ability to bear more load than previously possible. If, however, a proper rest period isn't taken and weighted training is applied too soon, the increased pressure on the disc annulus will cause the collagen fibers to rip away and the delamination process is then accelerated, causing painful injury. In these cases, additional fracturing and disc bulges commonly follow. Brian was successful in building the callous!

This story and accompanying images provide a background to guide young powerlifters. Either of two different scenarios can happen. One is a positive outcome, producing a stronger vertebra. The other ends in injury. The tipping point is different between individuals and is influenced by differences in anatomy, the extent of the damage, rest time taken to callous, genetics and luck. We have tried bone callousing approaches in powerlifters in our lab to determine how to influence the desired outcome – more on this later.

Spine Bending under large training loads: I have seen internet forums that argue that spine bending is OK, or that 'buttwink' is OK. It is important to note that this information is not coming from the scientists educated in the biological processes. There is no question that there are people who have been touched by the hand of God in terms of injury resilience and are less likely to experience bend-related injuries. These individuals, however, are the exception, not the rule. Many variables affect this predisposed tolerance level – differences in hip anatomy, leg to torso length levers, spine thickness, spine shape, genetics, rates of repair, and reaction to training progressions. Some coaches may be successful with themselves, or one or two athletes. This usually comes down to a very lucky accident in which the individual was already blessed with the ability to tolerate such spine abuse. In the vast majority of cases, these methods will not systematically produce high performance and endurable athletes. Spine bending, when under substantial load, may lead to enhanced athleticism in some, but it is usually temporary. They are not aware of the stresses and adaptation processes. Tragically, many eventually ruin their backs. These poor souls call me wanting to know why they are disabled after following a guru promoting buttwink, who is a good marketer and may have previously dismissed our work. Ignorance, impatience and poorly placed trust led to their grief.

The discs of the spine are not ball and socket joints like our hips and shoulders are, and therefore cannot be treated the same way. The outer rings forming the disc are strands of collagen held together with an adhesive "ground" substance. Adapting to motion (i.e. spine bending and more mobility) includes a softening of the collagen ground substance. This softening equates to a weakening, and is therefore the enemy of the strength athlete. In contrast, this softening is what makes gymnastics possible. It should come as a surprise to no one that the physical demands of a powerlifter are quite a different set of requirements than that of the gymnast. But, what this really means is that they must train differently.

Under compressive load, the nucleus gel in the middle core of the disc becomes pressurized. However, when the mobile spine adapted from mobility training has been stretched and bent, the collagen fibers will eventually delaminate under the hydraulic pressure built up in the nucleus, or inner disc. In contrast, a disc subjected to high compressive loads that do not involve bending (i.e. good form with the powerlifts) will get stiffer and resilient to delamination. This is what the strength athlete needs. Most athletes cannot have it both ways – that being a mobile spine that bears high load. Strength athletes should avoid yoga, and spine stretching. Buttwink, when squatting, will eventually cause problems in most people. Stay tight, "locked in," let the hips power the rigid torso.

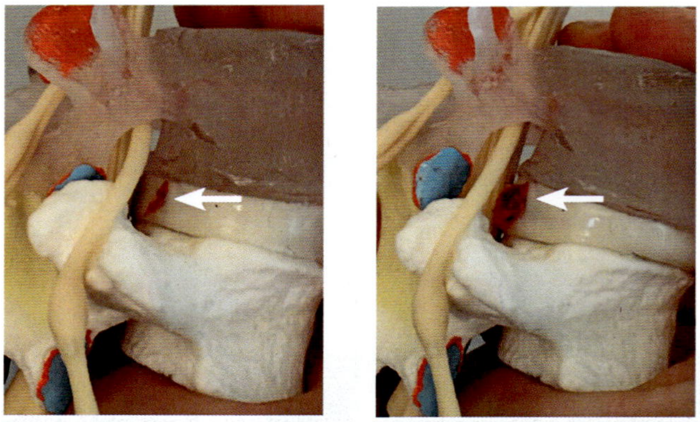

Left Panel: This spine had cumulative delamination of the posterior disc due to excessive bending and compression. But it remains non-problematic if it is not flexed forward. Right Panel: When the spine is flexed under compressive load, hydraulic pressure is directed posteriorly in the nucleus resulting in a visible bulge.

But this scenario can be avoided by the strength athlete. Lifting with a neutral spine, meaning the avoidance of spine flexion, or extension, results in even hydraulic pressure throughout the nucleus of the disc. This is its most load-resilient and strongest position. Flexing, or rounding the back, focuses hydraulic pressure to the posterior part of the disc. Slowly over time and with more repetition cycles, the movement will soften the collagen fibers in the disc annulus, so that the nucleus gel may seep through the cracks with more bending and loading resulting in a disc bulge.

CHAPTER 5

Disc bulges: Some clinicians tell patients that disc bulges just happen and are a process of growing old. This is not true. There is usually a combination of events that setup the collagen delamination, and eventual disc bulge. For example, the damage to the bone end-plate (described earlier) with excessive deadlifts to an untrained spine causes this delamination to occur sooner as the collagen fibers rip away from the end-plate since it has been weakened. Then, more bending of the spine under compressive loads allows the collagen fibers to delaminate further. Eventually, the nucleus material extrudes, firing off the familiar stabbing pain, as inflammation irritates nerves and/or compresses the nerve roots directly. Thus disc bulges are caused by poor training! The way to avoid this cascade is to allow the discs to stiffen by reducing spine bending throughout the day and training with minimal spine motion.

Brian recalls the visits to two surgeons and their reports:

Surgeon 1: "I don't see a solution for Brian's back. Lots going on there and regardless, he will need to stop lifting. A fusion is 100% in his near future either way, but anything other than a fusion won't really help him with all that is going on. The only procedure that will help him is a fusion, so I'll plan on seeing him in a few years either way."

Surgeon 2: "I can do a spinal fusion on him, but I won't agree to do it unless he promises to stop lifting and takes the steps to show me he's done. If he keeps lifting even with the surgery I can do, it's going to cause him some serious problems. Either way, he is done lifting with my surgical help, or with anyone's for that matter."

I was simply told to quit lifting competitively – that was THE solution. What sort of rehab solution is that? What sort of long term solution to pain and back problems is "just quit lifting?" In my mind, that was the same as quitting life too. It was obvious that my issues went beyond just lifting big weights, as we will discuss in this book. The bigger picture was never mentioned: the idea that I was causing a lot of my own pain and injury through repeated poor posture and movement patterns, all the while denying my body the healing time it needed. In other words, I had to earn a capacity to train pain-free, to use Dr. McGill's words.

PRE-REHABILITATION

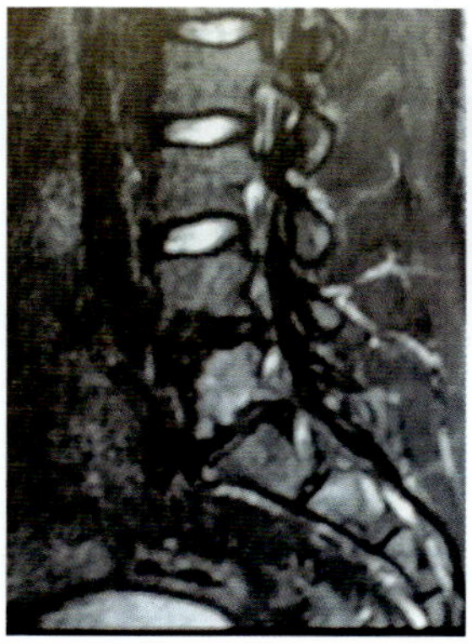

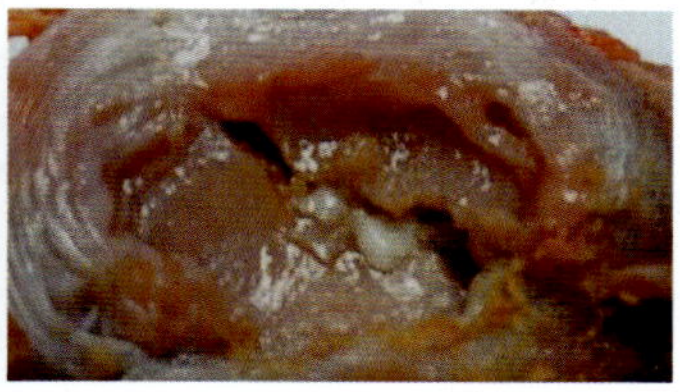

BRIAN'S INJURY:
(Left panel): The MRI shows a massive fracture of the endplate and sacrum – it is split open front to back. The fifth lumbar vertebra is crushed with massive damage to the discs above and below. The fourth vertebra is similarly broken. (Right Panel): We applied crush load to a cadaver spine to re-create the same fracture. This is a massive split in the end-plate with massive bone fracturing to the underlying vertebra.

POST-REHABILITATION

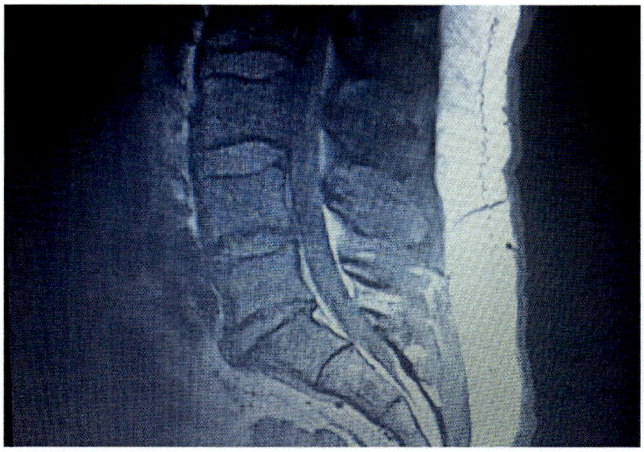

BRIAN'S SUCCESS:
The bony fracture splitting the sacrum is filled in with solid bone. The L5 vertebra has remodeled back into a solid block with heavy end-plates. The discs have only very small bulges.

CHAPTER 6
THE NEGOTIATION

STU:

Great athletes are not normal! Some have developed a killer instinct that, when trained and tapped into, can unleash a beast on competition days. Others are genetic mutants whose natural build lends itself to greatness in their particular sport. Most of the "greats" are a combination of both. Regardless of their predisposition, pure will is a critical factor on the path to success. That mental strength reassures them they will compete at their best and dominate the opposition, or in this case, the bar. Strongman Bill Kazmaier, just knew he would lift and move the load in front of him in strength and powerlifting competitions. There was no doubt. The great Russian Olympic lifter Vasily Alexeyev claimed he was the best. The best lifter, best cook, best singer and the best lover! For him, failure was never an option. He simply executed each lift he focused his mind on. There was no other option for him.

When talking to the great ones, I follow the advice from my father 50 years ago - "Whoever you are with, you treat them as your equal." This has always served me well. It makes conversation easy on both the other person and myself. It is equally important that I genuinely care about each patient as an individual. When someone in pain comes to see me, I can't help but become personally invested. I get genuinely upset when I see my colleagues treat patients as a commodity with which to spend a few minutes and then move on to the next billable entity. In my office, it is imperative that I direct every part of my brain to the patient and focus on giving them the most beneficial experience if they are to succeed in their recovery. I try and be realistic and truthful. I do not treat patients like 5 year olds and over simplify my descriptions, or predictions. I must maintain integrity. While many are quick to nod and agree to my recommendations, there are always some who are initially hesitant and may not agree with, or like my approach.

During the assessment, I had formed an opinion of Brian. Then I had to consider how I would approach this next conversation. I had to give advice in the best interest of Brian's health, yet still respect that athletes make compromises. In front of me was a great athlete who had mastered the mental game of willing the body to pull massive weight despite all of the sensors telling the body to shut down. To compete at his level, lifters must defy the evolutionary fuse box that has allowed the survival and preservation of our ancestors by steering them away from tearing their bodies apart. How would I deliver a "tough love" message to a mind so strong-willed that it can coax the body into pulling over half a ton from the floor? There was no question I had to reign in the element of his personality that was a big part of his success. I suspected I was in for a negotiation.

I opened the conversation by posing the hypothetical that if Brian were my son, I suggest he should listen to the advice of the orthopedic and neuro surgeons he had seen, and seriously reconsider the pursuit of powerlifting. They were unanimous in their message to him - he will never lift again and may never be out of pain. I did not believe the pain prognosis, but I did suggest he think deeply about the cost of returning to heavy training and sacrificing his prospects of a normal life. It was alright to find satisfaction in working to get out of pain and to find happiness elsewhere. It is the classic balance between risk and reward. If one is to take a big risk, then the potential reward must be equally big. Without hesitation, Brian responded he wanted to set the next record. I countered, "Let's see if we can work to get you out of pain first. I want you to feel and appreciate the value of feeling pain-free and able-bodied." Brian didn't budge. I reviewed again the significance and extent of the crush damage in his spine.

Maybe it has to do with our shared heritage – two Irish boys, one wanting to bull ahead, the other wanting to hold back, neither giving an inch. With all patients, getting rid of back pain is always a two stage process – first, focusing on reducing pain by eliminating the cause to allow the pain sensitivity to reduce, then second, shifting the movement approach to enhance ability and performance. I proposed that we must focus on reducing pain. I ultimately convinced him to ease off by explaining that if and when we achieved this, I would ask him and Ria to return to Canada for a follow-up meeting to make the big decision. Do we stop at that point and enjoy a pain-free and lower risk life? Or, do you want to risk it all and try to train and compete again?

The next appointment was scheduled after Brian called me to say he was pain-free doing daily activities. As we got down to business, Brian and I both acknowledged that he had done quite well thus far in recovery, despite his massive compression injury. I had worked with numerous elite powerlifters before and had an idea of how to restore the bone, and I had guided ordinary people with this kind of injury to become pain-free with modest load bearing ability sufficient to enjoy "normal activity," but had never attempted to restore championship load bearing ability with such a massive injury before. This spine had lifted to the edge of human capability – this was not exercising down at the neighborhood gym! I was well aware of the risks and conveyed this to Brian and Ria. As the surgeons rightly had told Brian, further bone crush could result in permanent disability, and worse. Brian did not capitulate. It was clear to me that he had made up his mind. And Ria was, as always, going to give her support to Brian. I told him that if he chose to resume training it would be at his own risk, and that I would advise him with reservation and reluctance and with no guarantees. By now I'm sure you can guess the decision he made.

Brian Carroll joined my list of athletes who I prayed for. Perform well and don't get hurt. Or, in plain English "Don't mess up."

BRIAN:

I was committed to following Dr. McGill's recovery instructions, but maintained that if I were to have any quality of life, abandoning lifting was not an option. I honestly didn't know how to define myself anymore outside of that world and I couldn't imagine simply giving up. As I listened to the fatherly advice from Dr. McGill and mulled things over, I vowed to control the risk of my comeback with some specific and strategic steps. My plan evolved into not only coming back from injury and returning to the highest level of competition, but coming back stronger while moving DOWN a weight class.

Ultimately, Dr. McGill convinced me to set some parameters that would help prevent me from total regression to the sorry state I was in when I met him. I pledged to myself that I wouldn't continue the comeback if the following were the case:

1. If I had any back pain return
2. If my lifts regressed and/or I was no longer a top 1-2 lifter in the world
3. If I needed pain medication for day to day activities

SECTION TWO

YOUR GUIDE: THE PATH FROM DISABLED BACK TO ULTIMATE STRENGTH AND INJURY RESILIENCE

– YOUR GUIDE

In this section, we begin to shift our focus from Brian to you, the reader, we provide the scientific context together with tools to help you organize your training.

We begin with issues to get the strength athlete out of pain. This is essential to build a foundation that eventually supports training. This is followed with a guide to an assessment that not only reveals why there is disabling pain, but also what is required to regain the ability to train. This is concluded with how you interpret your results and translate them into your own training program. We also show you how to assess the demands: meaning converging on and identifying your goals at hand. Then, we show how to put the demands of events and sports together with the assessment of your current capacity to create your custom training program. Finally, in this section we introduce several training drills that assist in reducing and eliminating specific pain triggers. Brian's actual program that returned him to the platform is shown in the next section (Section 3) together with drills to regain strength and performance.

SECTION TWO

CHAPTER 7
COMMITMENT AND RESOLVE TO GET BETTER

In essence, rebuilding an athlete requires two stages. The first stage is dedicated towards stabilizing the injury and relieving pain by approaches that allow desensitization and healing. The second stage, which focuses on developing strength and ability, only begins when the first has been achieved. Trying to perform the two stages in tandem will result in failure to reach either objective. Brian's success can be attributed in part to his professionalism and ability to hold back, using patience and restraint to abstain from strength training until he had achieved the pain free day-to-day foundation he needed before he could move forward.

First, movements must be relearned in order to avoid inflaming the pain triggers. Once this has been achieved, an athlete may begin to add strategic exercises to achieve the goals in each training cycle and avoid regression.

A CHAMPIONS DISCIPLINE

Brian: I can attest that changing a lifter's attitude towards training is easier said than done, but I am living proof that it is essential if progress is to be made in a recovery. This is something I see many other athletes really struggle with. I often try and impart the wisdom I have gained from Dr. McGill and urge them to hold back on their usual training regimen and focus on simple pain-reducing movements. It's always followed with "I'm not going to stop lifting because I'll go crazy/lose my gains/get worse etc." Or, most commonly, I can't start over because "..." or "I can beat this while lifting 'lighter' weight."

I would venture to say that so many people fail to regain their back health due in part to lack of knowledge but, perhaps even more sadly - their stubbornness and unwillingness to deviate from their usual training and failing to give themselves permission to heal. This breaks my heart. Their egos are simply too large to ever let themselves put the weight down.

You have to be mentally locked in, and fully committed to allowing your back to settle and heal. In one particular case, a few months after my first visit with Dr. McGill in 2013, while attending an athlete and coach instructional summit at EliteFTS, I had an experience that would have tested the resolve of many. To be clear, I couldn't have cared less what my powerlifting peers thought, or what I knew I'd hear from the many fans, friends and colleagues about my new program. I remember Dave Tate making a joke (he wasn't the only one) to the group that referenced my "Seal-Pilates on the ground," while I was working on the McGill Big 3, as everyone else was squatting, deadlifting and 'going big.' But, what he followed with stuck with me: "jokes aside, those following Brian's rehab... I believe this one ends with a successful outcome, this one could get interesting and one to follow for those who are injured." I was still early in my rehab stint, but this boosted my confidence even more. I was following the exact protocols required during this stage while teaching and instructing at this summit (a "giant" training session and learning weekend with many other great lifters). Regardless of who was lifting, I stuck to the plan I had laid out with Dr. McGill, indifferent to the background noise, and regardless of my ego. By this point, I had been noticing improvement and wasn't about to risk the progress I had made, just to impress those around me in a "gym" setting.

Sadly, many fail to maintain this perspective and are easily influenced by any buzz coming their way that threatens their path to recovery. Many would be embarrassed to be seen focusing on core work, air squats and 12kg kettlebell goblet squats while others were pushing serious mass around them, but not me. I could always rely on my inner monologue on such occasions to keep me on track. My mantra was as follows,

"I'll be back, stronger than ever, ready to smash every doubter and nay-sayer's face on the platform, just like I always had. And I'm going to do it with a smile on my face."

This narrative gave me permission to take things easy as my back settled, confident that in the long run, this calculated restraint was making me stronger.

CHAPTER 8
A GENERAL APPROACH TO GUIDE YOUR RECOVERY PLAN

STAGE 1:
GET RID OF DISABLING PAIN

STU: As we've established, all early recovery efforts should focus solely on identifying your pain triggers and eliminating them effectively.

Back pain and the associated uncomfortable radiations along the limbs can be wound up and wound down. Training through pain often winds up the pain sensitivity. It may also increase the tissue damage. The key during this first stage is to avoid any activity, posture, or movement that you have found painful in the past. This will allow the tissues to settle and the nerves to decrease their sensitivity. Allowing pain to aggravate in this stage is akin to picking a scab while it's trying to heal, or repeatedly hitting a body part with a hammer, expecting the pain to go away. Stop picking and take the hammer away! This sounds like a common-sense solution, as nobody chooses to be in pain. You would think everyone would do their best to avoid it. The catch is that many people simply aren't aware that some of the actions they're taking are contributing to their discomfort and inability to heal. The faster you are able to identify the cause, and stop painful triggers, the faster you will achieve a pain-free foundation. As you progress, you will find that any occasional relapse of pain will be less severe than before as your nerves continue to settle and adjust to your new movements.

The process begins with an assessment that includes pain provocation tests to create a precise diagnosis of the pain trigger. In my clinic, I test a variety of different postures, movements and loads with my patients to find exactly what it is that may be inflaming the spine. The majority of clinicians have never been trained to perform this type of assessment. It is not possible to thoroughly conduct an assessment of this nature within the 10-minute appointment usually allotted by a clinician for seeing a patient. The majority of injuries associated with strength athletes produce flexion-intolerant individuals, so this is the type of pain trigger we will focus on in this book. For the curious reader, or the athlete whose injuries don't fit this profile, a more complete self-assessment is explained in Dr. McGill's book "Back Mechanic." The clinicians guide is the more thorough and detailed book "Low Back Disorders."

MOVING WELL:

In Brian's case, as with many other powerlifters and athletes from a strength background, the assessment revealed that his casual day-to-day movement patterns included spine bending that stress the vertebrae and discs, picking the proverbial scab. Our lab-clinic studies revealed that the spine was most resilient to load when placed in an upright stacked posture. This posture, which preserves the natural curves of the lumbar and thoracic spine, is what we refer to as a neutral spine. When Brian would bend forwards or sideways, and his back would round, his familiar pain would return. This pain mechanism was triggered when getting in and out of a chair, tying shoes, and bending to the floor. In other words, his daily movements included a multitude of activities that perpetually picked the scab before it could heal. Teaching Brian the essential alternative to spine bending we call the "hip hinge," allowed him to begin winding down the pain immediately.

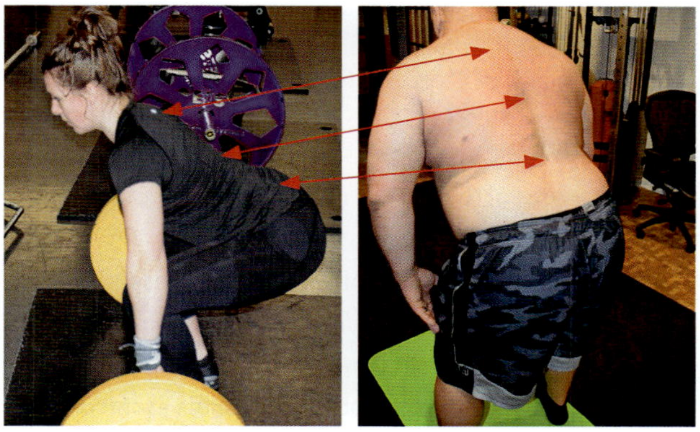

The spine has three natural curves. The strongest posture is when they are preserved. Top arrow: Cervical spine (cervical lordosis); middle arrow: Thoracic spine (kyphosis); Bottom arrow: Lumbar spine (lordosis).

The hip hinge: (left panel) Standing, suck in air to about 70% of full tide. (middle panel) Then run the hands down the thighs and the hands grab around the knees. The curves of the back are adjusted to neutral. The knees are over the balls of the feet. (Right panel) Now stiffen the back by pushing down on the hands through the arms. The pecs and lats are activated in the anti-shrug movement. To return to standing, keep the back stiffened and think simply pull the hips through, or, pull the hips forward. There should be no pain associated with this hip bending technique. Now use this technique to reach and flush the toilet, brush your teeth etc. and you will eventually use this as the springboard to re-establishing your deadlift.

MOVEMENT EXERCISES TO ELIMINATE:

Stop all torso stretching exercises. You need a stiffened spine to bear load. Pulling your knees to your chest is a dated and misinformed "cure" for back pain and should be the first thing to go!

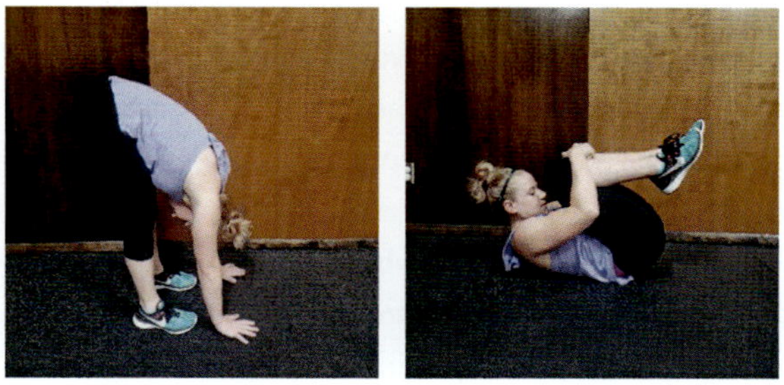

The silly stretches. Stop these and you will reduce your pain sensitivity. Don't add more hip mobility or stretch hamstrings- rather tune them to have "just enough" mobility and stiffness.These include toes touches, palms to the floor, and pulling the knees to the chest.

STIFFENING THE BACK FOR LOAD RESILIENCE:

Brian's program incorporated the "Big Three" spine stabilization exercises in a rep/set pattern following a Russian descending pyramid principle (four reps, short rest, then three reps, short rest, then two reps, finished). The Big Three exercises, as they have become known, are: The Modified Curl-up, the Side plank and the Birddog. This three-pronged stabilizing regimen involves highly studied exercises which complement each other and aid in creating a durable, healthy, desensitized spine. Not only do these exercises engrain healthy movement patterns and improve resilience over the long-term, but they have immediate short-term benefits as well. Our recent experimentation has revealed that the Big Three exercises provide a stiffened, bracing effect to the intricate muscle network that supports the spine, thus reducing the joint micro-movements that trigger pain, for a period of time after they are performed. This extra support will usually last for an hour or two. In the early stages of recovery, it is best to perform one session of the Big Three mid-morning, then again mid-afternoon, allowing for extra "spine coverage" throughout the day.

INTERVAL WALKING PROGRAM:

Also added to Brian's routine was a walking program based on short intervals. For him, it required a fast paced fifteen-minute walk, swinging arms from the shoulder joints, three times per day. He did this before breakfast, lunch and dinner. Walking is the best tool we have in the essential early training of the muscles in the frontal plane. In other words, this simple movement engages and exercises the core muscles required to counterbalance a recovering back, and takes some of the load off the body's rear muscles. A brisk walk activates the quadratus lumborum and abdominal oblique muscles, which are essential structural supports. Pained individuals tend to carry an unnatural tension in their shoulders, particularly so in the bulky strength athlete. Laxity is required in the shoulders to reduce spine load while walking, which is why we encourage a "jaunty" arm swing to loosen those shoulder muscles as you stride. This movement also enhances the storage and recovery of elastic energy in the muscles that criss-cross in an interlacing pattern across the back, further reducing the load on the spine.

Much to his credit, Brian was disciplined in executing the first stage of his recovery and eliminating his pain. He behaved like a real old pro as many cannot do this. They are encumbered with too much ego. He had stabilized his pained back far sooner than I had expected, and so, as I had promised, I invited Brian and Ria to return to Canada to talk potential athletic plans moving forward. My wife Kathryn, herself an elite international athlete, joined the Carroll's and myself for dinner at "Beertown," a great local restaurant that I take many visiting athletes to. We had a great social evening. Ria is fantastic and so is Kathryn. I think I said to Brian that neither of our wives have figured out that they could do so much better than either of us! In this department, we are very lucky. As you know by now, Brian wanted to attempt a comeback.

Ego: I will emphasize once again the role of ego as an impediment for pain desensitization. Ego for success is essential. One must disrespect the load enough to be assured that they will defeat it. They must have ego to defeat their heroes when competing against them. I see this when working with MMA athletes. Some athletes lose because their ego will not let them defeat the icons who were examples to them and their development. But this same ego won't allow them to start over, or back off. This is so important to heal, beat pain, avoid surgery, and prepare the foundation to rebuild strength later.

There are several reasons the rate of his recovery thus far had been a pleasant surprise to me, not the least of which was the massive injuries that had to heal as part of the process.

The broken and split vertebral end plate on the top of the sacrum needed to mend. Elite powerlifters, the grand old men and women of powerlifting, have had to callous their spines to endure. To reiterate: a broken bone forms a callous over the break line, resulting in a stronger bone when the healing is complete. Callousing a vertebral end-plate, on the other hand, is unusual and not as well recognized, or understood in medical circles. Strength athletes will often get a report from a radiologist that they have sclerotic bone over the endplates of their vertebrae. But the radiologists never see the person and have no context for what they report. The bone thickens with training sessions. Heavy lifting will cause micro-fracturing that heals, forming thicker bone. But my pioneering approaches to bone callousing remain experimental, and therefore those who are attempting to do so are straying into somewhat uncharted territory. I had given guidance to some athletes in the past about callousing an end-plate fracture and through trial periods, found several were successful following our specific protocol. All I can state in this regard is that we restored their careers.

Bone callousing: Our initial approach is this: Basically we challenge the fracture with a small load followed by four to five days of rest. The theory is that bone is a form of piezoelectric crystal, in other words the bone develops an electric charge when exposed to a load. The charge attracts other ionically charged minerals such as calcium and magnesium that build bone. Following the load with a period of a few days' rest, allows the minerals to deposit within the fracture and a stronger bone scaffold develops. The correct doses of load and rest are crucial and if this cycle is repeated over a series of months, a stronger callous should form over the break in the end-plate (the top and bottom of the vertebrae).

With Brian, we got lucky once again.

After a few weeks of minimal, but deliberate bone callousing loading followed by rest periods, he had progressed his training cycles to create a balance of stability-mobility and strength-endurance into his body. He patiently enhanced athletic abilities using the tricks picked up from our years of scientific investigation, coupled with wisdom of different successful programs throughout the world. These included the Russian approaches, documented by personalities such as Mel Siff, Jiri Verkohansky and Pavel Tsatsouline, Polish Olympic lifting techniques explained by athletes such as Jerzy Gregorek, Strongman training techniques from Bill Kazmaier, and techniques from the wide realm of martial arts training from many international colleagues. All of these people have been friends, mentors, teachers and students.

STAGE 2:
THE GENERAL APPROACH TO DETERMINE THE TRAINING PROGRAM

In order to reap the most benefit from Brian's story and begin to design your own recovery program, it is essential that you first understand the science of the neural, mechanical and psychological concepts that influence the design of a rehabilitation program. This foundation will assist you to make better decisions regarding your own programming and training techniques.

NEURAL:

We begin with the brain. That is the most critical part of the body when it comes to strength. What we perceive as strength, or powerful muscle activation, actually begins with a thought, or neural trigger, that produces a volley of nerve impulses in the brain that travel to the muscle. The denser the thought, the denser the neural drive or activation to the muscle.

This concept is much more easily grasped in theory than in practice. The masters of strength train these elements and harness their brain power to attain new heights in the weight room. The weaker athletes strictly train muscle.

Humans have more grey matter (the tissue that implies higher development) in the brain than our primate cousins. Like all of our bodily systems, this grey matter evolved with the purpose of aiding chances of survival. This makeup creates a fuse box that controls and puts limits upon maximum muscle activation. Another of its primary functions is to improve fine motor control. True strength training involves grooming the brain to override these natural limits on activation and control what can otherwise limit an athlete and cost them their ability to lift seemingly impossible weights. Strength athletes learn to subdue the natural tendency of the body to choose endurance over strength efforts, and instead, unleash highly concentrated amounts of neural drive and muscle activation all at once. It is in this "red zone" that the ability for super-strength becomes available. Survival situations are well documented where people have unleashed this fuse box to perform feats of Herculean strength. Consider a mother who lifts the front end of a car off her trapped child. She rips muscle from the bone and crushes her vertebrae. In these moments of extreme necessity, the brain chooses maximum exertion over self-preservation. The strength athlete must learn to summon this type of unbridled strength without surpassing the limits of breaking strain that destroy the body in the process.

Strength and endurance are two distinct athletic aspects and are controlled differently. The brain decides which muscle motor units are recruited, their firing rate, and which neuromuscular compartments within muscles will be the focus of activation. To get high recruitment and neural drive in non-life threatening situations to the muscle, the brain must unleash the fuse box and force itself to experience a similar stimulus to that of the mother desperate to rescue her child from under the car. The athlete invokes a flight or fight response. While introducing this "fury" into training, an athlete must ensure that in the early stages, the exercise of choice is low risk. The techniques needed to train this neural strength are explained in the next pages.

LIMITS ON MUSCLE ACTIVATION:

Most muscles in the human body span across multiple joints. While this interconnectivity creates movement efficiency, it also reduces the ability to create maximum force. For example, consider the oblique muscles of the abdomen. The right external oblique causes a right rotation, right lateral bend and some torso flexion. Thus, if only flexion torque is required, the excess bending and twisting forces from the oblique muscle can be problematic. In some cases, these unwanted movements can be nullified by other muscles, but this limits the activation of the external oblique towards the sole purpose of flexion torque. Think of the simplistic joint linkage found in some heavy machinery such as a backhoe. The long reach of the "arm" is an articulated linkage where the hydraulic cylinders (muscles) only cross one joint. Full power can be given to the cylinder. But if the cylinder crossed two joints, additional cylinders (muscles) would be needed to control the other joint. Here, the brain must limit the force. The challenge to humans is that our muscles often span several joints. On one hand, this intricate linkage is a beautiful thing that allows us to create complex and dynamic motions in multiple planes, but on the other, the more joints a muscle traverses, the less it is able to focus its power on one specific motion. This is a challenge for training.

The implication is that ultimate strength comes from training the entire body and integrating complex movements, rather than exercises that isolate one muscle group. Stabilizing some joints allows more force to concentrate around other joints effectively strengthening them. Some refer to this idea as "Farmboy Strength" or "Functional Strength."

Thus, the principles of joint stability influence the brain's ability to fully activate muscle. Let me explain.

CORE STABILITY AND INSTABILITY:

There are several components in creating core stability, or core stiffness. On the performance side, the ability to activate "core stiffness" is mandatory. This type of engagement is absolutely essential for carrying heavy loads, running fast and changing direction quickly, for example. It determines the rate of speed for movement of the arms and legs. There are those people who state they do not need dedicated core training because they lift and squat. Yet, when I assess their strength ability, I often find they are unable to translate their strength to sport performance. Pointing out their weak links brings them to the realization that training the core is non-negotiable.

How does core stiffness enhance leg and arm strength? Consider the pectoralis major muscle. It crosses only one joint, the shoulder. It attaches the rib cage at its proximal end, crosses the shoulder joint, and attaches to the humerus of the upper arm at its distal end. When muscles contract they try to shorten. Pec major shortens and flexes the arm around the shoulder joint at the distal end. But the same shortening also bends the rib cage towards the arm at the proximal end of the muscle. Thus, isolating the pec muscle in an attempt to create motion would not result in a fast, nor forceful pushing movement like a punch. If, however, you stiffen the proximal end of pec muscle attachment – meaning stiffen the core and ribcage, so it can't move, you drive your force through the desired linkage to maximize your results. In this way, 100% of pec muscle shortening is directed to action at its distal end, producing fast and forceful motion in the arm. This "locking and loading" is comparable to the way a strong and engaged core stiffens and holds the proximal ends of the hip muscles on the pelvis, producing faster leg motion. A loss of core stiffness causes the torso to bend when sprinting, resulting in what are known as "energy leaks" and a loss of speed. Some of the force that could have been used to propel the leg and increase velocity is dissipated into the bending torso. This example perfectly illustrates a universal law of human movement – "proximal stiffness enhances distal mobility and athleticism."

Pec Major is an example of a single joint muscle. It flexes the arm at the distal end, but bends the rib cage towards the shoulder at its proximal end. Eliminating the proximal effect with core stiffness directs 100 % of the muscle action towards the goal: to move the arm. Core stiffness was essential for effective movement.

Bracing: Finding the best bracing pattern requires experimentation. We begin by poking the fingers into the obliques lateral to the navel and lateral to the rectus abdominis. Then, instruct the person to push the fingers out laterally. The exertion effort is tuned to the task. It may be mild to control torso movement, or it may be very substantial to prevent the spine from experiencing micro movements under heavy load.

Other forms of bracing place more emphasis on upper torso muscle to create torso compression. Here, the pecs and lats are activated, compressing the shoulder girdle down into the torso. Sometimes combinations of abdominal muscle and upper torso muscle strategies form the best bracing strategy to enhance performance and pain resilience.

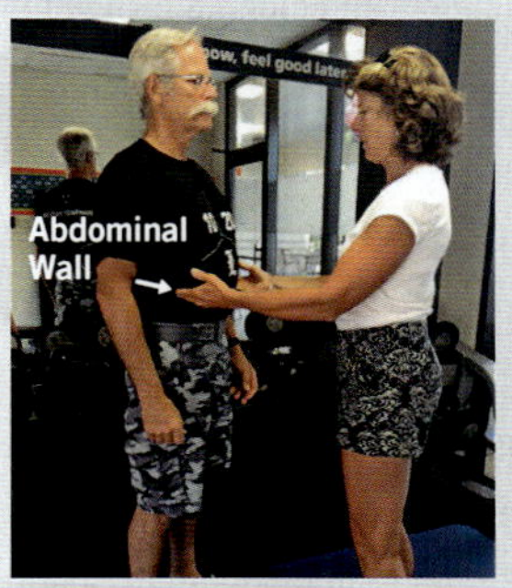

The abdominal brace is coached by pushing the fingers out laterally.

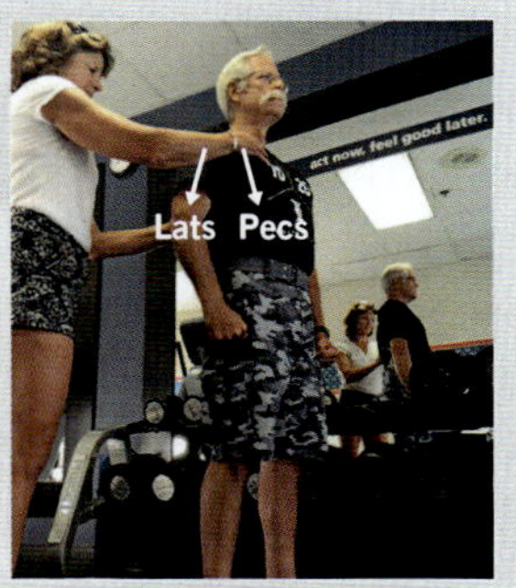

The torso brace is coached by cuing the pecs and lats to compress the shoulder girdle down into the torso. Various combinations of these efforts are perfected for optimal resilience and performance.

Consider a 340 pound NFL lineman, who has strength trained in the weight room using deadlifts, squats and Olympic lifts. Although his coaches believe he is well trained, the athlete experiences back pain that he finds limiting. When we assess his cutting speed – we find a relative weakness in his ability to take 5 fast strides forward, plant his left foot and cut to the right. What does this mean? Simply put, we have determined that this individual has a strength imbalance that limits his overall athleticism. The pelvis drops on the swing leg side and the spine bends laterally. He reports a twinge of pain. Consider that all of his strength training has been performed with two legs on the ground. All of the pulls, lifts and presses never trained the core for movements in three dimensions. Too many powerlifters experience this pain when un-racking a heavy bar and taking a step back. They fail to create sufficient frontal plane stiffness, lateral torso strength. Consequently when walking or running, the stepping leg side of the pelvis drops and stresses the low back. This deficit could have been eliminated with loaded carrying exercises that involve a weighted walk. The target muscles that prove most influential in this type of core training are the quadratus lumborum and lateral abdominal obliques. When properly trained and engaged, they prevent the pelvis from tilting and the spine from bending when the legs move. It's this sloppy tilting of the pelvis that creates painful stress concentrations in many backs. When the stress concentration at the joint is eliminated, performance is enhanced and the pain is gone. Good training always addresses the components that assist and potentiate one another throughout the body linkage. This means limb movement requires proximal stiffness and stability. Clearly, the core is home base for all strength and speed.

The second essential mechanism of core stiffness is the formation of a muscular guy wire system around the spine. Consider the spine as a stack of bony blocks. This stack will buckle and collapse without the stiffening action of the muscles to buttress the column. This stiffening occurs when the athlete creates torso "compression" with conscious muscular bracing. The effort of the muscular brace is tuned to the stability demand. Lighter loads just need a mild brace to control motion and ensure sufficient support of the spine. Lifting heavier loads demands mustering greater stiffness. Here the lungs are inflated to about 70% of maximum volume, and the breath is held while muscular compression is created. Further muscle activation technique enhances the stiffness (such as the "double cam" which is described later).

The third way in which stiffness/stability bracing techniques enhance movement is through the arrest of joint micro-movements. These micro-movements are detrimental on several levels. Micro-movements between vertebrae cause pain and inhibition of muscle force. But, muscle bracing adds a stiffening girdle around the spine to eliminate these micro-movements. These uncontrolled joint movements also can create tissue strain that are at the root of many injuries. Again, these are addressed by adding stiffening muscle bracing efforts.

Core training, and the employment of core stiffness are non-negotiable to injury resilience and performance enhancement. I know of no other athletic variable that measurably enhances athleticism so immediately. Although many athletes think they know the tenets of core and "ab" exercises, many of the classics such as the traditional curl-up or "crunch" can be quite detrimental for the strength athlete. We will discuss healthy and proven alternatives to these exercises throughout this book.

MINDFUL TRAINING:

Over the years I have had very candid discussions about strength training with several of the very best strength athletes in the world. I have investigated and quantified many of their successful techniques in our research lab. Every single one of these "masters of strength" discussed the psychological aspect of their sport and specifically the importance of mindful training: the concept of focusing the brain on the movements and the muscles in play to enhance "neural drive." Neural drive is a term for the nerve pulses reaching the muscle causing contraction. Thus, to create maximum strength, one must create maximum neural drive. There are several factors that can limit neural drive: 1) the strength of the mindful thought; 2) the ability of a neuron to carry many pulses; 3) the subduing of the inhibitory neurons along the neural path; 4) the efficiency of the muscle to respond to the stimulus.

The same mindset with 100lbs or 1000lbs – treat every load as equal

Vasili Alexeyev emphasized how he trained the mind and nerves, rather than individual muscles as a body builder would. Bill Kazmaier trained his mind to skillfully connect and control the various neuromuscular compartments of his back muscles. Brian Carroll treats every load the same, no matter if the load is 100lbs or 1000lbs (this was not always the case). Thus, mindful focus is essential. I do not allow music, or gum chewing when I ask an athlete to perform their lifts in our lab-clinic, as I believe these habits can be distracting and can compromise the skill development needed to add density to the neural drive. At the least, I insist on this in the early stages of learning new skills. I also assess the attention span of an athlete and arrange the training sessions accordingly into short blocks to maintain mindful focus. I am often asked about rest periods. For strength technique, the answer is that brief intermittent periods of rest are required in between exercises to restore mindful focus. Here are a few mindful training techniques:

Game Face: Jerzy Gregorek (3-time record setter in Olympic lifts) tells a story about a championship meet in the clean and jerk event and being on the brink of another world record. After successfully completing the clean component, he knew he was about to beat the previous holder's number and allowed an internal "smile" to creep into his physicality. This brief flicker of contentment slightly reduced neural drive and cost him the lift. He missed the final jerk component to complete the lift. Dense neural drive requires a grim game face with intense focus on the goal. Happiness will ruin the drive. You cannot smile and expect to simultaneously initiate your maximum strength.

Powerlifting champion Clint Smith still fired up after smashing an 800lbs bench press! Save the smiling for after the lift – or for your coach!

Fight or flight: The athlete is trying to create a high stakes scenario that triggers the body's primitive and instinctual reaction and in turn, prime the delivery of optimal neural drive. Setting the mindful state, the hormonal state, the blood pressure etc. are all accomplished by triggering this response. It is impossible to "see red" and feel joyful at the same time. In the crucial moment of competition, the former is the key to shattering records.

Flipping the switch: The great strength athletes, for the most part, are calm and in control. But every one of them has the ability to "flip the switch" into the state of "strength rage." In that moment, do not cross their line - it will not be a pleasant intervention. This is an ability that comes more naturally to some than to others but it can be trained and developed over time and through repetition.

USING SPEED TO REACH 100% NEURAL DRIVE:

I have heard trainers state that to maximally strengthen the back one should deadlift. We have measured many athlete's abilities and technique when performing a single deadlift: Olympic swimmers, rowers, track and field, ice hockey, skiers, American footballers, and powerlifters, among others. Maximum effort deadlift usually produces about 65 to 70% of max neural drive to the back muscles, even in these athletes who are skilled at producing 100%. Deadlifting will not recruit and challenge the back muscles to 100% of their capacity. (NOTE: deadlifting will create whole body strength and stiffness in a balanced fashion between the various parts that form the body linkage).

The question is, how can more neural drive be achieved? We have found that speed of effort (lifting in this case) is needed to achieve 100%. For example, Alexeyev would load the bar to about 30% of his competitive load, set the lifter's wedge and rip the bar upwards at high velocity, the feet leaving the ground and the bar travelling high into the air. (Caution when trying this one at home: realize that the bar is going to come down somewhere!) This max effort to create speed was his attempt to achieve 100% neural drive. He did not think of his training in terms of heavy load days and light load training days – instead he created high load and high speed days.

Another technique used by Alexeyev to create enhanced neural drive, muscle length change and strength involved the Roman Chair. Note that it provided temporary success, but is one I don't often recommend personally, as it creates a high risk of injury in most people. He happened to be one of those great athletes who won the genetic lottery and possessed that freakish injury resilience. Climbing onto the Roman Chair, he would intentionally flex and extend the low back while holding a heavy plate held with criss-crossed arms across the chest. Over time, his injury resilience did wear thin and he finally paid the price for this exercise when he experienced severe and debilitating back pain after his lifting career. As we've established, moving the spine out of its neutral position while under load uses up a lot of training capacity and must be carefully considered before incorporating it into a training regimen. Alexeyev's precarious exercise of choice is one of several examples I have studied that confirm that changing the lumbar lordosis curve under load creates high neural drive to the low back muscles. This being said, the cost does not outweigh the benefit for the vast majority of athletes. Instead, it's best to maintain a locked neutral spine position while under load, and call upon the other tools we've discussed to summon maximum neural drive.

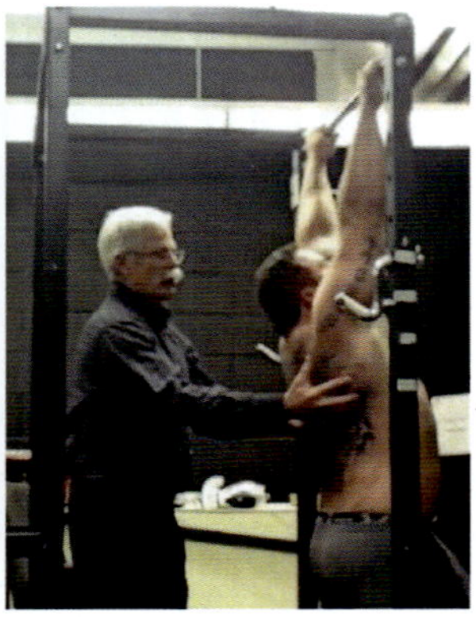

SUPERSETS OF 1 REP:

Another neural trick I gleaned from one of the strength greats came to me from Pavel Tsatsouline many years ago. Consider the athlete who trains pull-ups in sets of ten. They are training at 60% of maximum neural drive and will therefore find it very hard to make progress. Instead, Pavel restructured his training to do a single maximum effort pull-up, dismount the bar and repeat this ten times. This technique of single efforts does not create the fatigue of performing 10 reps in a row. Further, a single maximum exertion pull-up at 100% of neural drive is achieved every time. Curiously, the athlete walks away from doing 10 single reps feeling energized, not tired. By training in this way, a large boost in progress is inevitable and training under full neural drive begins to become habit. Soon, the ability to perform pull-ups for reps increases substantially.

(Note: this what Brian refers to as the "McGill pull-up. - Perhaps he should call it the Pavel pullup!")

CHAPTER 9
ASSESSMENT: TESTING YOURSELF – THE KEY TO DESIGNING YOUR REHAB-TRAINING PROGRAM

We are assuming that you have had a detailed assessment with a trained clinician following the approach from the book *Low Back Disorders* to reach a precise diagnosis of your pain triggers. At the very least you have followed the self-assessment of your specific pain triggers from the book *Back Mechanic*. That information will guide you on what to do, and not do, to wind down the pain sensitivity. Now we progress with the recovery.

Weaknesses must be addressed as part of a complete rehabilitation program. Although our focus of this book is obviously the spine, assessing proficiencies and deficiencies across multiple athletic measures is helpful to ensure progress and a complete recovery from one's initial back injury.

People are different. Age, injury history, movement competency, body type, and variations in fitness levels mean that no single training program can be the solution for all pained individuals. Whatever your goals, you will find that a good starting point in designing your best program is to follow these three steps:

1. *List the demands of the sport*
2. *List your current capabilities (and deficits)*
3. *Design a program to address the mismatches in demand and capability*

Here's how:

STEP 1: WHAT ARE THE DEMANDS OF THE SPORT/ACTIVITY?

Document the demands of the sport. (NOTE: there is a table to assist with this exercise in the last section of this book.) These may be basic demands (eg. pick up a heavy weight and put it down), or they may be specific demands (eg. stiffen the neck to enhance a pulling pulse). Catalogue the demands and organize them in order of importance and necessity to the sport.

(USING A DEADLIFT AS AN EXAMPLE) DEMANDS OF THE ACTIVITY - WHAT IS REQUIRED:

Balance: Ability to find an equilibrium amongst the body center of mass and load within the foot base of support. Ability to have a balance between fitness variables such as whole body strength, mobility, and stability throughout the linkage.

Motor control to steer forces through the body linkage: The ability to recover from movement errors and steer force through the body linkage to reduce joint stress.

The cohesive and synchronized use of strength initiators: No weak links – all strengths in balance - the ability to block excessive muscle lengthening around weaker joints.

Grip strength: Achieved through training with wider grips on bars/handles (more info later), NOT by using straps. This element is particularly crucial as low grip strength is a severe hindrance to an otherwise strong body.

Torso isometric compression with breath held: A stiff torso, which allows more strength to be transferred across the hips and shoulders, sharing the load.

Joint positions to optimize dense neural drive: Proper set up; setting the head/neck posture, aligning the ankle-knee-hip hinge etc. Some postures reduce neural drive.

Establishing a lifter's wedge: The lifter "pulls" themselves down to the bar. Constrained mobility (tightness) is necessary as the lifter's wedge is formed. Use cues such as "bend the bar" and "spread the floor" to create optimal stiffness and strategic mobility.

Hip extensor strength and spine stiffness: Power about the ball and socket joint of the hip is transmitted efficiently up the torso with a stiff spine, and then down the arms to the bar. There is no risk of the spine buckling.

"Tuned" Mobility: Limited mobility in the hips is controlled by the hamstring muscles. This mobility is adjusted to increase elastic force at the beginning of lifting the bar. Too much mobility (from over stretching the hamstrings) will remove the passive elasticity limiting the muscle tension. Too little will only constrict motion and prevent the full range required for the sport from being realized.

A mind-body connection to create the densest neural drive to muscle: An approach that comes from mental drills to create neural excitement and more neural drive output from the brain.

WHAT YOU DO NOT NEED:

Excessive Mobility: Stretched hamstrings, loose ankles, floppy feet, a deeper than legal squat.

High Endurance: Endurance is a double-edged sword. This athletic attribute is needed for an injury recovery program only to allow repeated spine hygiene moves, and for repeating other joint sparing movements with precision. The problem lies in the fact that training endurance means also training aerobic metabolism, which competes with strength. Therefore, endurance and the aerobic metabolism must be sacrificed when training to achieve maximum strength. It is best to develop an endurance base during the rehabilitation phase, but eliminate this type of work once the pain has subsided, leaving only the bare minimum that is sufficient endurance to allow good form during all daily movement. Walking seems to be a gentle enough activity that many strength athletes can incorporate long bouts of this activity without adding unwanted aerobic metabolism. Marty Gallagher walks his mountain for two hours each day and has deadlifted 500 pounds for 5 consecutive decades! While walking creates endurance, it also creates a frontal plane athleticism often neglected in powerlifting. Every athlete must refine his, or her own strength-endurance balance (more on this later).

Endurance is a double-edged sword for the strength athlete: Endurance drills create an aerobic metabolism and limit the number of motor units that can become fast twitch strength motor units. But there are a finite number of motor units and the strength athlete would want the maximum number of fast twitch anaerobic units. Thus, endurance training limits potential ultimate strength. In contrast, the strength athlete needs to perform perfectly executed repetitions. This requires endurance. The balance between these two mechanisms must be found by the athlete.

Pre-existing structural weakness: This is self-explanatory and needs to be addressed per individual case.

STEP 2: ASSESS THE ATHLETE: WHAT ARE THE CAPABILITIES AND DEFICITS OF THE ATHLETE?

Now, document the athletes' existing capabilities of the sport demands identified in Step 1. By this point, we have also cleared the athlete of any specific pain triggers, or at least have them well managed. There will be some athletes at this stage still suffering substantial inhibition and with perturbed patterns due to pain. To recover well, these people must be regressed back to the program outlined in *Back Mechanic* (for lay readers), or *Low Back Disorders* (for clinicians).

Example: Assessment of Athlete (specific attribute and test):

Isometric core endurance: Big 3 endurance test times

Whole body endurance with relaxation pulses: Push-up tests with 1 hand to elbow

Explosive speed: Twitch speed test

Grip strength competency: Maximum hand shake assessment

Mobility Hip and shoulder: Tri-planar assessments, pelvic rock, hip exam

In the previous pages, the essential athletic "demands" were revealed which become the content of the "capabilities" assessment. In this case, the demands are ranked by the coach for importance and then the appropriate tests are determined. Here are just a few examples using the previously selected deadlift.

THE ASSESSMENT AND DRILLS TO CORRECT FLAWS

Every exercise, and every movement task is both an assessment and a training exercise. For this reason, this section is organized to step the athlete through some movements and drills. Some will reveal flaws and weaknesses that need to be corrected. The flaws may be part of the pain causing mechanism, or the athlete and coach may feel resilient from pain. The drills remain to tune ultimate performance, in the never-ending quest to achieve the biological limit without crossing the tipping point. A few special strength topics are discussed here.

General movement screens are not appropriate for strength performance: There is no such thing as an ideal assessment for everyone, nor are general assessments, or movement screens appropriate for powerlifting. These types of diagnostics can actually lead an athlete down the wrong path and cause further confusion. Let's take, for example, the commonly used assessment of the deep squat to determine mobility. Failing to reach full depth is often blamed on stiffer ankles, and in these cases, ankle mobility corrective exercises are suggested. This can be problematic on two levels. The deep squat is actually more influenced by the shape of the hip socket and the length of the thigh relative to the lower leg and torso, two genetic aspects over which the athlete has no control. Further, deeper hip sockets do not allow a deep squat as the femur (thigh bone) collides with the hip socket labrum (rim of cartilage at the front of the socket), causing femoral acetabular impingement (FAI). The solution here is to modify the squat style rather than employ a corrective exercise that may ruin performance for a specific sport. Another common assessment is the toe touch. Scoring well in this test of mobility is actually a detriment to a powerlifter. A better score in toe touching will compromise performance– a lifter needs tight hamstrings that will contribute elastic forces to the lift. A lack of stiffness in the hamstrings and back will work against heavier lifts. In summary, scoring movement in standard tests is not appropriate for high performance athletes from certain sports. The assessment for the application of strength, such as in powerlifting, strongman, and Olympic lifting all require a specific assessment of the variables that matter. The ideal assessments for athletes change to reveal the specific deficiencies and capabilities demanded of them by each event.

Let's examine some of the assessments that count:

Standing core control: Knee circles performed well and poorly. Good core control is demonstrated with a locked torso and the only movement occurring about the hip joint (two left panels). Coaching cues to enhance competency would include torso muscle stiffness by pushing the fingers out with abdominal wall stiffness, and breath control. Start with small circles and grip the ground with the stance foot. Poor control is illustrated with reduced hip motion and more spine motion (two right panels).

Torsion control: While in the pushup position, lift each leg, then place the hand on the opposite elbow. A pass is awarded when this position is achieved without a spine twist. A fail is demonstrated by the position shown in the right panel. Notice how in the correct position the athlete's hips are parallel to the floor, as are her shoulders.

CORE STIFFNESS AND CONTROL:

Simply observing an athlete moving will reveal competency, or a lack of core control. This can be monitored during specific tests, or during performance. For example, simply standing on one leg while drawing circles with the opposite knee will reveal core control.

Front and side planks timed tests. Note the technique. No sagging of the body is allowed. One verbal warning to correct the alignment is allowed and failure is marked if another warning is needed or the athlete simply stops.

CORE ENDURANCE:

This is essential to allow you to train strength in repetitions with flawless technique. Hold the front plank, then both the right and left side plank. For calibration sake, professional hockey players need to hold all three for a minimum of 2 minutes each. In particular, failing to hold less than one minute marks an injury risk indicator.

Restricted shoulder and thoracic spine mobility compromise optimal positioning under the bar. The elbows are not centered beneath the bar, the head/neck is down and the torso is pitched too far forward. All of these will rob performance. B. Thoracic spine stretch performed with 10 second holds and releases. C. This thoracic spine exercise creates an immediate reset to posture that allows the elbows to come under the bar, a better grip on the bar to stiffen the back and shoulders, and a more upright torso to enhance leverage and the "line of drive" under the bar.

SUFFICIENT MOBILITY:

You are now understanding that too many lifters compromise their performance through inappropriate stretching and mobilizing in an effort to meet some mythical standard. *More is not better.* "Tuned" mobility, or sufficient mobility and stiffness, is the key to higher performance and injury resilience.

When training to prevent physical trauma and injury, an increased stiffness in the core and in the hands, proves very beneficial. When training for maximum performance however, tuned stiffness in the shoulders, hamstring muscles, ankles and feet should take priority. The athlete must decide the optimum for the event. For lifting, when descending to the bar, the hamstrings should be stretching to their limits. Some of the great lifters can only achieve a starting position on the deadlift with heavy load to "pull" them into position. If an athlete feels he/she could continue to descend lower after reaching the bottom of their descent with proper form, the hips and hamstrings are too loose. A set of tight hamstrings will produce the highest force, as the elastic stretch is added to the neural activation of contraction. Would you rather be working with a stiff and "fully loaded" spring, or a loose weak one? Do not try and stretch outside of the squat range. This limited hamstring mobility needed for lifting strength is why many of the great lifters have difficulty tying their shoes, and choose to wear slip-on shoes instead! A small sacrifice compared to the exponentially increased leg-drive that accompanies this inflexibility.

Some finite mobility is also required in the shoulders to rack a bar and effectively drive more upward force. It is important to note, however, that many factors must be considered for upward drive beyond the shoulders. Sometimes lack of thoracic spine extension mobility will masquerade as shoulder deficits. If you feel your upper back (also known as the thoracic spine) may be the source of tension, a gentle stretch, such as the one demonstrated on this page, can help loosen the area and free the shoulders. The key is to be able to comfortably extend each joint up to the position it needs to be in to execute the lift, but no further. We are attempting to safely increase the muscles' mobility without stretching them to the point of weakening them.

Assess the "lifter's wedge" for the pull and the squat to determine your own limits of stiffness, optimal foot width and turnout, head posture and establishment of a focus point for eye gaze.

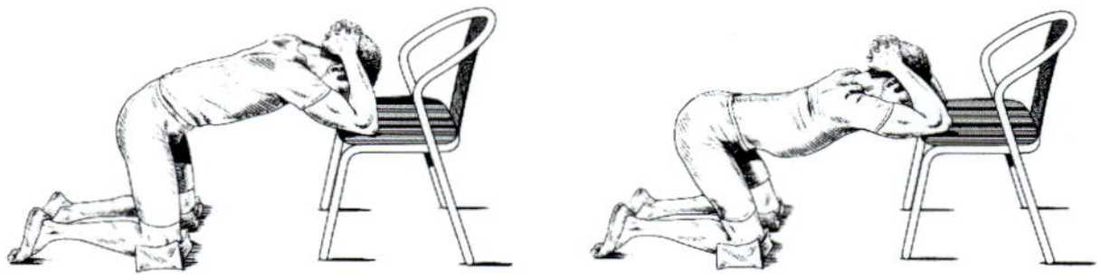

Thoracic spine mobility self-administered: Here the drill can be performed using a bench or chair. (left panel) The fingers are interlaced behind the head. The elbows are supported on the bench with a relaxed tone to the body. The elbow width is adjusted to create a "balanced" stretch feeling shared between the lats, spine and shoulders. The drill begins by gently pushing the elbows down into the bench with an additional force of about 2kg per elbow – no more. Hold for 10 seconds. (right panel) Now relax, and allow the hips to pull back towards the ankles creating an extension in the thoracic spine. Repeat this cycle another couple of times. Then stand up. You will notice almost immediate improved leverage in your lifting posture that will only continue to improve if repeated over time.

Bar carriage and leverage is improved by using the thoracic spine extension stretch (left panel) to reduce the "chest proud" posture from lower thoracic extension, and enhance mid to upper thoracic spine extension (right panel). Also notice improved wrist alignment to direct more "twist" and drive into the bar.Here the athlete performs the drill on a bench.

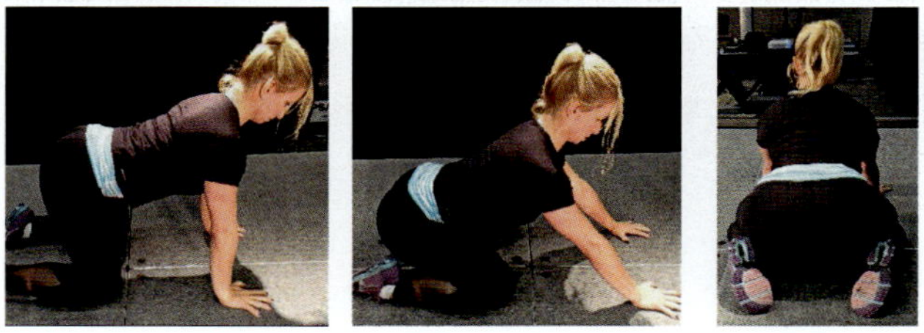

Observe the pelvic rock motion from the back and side views. Starting on all fours the athlete rocks the hips back to the ankles while trying to maintain a neutral spine curve. The break in spine angle will reveal the squat depth determined by the shape of the hip socket (acetabulum and femur contact). Adjust the knee width and repeat to determine the best knee width and hip turnout angles to achieve a legal squat. For powerlifting do not go any deeper than you're able to from this position. For Olympic lifting full depth is necessary. If a full squat cannot be achieved, Olympic lifting is not for you.

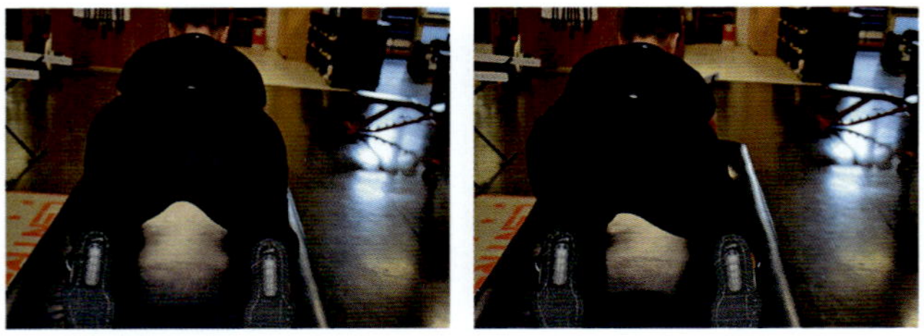

Next, observe from behind (left panel) as the focus is on hip symmetry, spine bending, and shifts to the right or left. Asymmetry (right panel) means that there is a limitation and should be followed up on to understand the mechanism. This may require more expertise (see *Low Back Disorders* by McGill, 2016 for more detailed guidance).

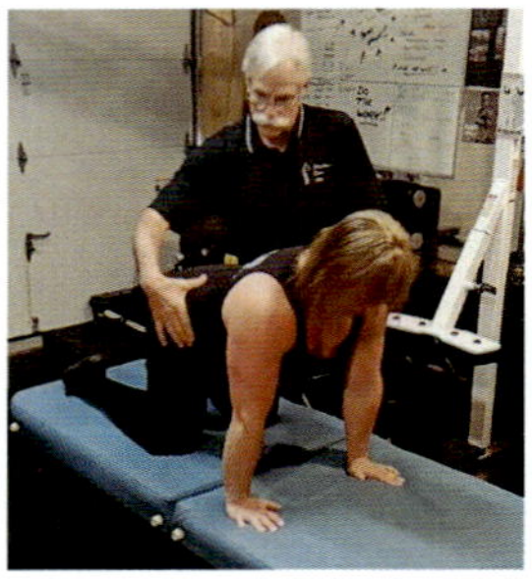

For the bigger, stiffer lifters coaching emphasis is on core stiffness and "pulling" back down into the squat depth with the hip flexors, while pushing the knees out. This creates a "muscle memory" to transfer to the platform.

The hip scour test is helpful for following up any impingements or pain sensitivities. More information is gathered about the shape of the hip socket and femur interface. The knee and thigh is guided around the hip joint in a circular pattern looking for the optimal squat depth and comfort for the athlete.

Three-time world record holder Jerzy Gregorek demonstrates magnificent hip, ankle and shoulder mobility, combined with perfect core stiffness and control. This is not ideal for everyone!

HIP MOBILITY:

Several tests reveal the lifter's natural hip anatomy. We use this information to match them to the appropriate squat style (such as foot width, foot/knee turn-out, squat depth).

These tests will reveal God-given hip anatomy and guide choices regarding pulling style, such as whether a sumo lift is appropriate.

So, you want to be an Olympic style lifter? Olympic lifting demands very special gifts in terms of shoulder and hip anatomy. The body must remain stacked under the load. If a person lacks this mobility they will either injure their joints, or fail to lift competitive loads. Obviously, this should be a flag for Olympic lifting.

OTHER MOVEMENT TESTS WHEN UNDER COMPRESSIVE LOAD:

The joints are assessed for pain triggers and mechanical advantages (disadvantages). A complete assessment of pain triggers (for example compression, shear, tension, bending, twist, and specific tissues such as disc, nerve, Sacro-iliac joint, hips etc.) is explained in detail in my clinical textbook *Low Back Disorders* (there are just too many to include here). For our purposes in this book, we will assume that most strength athletes' pain triggers can be associated with spine compression (or bending) under load.

The "midnight movement" test begins with an unloaded bar. Standing upright, pelvic tilt anteriorly and posteriorly. Assess whether any pain or discomfort occurs. 3 or 4 cycles is sufficient (additional cycles will generate pain in many people). Note if any discomfort is experienced during a specific direction of motion (for example from extended postures into flexion postures), or as a specific posture is reached. This information is used to "fine-tune" lifting positioning.

Here we use the "midnight movement test" to reveal postures and motions that create discomfort, or pain. Once the pain mechanism has been confirmed, the program is adjusted to avoid the trigger and allow pain desensitization.

ASSESSING THE NECK FOR MECHANICAL ADVANTAGE:

The neck is the supporting derrick from which all pulling muscles hang. The trapezius muscles connect the neck to the shoulders. An insufficient trapezius muscle defines the limit for a vertical pull. Thus, the balanced guy wire system stiffened to support the stack of vertebrae begins with neck muscles together with good mechanics in order to be utilized properly. Many strength athletes underestimate the importance of the neck, and suffer because of it. Once again, it is not about neck mobility but rather strengthening and stiffening the muscular guy wires.

There is always discussion about ideal neck posture. To find the answer for the individual, natural neck length matters. Those with a shorter neck and limited neck mobility, usually due to muscle bulk, do better with a "packed" neck. In contrast, those with a longer neck can use technique to generate a pulse to initiate movement.

(left panel) Those with a thicker, or shorter neck do better with a packed neck fixing the gaze on a reference point. (right panel) Those lifters with longer necks can create additional power. To achieve this, the lifter images the neck and head being set up tall then stiffened. The head and neck creates a very small amplitude pulse to initiate the upwards drive. Note the pulse is barely perceptible to the observer. But it creates a shockwave that travels through the stiffened body linkage to the bar.

Assessing daily habits - Gum chewing: Did you know that chewing gum might be inhibiting your neck flexors? This is because the continued jaw clenching associated with this habit builds strength in these jaw muscles. When a gum-chewer then tries a challenging lift in which their neck is engaged and their jaw is tight, the overused jaw muscles spring into action and compensate for the duties regularly required of the neck muscles. In addition, continued slack-jawed chewing may further limit their activation. Over time, this allows the neck flexors to become weak.

Neck pre-habilitation begins while standing. Posturing the head in a neutral pose looking straight ahead, place the fists under the chin. Touch the teeth lightly together and place the tongue to the roof of the mouth behind the teeth. Now push the tongue up and place pressure on the roof, stiffening the front of the neck. Gently push the fists upwards while resisting with the neck muscles. No motion should occur.

Do this with enough effort to engage the muscles, but not to create discomfort, or pain. Build the capacity to support your neck in a pain-free manner as you slowly increase the effort. This type of engagement should then easily translate in to the Big Three curl-up and further into lifts.

REMEDIAL NECK EXERCISES FOR RESILIENCE:

A healthy neck, able to bear load, is essential for all types of lifting. Any neck pain, dysfunction or discomfort will compromise the essential pulling muscles and inhibit the lift. The key is to build the neck rather than sensitizing it with more inappropriate exercise. Try the technique shown in the sidebar.

ASSESSING THE FEET FOR ADVANTAGE AND INJURY RESILIENCE:

Stiffer feet enhance the ability to root and grip the ground. This is essential when creating full power from the hips and the gluteal complex. Stiffer, stronger feet also assist with correcting flaws in the line of drive and the thrust lines which connect the load to the base of the body. This is achieved with control of the center of pressure within the foot. Centering this pressure and using it to "grip" the floor is actually the best strategy to adjust how the weight is loading the body when under very heavy loads because it is not possible to realign the spine, or hips. Here we assess the ability to spread the toes, create a "big foot" for foot grip and create more foot stiffness.

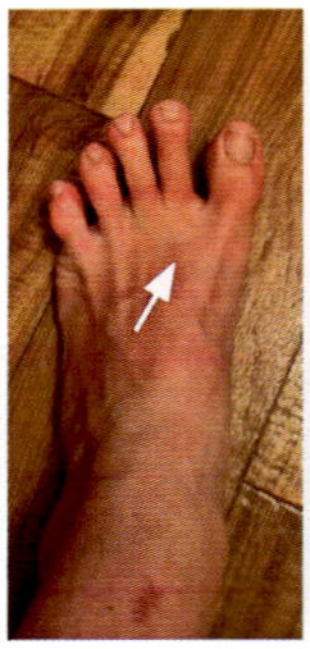

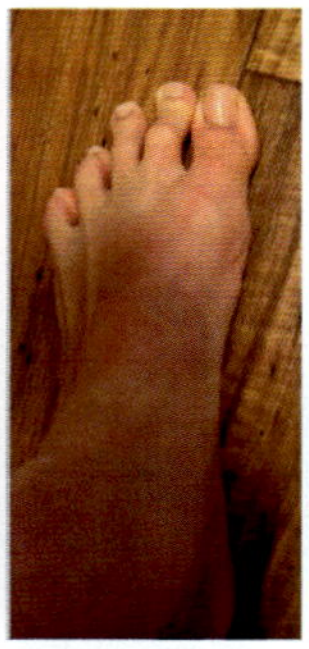

"Big foot" drills enhance the size of the base of support. This allows the lifter to migrate the center of pressure under the foot to make correction to the line of drive to the bar allowing the exertion of full power. Practice spreading the toes. Then grip the ground with the heel and toes.

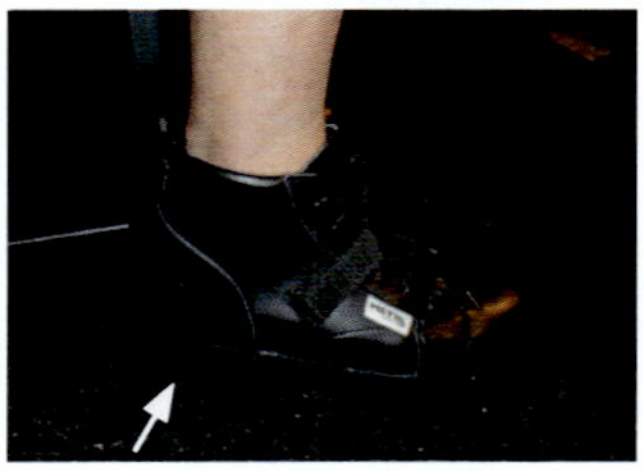

Bounce on the ball of the foot adjusting the stiffness in the ankle with co-activation of the soleus and grastrocnemius posteriorly and tibialis anterior muscles. Ankle motion is small but slightly elastic.

FOOTWEAR ASSESSMENT:

Another discussion regarding the feet has to do with the choice of footwear and the tightness with which the shoes are tied. Again, we respect the individual differences of neural acuity, joint mobility, and body segment lever lengths. Having shorter legs and more mobile hips allows the lifter to use stiff lifting shoes with elevated heels. Limited hip mobility and longer legs usually favor footwear that lowers the heel to the ground as far as possible (barefoot or ballet slippers). Some athletes have neural acuity that favors a tightly bound foot, while others enhance performance with non-restrictive footwear allowing foot athleticism to add control to the lift.

To assess your best choice of footwear and lifting technique, try the following assessment. Start with shoes with a low heel such as classic converse shoes. Bind them tightly and lift. Then loosen the shoe and compare the performance and comfort. Repeat with various heel lifts. Through trial and error, you will find your optimum shoe and technique.

Body segment proportions (influence style): Leverage for a construction crane is adjusted by changing the length of the linkage arms. Every athlete has a gearing ratio determined by the length of their body segments, muscle insertion lengths, tendon lengths etc. While these genetic predispositions cannot be changed, they should be assessed and noted in order to determine which training techniques best suit their natural gearing. For example, a long-legged lifter will lift more by concentrating a higher torque about the hips, lessening the torque about knees. A short legged, but longer bodied lifter will find greater leverage by placing an emphasis on a more upright torso posture and the assertion of more knee torque. A study from our lab about 30 years ago noted that those who deadlifted closer to world record levels had less back load. This was primarily due to their relatively shorter femurs allowing a more upright posture. This was a great leverage advantage. There is no pass/fail. Adjust technique and tune to fit the body type.

Lifter with shorter femurs and appropriate ankle mobility in lifting shoes (left) and flat shoes (right). There is little difference.

This lifter has longer femurs. The lifting shoes elevated the heel (left), reduced ankle and hip flexion slightly lowering the hips. Flat shoes (right) reduced the squat depth. This produces less back load but requires more leg strength. Flat shoes (right) increase back load.

Lifting shoes made the difference to a legal squat (left) and improved line of drive. The torso is slightly more upright, the leg load slightly higher and the back and hip load slightly lower. (right) Flat shoes.

This athlete is setting up for a front squat, but his forearms are too long to allow the bar to rest across the shelf created by the upper chest. This will result in poor form, performance and more joint stress. However, the bar shelf can be created with a crossed arm position. The front squat exercise becomes a tool to assist leg power development.

OBSERVE THE LIFTER'S WEDGE:

Once again this drill is helpful for both assessment and training. Now the athlete has a good understanding of their anatomy, mobility, stability, stiffness and control. These are refined in the wedge.

OBSERVE THE HIP-KNEE-ANKLE HINGE:

Flaws in the plane of the hinge formed by the hip-knee-ankle will limit performance and increase potential for injury. Buckling inwards (valgus) strains knee ligaments and is a predictor of potential ACL injury. Buckling outwards is a common flaw associated with those trying to protect an ACL deficient knee.

Another helpful assessment and training drill is the "Dan John goblet squat." This involves cuing the elbows so that they are the first linkage to engage when gripping the bar. Then spread the knees, and using a slight side to side waver shift to ease into a deeper squat. Caution: avoid overtaxing the hip labrum. Another helpful cue is to pursue a "spreading the floor" pressure through the feet, to reduce anterior hip socket loading.

If cues to achieve hinge alignment are not successful, try some "internal" and "external" coaching cues that facilitate "imaging" specific muscles and isometric efforts.

(left panel) The athlete begins in an upright posture, hands on the thighs, neutral neck and gaze fixed ahead. (middle panel) They descend by moving the hips back, as the hands slide down the thighs, gripping just above the knees very robustly. The knees are adjusted to hover right over the balls of the feet. The spine curves are adjusted to neutral. More load is carried down the arms as the athlete does the opposite of a "shrug." This "anti-shrug" is essentially a push down through the arms carrying as much weight as possible down the arms. Some athletes fall back onto their heels at this point. Use the "leaning tower drill" to move the center of pressure to the middle of the foot. (right panel) Now slide the hands down to the bar. Grip robustly and push the bar away. Try to "bend the bar" by activating the lats as they stiffen down. This is the wedge.

The leaning tower drill: This drill enhances foot athleticism to assist recovery of balance under load, together with aligning the body segments into a stack to increase load bearing. Standing tall, lean forward using as much toe pressure as possible. Then lean back using as much heel pressure as possible. Then go to hands on knees squat position and repeat. Enhance your foot athleticism and strategies to correct misdirected line of drive forces.

(left panel) "Leaning Tower" is a drill to correct the center of pressure under the foot to allow full power development and upward drive on the bar. Assume the "short-stop squat" and stiffen down in an "anti-shrug" with the lats pulled down and a neutral spine. (right panel) Now lean forward moving only about the ankles. Spread the toes and try to focus the center of pressure to the front of the foot as far as possible. While this is not an ideal lifting posture, it is a drill to help corrections in the center of foot pressure.

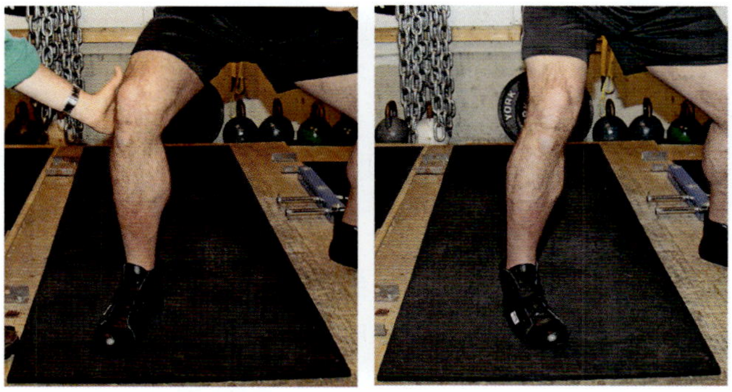

Correcting ankle-knee alignment: (left panel) The coach positions themselves in-line with the hip-knee-ankle hinge. (right panel) Buckling inwards can be coached with a cue placing the hand lateral to the knee and asking the athlete to push the knee into correction.

Drills to encode muscle memory into the patterns of lifters with knee valgus flaws can include cuing the upper gluteal muscles in the clamshell drill. (right panel) Place the thumb on the ASIS (anterior superior iliac spine) of the iliac crest, also known as the upper-most curve of the hip bone. Then reach with the fingers to the high gluteal muscle (the thumb acting as a target position anchor). (right panel) Coach the athlete to perform the clamshell while mentally focusing on stiffening the core first then activating the gluteal muscles. Then transfer the focus to the upright squat.

Dan John's goblet squat is a drill to practice "pulling" into the legal squat, and for fine tuning foot placement.

It is also an excellent assessment. Observe any asymmetries or poor hinge alignment of the hip-knee-ankle. (middle panel) The foot is turned inwards, or inverted. This is a common strategy used by those with insufficient ACL's. However, this results in forces buckling the knee over the foot.

The opposite is when the feet are rotated out, or everted (bottom panel). This adds more stress to the ACL and medial collateral ligament and is a predictor of injury to the knee and associated ligaments.

Corrections begin by adjusting foot placement to improve alignment of the hinge. Use this drill for coaching these finer points to achieve higher load bearing capabilities.

STRENGTH:

It seems obvious in strength sports and in powerlifting in particular, that "stronger is better." But there is a skill needed to convert the muscle force working on a skeletal linkage into force focused on moving an object. Observing the principles of leverage, overcoming sticking points, buttressing weaker joints, and training the weak link will define success or failure, and realistically, injury limits. Assessing strength is more than simply watching an athlete pull on a machine. Here are a few suggestions related to strength assessment that consider assessing the balance of strength throughout the body and the identification of weak links. Remember that "neural" power and wisdom will always play a part in any athlete's ability to direct focused exertions of strength.

RECOVERY FROM MISDIRECTED FORCE:

A skilled lifter likely already has several tools he or she relies upon to make minor adjustments to their movement. For example, recovering the line of drive through the body linkage requires an interplay between the intrinsic and extrinsic muscles. In other words, the small muscles responsible for fine tuning movements around the joints must work with the larger muscles that span limbs and the core, such as biceps and lats. Consider the example using a bench press. Suppose the person can press 200kg. You would say they're pretty strong. Yet this same athlete has difficulty pressing a single kettlebell and maintaining its "bottoms-up" position while lying on their back. They blame the failure on a lack of grip strength. The source of the failure may not have been a lack of strength, but rather, a lack of "strength wisdom." Try this kettlebell drill on your own while lying on a bench to test your current "strength skill." If you are strong, but lack the necessary communication between muscle groups, the lift will suffer from lack of motor control wisdom. In this scenario, the kettlebell may shake, or sway side to side on the way up. If this happens and you are unable to accomplish the press smoothly and deliberately, try the following single kettlebell floor press and roll.

Other drills to enhance bench press strength wisdom include pressing with the bandbell bar loaded with weight on elastics. Be prepared to only be able to lift very small weights.

Standing squat drills are similarly challenged with swinging weights suspended on elastics. Another drill to train more control is to use asymmetric weights on the bar. Failure to control the force is indicative of potential future losses on the platform. Learn feet control and "leaning tower" strategies.

No weak links – all strengths in balance: Powerlifting by its very nature creates imbalances in the body. Let's look, for example, at the difference between sagittal strength requirements and frontal plane strength requirements in a standard lift. Typically, since both feet remain on the ground for the duration of the lift, sagittal strength, or in other words the strength that drives a load vertically through the body with the pelvis and hips parallel to the floor, is the type that is primarily utilized. Frontal plane strength, the type that is required to brace the body when the hips swivel side to side as they do when walking, is not challenged at all. Over time, this imbalance allows a weakness in stability that impairs the capacity to recover from any lift that loses center. This also impairs spine stability by failing to enhance the lateral guy wire system. The proper way to train this imbalance is to add carries to your routine. Strongman

A test for strength and motor wisdom. Position the torso with only one half on the bench. Press a kettlebell racked on the back of the arm to get the movement and core engaged. Now, press a kettlebell in bottoms-up position. If the person can bench press 100kg but cannot bottoms-up press a single 20kg kettlebell without losing the bottoms-up, then most likely there is a lack of "strength wisdom."

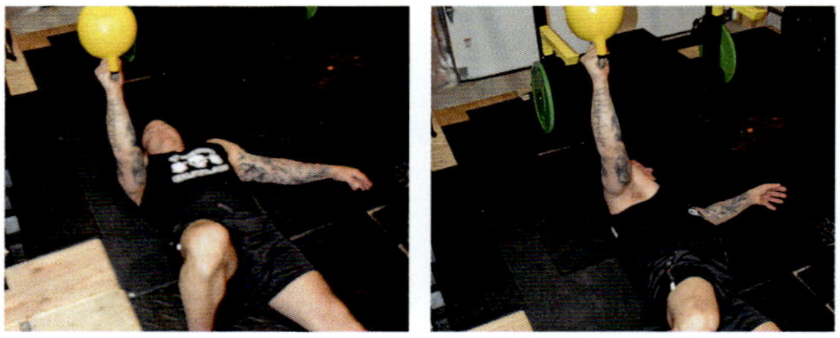

Here is a drill for those lacking strength wisdom on the bench press, indicated by the previous loss in the bottoms-up kettlebell push. (left panel) A good corrective drill begins by lying on the floor and "checking-in" to control stiffness. The core is stiffened, locking the ribcage and pelvis together. Here, the left knee is flexed and the left hip extensors drive the torso rotation. (right panel) The shoulder rotates to allow the arm to remain straight in the air and maintain the bottoms-up position of the kettlebell. This trains the wisdom of control by deliberately facilitating coordination between the larger strength muscles and the small intrinsic muscles.

Squat drills using asymmetric loads on the bar create "wisdom" to assist recovery from small flaws on force projection.

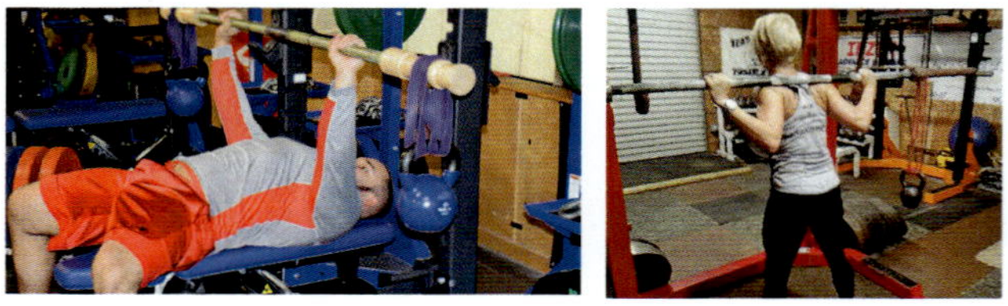

Make the load "labile" by hanging weights on elastics and deliberately creating some swing and bounce movements. Controlling this lability will add motor control wisdom and enhance recovery when under bigger loads.

carries such as the Farmers, Suitcase and Bottoms-up kettlebell carries should be in every powerlifters workout regimen and are essential to keeping a balance in muscle development and control. Assess competency in carry technique together with sufficient duration and load magnitude. A common "minimum strength" standard would be half bodyweight per hand. More on carries later.

GRIP STRENGTH:

Grip strength is an essential element when trying to transmit body strength into performance, yet it is one that is often neglected in training. The coach who teaches clients to use a mixed grip aka over-under grip during the deadlift is one of the most common examples I see of blatant disregard for the importance of this component. The truth is that a standard double-overhand aka hook grip is imperative when linking the engagement and stiffness in the back (particularly the lats) down the arms and through the hands to the bar. A mixed grip (one arm under and one arm over) breaks this linkage and weakens the lift.

When assessing grip strength on an individual, start with this simple test: Ask the trainee to grip your hand and squeeze hard, as if their life depended on it. Many do not understand this concept and have no clue how to muster full strength. They laugh, and try and squeeze with their forearm. This should be a whole-body task. Remember that the more muscle linkages you can incorporate into a task, the greater the mechanical composite stiffness and strength. Isolating muscles and body parts limits you to only a fraction of your full capacity.

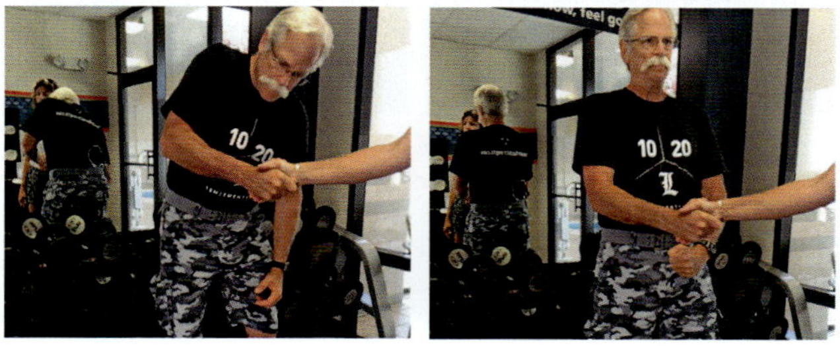

(left panel) The maximum "hand squeeze test" reveals many flaws. Many have weak outer hands with lesser strength through the third and fourth fingers. This can occur when the main strength exercises are performed with barbells and dumbbells. They fail to root pressure through the ground and harden their bodies. They smile. All weakening strategies!

(right panel) Now repeat the test after some strength coaching. Grip and root the ground, spread the floor, and compress the torso with abdominal and latissimus contraction. Stiffen the neck to create a "killer" mental attitude and appropriate facial expression. Squeeze the left hand hard with the elbow held against the side of the torso, creating a much more competent grip strength.

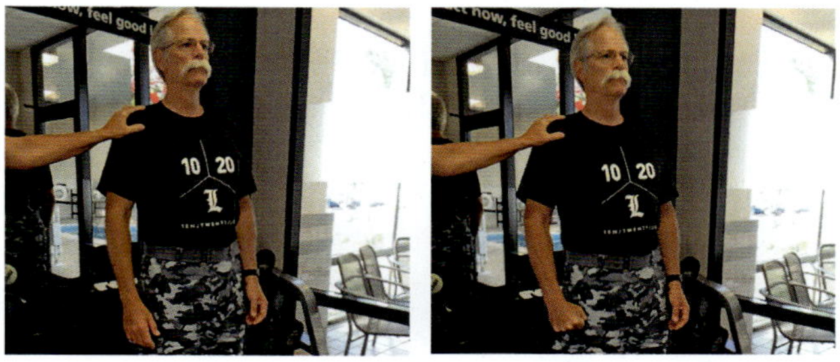

Ask your trainee to feel your shoulder girdle. Now slowly increase the grip effort to maximum and feel the contraction and stiffness radiate up the arm, into the shoulder and throughout the torso. This is how real strength is created. This method is a good opportunity to show the intensity and mind power needed for optimal strength.

Here is how to create competent grip strength.

(left panel) "The Lobster Claw" First, we teach how to use the strongest part of the hand. Make the hand stiff, reinforcing the action with full body contraction. (right panel) Now flex the fingers on the hand only at the finger/hand joint as if you were cracking a walnut. Use stiffness and high effort. This is the first source of strength required to establish control on any object.

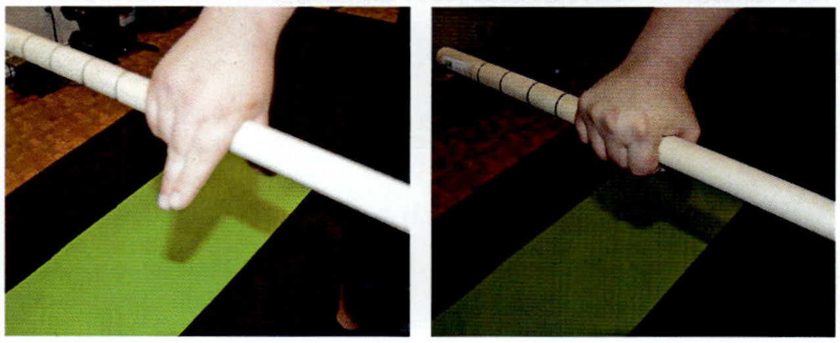

Now practice wrapping each finger, focusing the mind to achieve full grip power. Begin with the little finger, then add the third, the second then all fingers. Focus on each digit individually first, then combine the effort for maximum crush.

Now put this skill into practice with different grip drills using difficult objects such as two bare plates, and over-sized grips requiring isometric effort. Once those begin to feel more comfortable move on to dynamic grip work such as pulling heavy rope hand over hand. Over time these exercises will improve grip strength and the results will become noticeable when applying these newfound techniques to big bar pulls.

Grip and squeeze various objects focusing on the full hand and all fingers, while engaging full body compression. Use different object sizes. Here Ria is using rubber "Fat gripz" covers to thicken the bar diameter.

Squeeze two plates together to add to the challenge, then go for a good carry.

Hand over hand rope pulls build dynamic grip competency. Yes, I believe there were two cars on the end of that rope!

Now practice overhand grips on bars, crushing the bar, posting down with latissimus dorsi using the cue to "bend the bar." Here effort should be seen with the outside of the hand turning white.

NEURAL CONTROL VARIABLES:

Motor control to steer forces through the body linkage: As the load increases, so does the challenge to steer the line of drive through the body linkage from the bar to the feet. The exercises used earlier in this chapter (recovery from misdirected force) will help. Here are a few more drills that use instability of the bar or purposeful asymmetric loading. For example, bands on the bar are tethered to dumbbells or kettlebells and swung and bounced during the lifts. Other "tricks" include adding some load just on one side of the bar. The lifter will need to enhance stiffness and motor wisdom to correct and compensate for the asymmetry. This type of exercise should of course be performed whilst switching sides in between sets to ensure balance in muscle and motor development. The notions of maintaining "big feet," and "spreading the floor" are commonly used coaching cues to maximize results. Later, drills are introduced to create more balance between the small intrinsic muscles and the larger extrinsic muscles around the joint. Correction strategies should emphasize the ball and socket joints first (such as the hips and shoulders), and the hinge joints second (such as the elbows and knees), all the while avoiding spine curvature, choosing to use it only as a last resort.

Spend more time training skills to recover from minor movement mistakes. This will enable progression to higher loads.

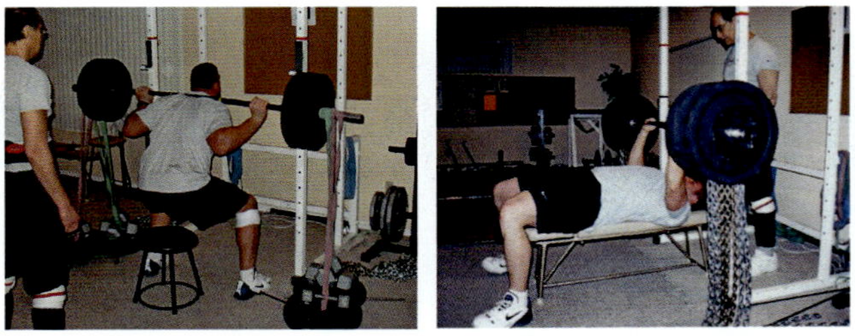

A historic pic training with Mel Siff at his place in Colorado – an NFL lineman using bands and chains to add instability to the load forcing the body to work in new ways to maintain control of the bar. This loading trains the body's motor wisdom to make skilled corrections "steering" the forces through the body linkage.

ENHANCING THE ABILITY TO CARRY NERVE IMPULSES:

Once the strength of mind and thought has created a dense neural stimulus, it must be transmitted to the muscles via the nerves. Assess where sticking points occur in lifts.

Here the "grinding" exercises are employed, enhancing nerve fitness to carry high density signals. Take the bench press, for example. When the sticking point is reached about two thirds through the lift, the motor strategy shifts from the initial pec major and anterior deltoid to direct the body's energy towards the triceps and arm lockout. At this point, mental focus is redirected into creating sensation of bending the bar using external shoulder rotation to put pressure on the outside of the hand. This is more of a latissimus dorsi "post" than a "twist" through the shoulder joint itself. "Spreading the bar" and "collapsing the bar" at the sticking point are grinding drills, conditioning the motor cortex to generate more signal and the nerves to carry them. Each mental cue involves a visualization of moving, or spreading the weight, or lifting surface that may not be visible to an onlooker, but is distinctly felt and controlled by the athlete. Each sticking point can be handled with a similar strategy.

Grinding drills focus training on producing more neural drive. That includes enhancing "strength of thought," enhanced density output by the brain, and enhanced carrying capacity of the motor nerves.

POWER ROBBING MOVEMENTS:

Most lifters do best by setting the neck posture in the wedge, and then maintaining it throughout the movement. It is understood that this may not be true for all lifters. Here is a discussion that will guide your technique.

Extending, or flexing the neck during a lift has been shown to cost some lifters their back and muscle stiffness, robbing their performance of much of its potential power. When a body part undergoes unnecessary motion, it loses its stiffness. Our research shows that a neutral neck position, or one that is in a very slight extension, is best for back muscle recruitment in most people. Extending the neck particularly at the finish gives some lifters a sense of "drive." The disadvantage is the shortening of the spine extensor muscles reducing force. Also, the bar is lifted to a slightly higher finish position. Finishing with a flexed neck reduces neural drive in some, but lengthens the spine erector muscles assisting in more force in others. It can also reduce the final bar height depending on lifting style. Eye gaze should be fixed on a determined point in front of the lifter. Coach the body to allow no movement, or deviation through the spine and neck once the load bearing posture has been set to find what works. But from an injury perspective, a neutral neck throughout the lift is best.

Some lifters raise or lower the heads before the lift is complete. This changes elastic contributions to extension power and can also affect neural drive. It may also influence the final bar height. Start with a neutral postured and stiffened neck. Then try different finishing posture strategies to see if you are enhancing, or robbing your body of power.

TORSO ISOMETRIC COMPRESSION WITH BREATH HELD:

Assessment of breath when under load is very revealing for injury resiliency and skilled strength development. Progressions to enhance torso compression involve training breath control and muscular bracing. Here's a simple assessment/exercise: Begin in a standing posture and simply compress the torso by holding the breath and engaging the abdominal muscles and pecs as well as the lats by pulling down. The cue for the abdominals is to push out laterally. Think in a sideways direction, not forward. Here, expel the breath with a slow controlled "hissing" to potentiate the compression. Next, fill the lungs with 70% of total capacity (similar to a lift) then practice quickly "sipping" the air in and out, almost like a controlled hyperventilation. Ensure the torso does not move. The breathing is accomplished with the diaphragm, not the abdominals.

In the next stage, load can be added to the standing compression by finding an immoveable object, such as a racked and heavily loaded bar, or in a pinch, the underside of a porch. Pull up in an "attempt" to lift the object without actually moving it. The cue for mental focus is to push the earth away under the feet. This initiates stiffening and discourages softness, or the "giving way" of a poorly stiffened region.

Practicing Okinawan strength: "sipping" the air in small, sharp pulses while building effort upon the immoveable object. There is no slack anywhere in the body. There is no relaxation, or softening of the abdominal wall. Training full torso compression builds more strength.

Nothing in the body can be allowed to feel "casual" while training isometric holds.

The entire body must be focused and hardened when performing these types of exercises. To an onlooker observing these postures, it may seem at first glance that the arm is doing all the work to pinch these two plates together. On closer inspection, you'll see that the engagement actually begins through the floor and invokes a stiffening of the whole body that supports and reinforces the grip action. Feet are rooted like the roots of a tree, both sides of the torso are in full "lockdown" position with the lats bracing the core and back, and with the head, neck, and spine braced in a strong neutral position. The mental focus is apparent in the "gameface." Superstiffness begins in the brain.

THE MENTAL GAME:

Assessment of mental aspects is very important for the strength athlete.

A mind-body connection to create the densest neural drive and the hardware to transmit to muscle: Mustering maximum strength potential is a skill and can be assessed. Stronger athletes achieve a mental state to create and send denser signals from the motor cortex, along the nerves, to the muscle. Density is enhanced when the fight/flight response is activated. Density suffers with a lackadaisical, or satisfied demeanor. This mental variable is actually quantifiable and we have measured its effects in several experiments that support this idea. Some lifters reach this competitive state by physically "shocking" the system with self-inflicted triggers, such as face slaps. Others can create this state with expert concentration and mind control. Watching Bill Kazmaier prepare using mental focus as he mindfully creates appropriate internal rage, the symptoms become evident. Sweat begins to appear on his brow, goosebumps begin to cover the skin and an unwavering focus and drive comes over his face as the mindful focus manifests itself and he trusts that he will not only achieve the lift, but destroy it. The great ones share this trait.

"Train zee brain, train zee nerves. I do not train zee muuuuscles."

Vasili Alexeyev - Most records as Olympic super-heavyweight

Eugene Sandow in 1904: "You may go through the list of exercises with dumb-bells [sic] a hundred times a day, but unless you fix your mind pon those muscles to which the work is applied, such exercise will bring but little, if any, benefit. If, upon the other hand, you concentrate your mind upon the muscles in use, then immediately development begins."

"I can, I will." A favorite quote that pervades Bill's mentality and expression of strength. Of course he has a lighter tone when not needing strength!

Bill Kazmaier – 3 time World's Strongest Man

FACE AND EXPRESSION DRILLS:

Simply observe the intensity and facial expression. Face exercises, to create an expression of hate and the want to kill, can be practiced in front of the mirror. Learn to stare yourself down.

The facial expression must reflect the dominant thought which must be to dominate.

Who will give in?

After a big lift and winning at the 2017 Arnold with All-Time World Record holder Shawn Frankl. There is no smiling before, or during a lift, but after the fight is over, you may see one come out – especially for the naysayers.

Consider metabolism influenced by other daily activity (white vs. red metabolism, or fast twitch vs. slow twitch motor units):

Assess the athlete's metabolism. Obviously, a marathon runner will never be a strength athlete. Consider first the daily training program. While working with strength athletes from a variety of training cultures around the world, the difference in commitment to manipulating their metabolism became apparent. For example, while in Poland I noted that the weightlifters avoided all aerobic, or repetitive movements. This extended beyond the weight room and became a fixture of their lifestyles. The group I was working with would choose to take an elevator rather than the stairs, even for one story just to avoid any stimulus that could turn a white muscle fiber into a red one. In a nutshell, this idea comes from research that shows that fibers can be trained and tuned to specialize in one of two attributes: fast twitch explosive force (which makes a fiber white) and a slow-burn endurance (which makes a fiber red.) The daily plan was to keep building a fast twitch anaerobic metabolism and avoid any activity that geared the body towards an endurance machine. They didn't risk turning a white fiber to a red fiber. The science on transforming muscle fibers is clear on this great ability to "teach" strength to a muscle fiber. This training also benefits the explosive abilities of the nerves of the motor unit associated with a specific fiber type, as well as metabolism in general.

The next level of assessment is very qualitative. A coach knows which players/athletes are explosive and which are endurable – notice they are never the same athlete. A decision must be made regarding the balance between strength, power and explosiveness versus endurance and ability to endure during a strength exertion. Endurance must be sufficient to enable flawless rehab exercise and then eventual strength repetitions. This "tuning" is what makes the great coaches, great.

CONVERSATIONS DURING ASSESSMENT:

During assessments, I have found that simply asking the athlete a few key questions can produce results that are surprisingly accurate and self-aware. Obviously, questions about injury history and pain mechanisms are essential. There are many other questions that will guide your programming. For example, I ask, "Are you naturally quick, or naturally strong?" They will know. Then I might ask, "Are you explosive, or endurable?" Hopefully they would not answer they are weak and endurable – you would have a long uphill climb ahead! If you are a coach, or a physician yourself, you will find that this direct approach will help you get a truthful evaluation of where the athlete thinks their strengths and weaknesses lie, which you can then follow-up through clinical testing.

Assessment or training? Every training drill should be thought of as an assessment. Go back to these drills and movements and look for improvement, or perhaps the need to regress. Continually hone competency in execution. Your resilience and performance will be determined by considering these attributes and in creating the balance between them.

STEP 3: DESIGN THE PROGRAM

We have now compiled a list of the demands of the sport (powerlifting in the previous example) and have also assessed the individual's notable areas of potential physical competence and deficiency. Now, we must compare the two lists from Steps 1 and 2. We are looking for the essential demands of the sport for which the athlete does not have the current necessary capabilities. These weaknesses become high priority in the training program. In addition, we provide some training drills that will enhance the foundation for pain-free and injury resilient strength training. In order to choose the best exercise tools for your own program, several factors must be taken into account, including personal goals, efficiency, injury history, age and fitness level. Tailor the program to be both practical and personal with room for progressions as you strengthen your body's weak links.

It is worth noting at this point that the assumption that enhancing one athletic variable will translate into better overall sport performance is not always accurate. For example, our work (Moreside and McGill, 2013) showed that training hip mobility through standard static exercises did not translate into more hip mobility in the required sporting movement patterns. Rather, the movement itself must be re-patterned. This means that most mobility programs must be coupled with movement skill programming to be effective. Specific strategies for program design are discussed later.

Example

Skills Needing Priority	Effective Exercises
Balance:	One leg stand, leaning tower, asymmetric bar right/left loading, swinging bands
Isometric core endurance:	Big 3, stir the pot, pushups with walkouts, bottoms up KB carries
Whole body endurance with relaxation pulses:	Slamball helicopters, skipping drills, grinder bench press, isometric wedge drills, thoracic spine extension
Explosive speed:	Twitch drills, strike/relax pulsing, Olympic snatch
Footwork:	Cross-chest goat bag carries
Grip strength competency:	Hand over hand rope pull
Mobility:	PNF* ball and socket joint work, integrate fascial trains
Appropriate sparing drills:	Designed to challenge the weaknesses

WORK THE LIFTS

The basis for the program is determined by establishing what the sport demands, then seeing if the athlete has sufficient capabilities to meet these specific demands. Train the difference between what the sport requires and what the athlete is most deficient in. This will create the greatest performance enhancement. This is in contrast to a program that has standard drill for strength, endurance, mobility etc.

*PNF: Proprioceptive Neuromuscular Facilitation

A final note on qualifying the athlete for specific training exercises and optimal program design:

The injury risk level associated with performing any exercise depends on the current ability of the athlete. The techniques described previously in this chapter will help uncover some of the current capabilities and deficits of the athlete. The intention is to match an exercise that helps the body meet the lacking requirements of the sport. Although there is no magical formula to guide this process – the best consultants are able to use science together with their own experience to know when, and how much, an athlete should attempt in terms of repetitions, load, and frequency of training. Other chapters provide insight on crafting this progressive training.

The following are pieces of wisdom that Brian and I have gained, through both research and trial and error, that will help maximize your training to target your weak links, and transition from rehab to performance training:

1. Train shorter periods when recovering from injury. Once the pain from the injury has been eliminated and an athlete begins to reintroduce strength training into their schedules, the temptation is to try to immediately resume the program and intensity with which they were training before. Resist this urge and be realistic. The early weeks back in the gym are crucial to reestablishing healthy, body sparing habits that will prevent future relapses while strengthening the body. Short but intense sessions are useful ways to introduce new exercises into performance training. Consider honing the quality of a training session before adding quantity in terms of load and reps. There is an exception to this truism practiced in the Soviet system. Add load and just do a single rep. Then, rest for a minute before performing another single rep. Repeat this sequence four to six times. Surprisingly, this method will help some athletes. Here, it is crucial that the injured athlete attempting this method avoid the primary injury mechanism. For example, if the athlete has compression-sensitized pain, which is common in powerlifters and occurs as the spine is loaded vertically, the load must be significantly reduced to lie below the threshold of the pain trigger. For these athletes, the focus in the early stages should be on maintaining pristine technical form during the single rep sequence.

2. Optimal training volume, whether for rehab, or performance, varies widely among individuals. Avoid adhering to a program in which all members of a team are expected to train at the same numbers. Remember, each person's baseline and needs should be and will be different. One athlete's "builder" movement could be the next athlete's "undoing."

3. A keen sense of physical awareness (or even better, a trained spotter) is needed to observe technique deterioration within a training session. Record every training session and review. When form begins to give way, this is usually an indication to stop. When fatigue sets in, form breaks down. When form breaks down, injuries happen. Keep in mind capacity changes from day to day and so should the program.

4. Plan training cycles. If the purpose is to reduce pain, the cycles should be 2 weeks in length. This ensures that progress is systematically monitored and the appropriate adjustments made. As the person moves to performance enhancement, try cycles of 3 weeks (for 3 weeks totaling 9 weeks). For example, try 3 mini waves – 3, 3 week mini-waves. Week 1: Load; Week 2: Load increased and/or volume; week 3 – light deload week. In summary, 2 weeks up and one week down to reevaluate and sharpen up the mind and body.

5. Consider your age and the mileage on your body. The harder you train earlier in your athletic career; the less gas you will likely have in the body's proverbial tank in later years. Of course, this variable is more highly influenced by the training extremes. If you remain skeptical, assess the people waiting for joint replacement – either they trained too hard, or too little. Either way, their

training age is older than their biological age. Remember training age, and biological age are much different. Know the difference.

6. Keep your goals realistic. You will never train a St. Bernard to win against a Greyhound on the racetrack, you will only get a broken dog. If you don't have the right body proportions and joint conformations, adding more load will only result in injury. Know that the top athletes have been touched by the hand of God in terms of their genetics! The wise person trains for health and once achieved, shifts to maintenance.

7. It's not where you start, but where you finish. We all wish we knew 'back then' what we know now. Strive for steady, continual improvement.

8. Decide if you want to train fitness, or train to be an athlete. Your health and injury rate will depend heavily on the path you choose. Athletes sacrifice a lot more than the average 'fit' person thinks, or will ever know. It's much more than just physical sacrifice and discipline. Those who have lived with an athlete, both in and out of season, can attest to this and know that it is a 24-hour-a-day job. It is a lifestyle. If you choose to be an athlete, be one 24/7, there is no other way.

9. Time spent in assessment will save you time in training (quote from Vladimir Janda).

10. Measure the strength of the great ones – There is a "minimal strength." After that has been reached, technique and skill matter even more. Make sure you have minimal strength.

11. Assessment never stops – it is done daily (quote from Dan John).

12. The guy with the biggest butt lifts the most weight (quote attributed to Paul Anderson).

13. On the Art and Science of training: "Use research wisely, but trust your grand-parents first." (Dan John) Few people have done more science and published more in the scientific literature than me. Few have rehabilitated more back-injured athletes to return to top level competition than me. I have made mistakes. I have learned from the successes and failures of other scientists, doctors and coaches. I will state that I would not have been successful without extensive experience in both practical clinical/coaching and in doing the science. There is a tendency for some to quote a scientific study, but the real wisdom and path to mastery comes from considering many studies and many real world experiences.

14. You cannot train on tough diets and tough workouts – you can only do one at a time. That being said, the time leading up to competition should not be an opportunity to experiment with either. Stick with what has worked for you up to that point!

CHAPTER 10
PROGRAMING: BUILDING THE FOUNDATION FOR PAIN-FREE AND RESILIENT TRAINING

Every strength athlete must possess the ability to stiffen the torso while simultaneously unleashing powerful limb movement. This type of synchronicity is developed by foundational core training, combined with pattern-based strength training (push, pull, carry, squat, grip etc.). For some athletes, athletic breathing and the ability to endure and sustain form under heavy load will be important. For others, holding the breath and creating torso compression will be the key. There are many other elements to consider. In this last chapter of Section 2, we present thoughts and exercises to enhance these foundational abilities.

On powerlifting and strongman training – Everything is a tradeoff: Realize that you cannot have it all. Powerlifting requires that you enhance the body's natural ability to bear load – this requires stiffness. A stiffened joint is a strong joint. That means that as a strength athlete, not only will you be poorer at yoga and other flexibility-based activities, but that doing yoga will increase your risk of injury. Yoga softens the connective collagen around a joint to allow pliability and mobility, the exact opposite of what is required for strength. The truth is that any elite athlete must forgo competence in one, or more areas of overall athleticism to optimize the specific skillset required by their own sport. The largest sacrifice made by the powerlifter on the road to greatness is flexibility.

Strongman athletes experience added challenges when seeking the optimal tradeoff. More endurance is needed to accomplish the loaded carries and strength tasks for reps. The paradox here is that aerobic endurance metabolism develops slow-twitch motor units at the expense of fast twitch strength units. The objective for these athletes is to enhance just enough aerobic metabolism to endure, without slowing the reflexes required for explosive lifts. It takes a special kind of athlete to master this balance. We have already touched on one of the great methods of achieving this: The Russian and Polish training systems that are designed to maximize single-rep strength involve one training session in the morning and another in the afternoon. These are very short, building to a one-rep high load exercise. Adding more endurance is done later in the training progression by condensing to a single training session of longer duration. This style of training increases an athlete's ability to succeed in multiple Strongman events by emphasizing the durability of the slow-twitch muscle fibers without overly compromising the fast-twitch fibers' ability to activate and release quickly for power production.

ESSENTIAL EXERCISES FOR EVERYONE

Building a foundation: Stiffness and torso compression:

Exercises that enhance training capacity by "prepping" the body for a lifting session are essential components to every lifter's program. Instead of choosing exercises that "use up" some of the body's available capacity, here we adapt the Big Three to create training capacity. Instead of tiring the body, these exercises energize the body linkage. Specifically, they stiffen the body, allowing it to support more load driving through the thrust lines down the body linkage and particularly, through the torso. Our studies have shown that they add a natural bracing effect to the core that lasts for a number of hours following completion of the exercises.

The modified Big Three are:

1. The modified curl-up
2. The side bridge
3. The birddog/quadruped

Our research has shown that the standard Big Three exercises were superior to other practices for their ability to spare the back while building muscular fitness and maintaining stability and control. They contribute to a lasting stiffness that acts as a girdle to reduce/prevent painful joint micro-movements for several hours after they were performed, in some people. Here we adapt these motions specifically for the strength athlete.

While performing the following "routine," it is essential that you find your appropriate starting level of holds, reps, and sets, then progress from there. Training times begin with ten second position holds. Use my "descending pyramid" model to guide your repetitions and sets. Work to build up endurance with repeated, short, isometric holds: this means avoiding holding times longer than 10-15 seconds.

Once you've mastered the "Big Three," you can progress to more difficult versions of these three exercises. As I'm sure you've discovered by now, each chapter sets a base knowledge in order to continue to the next. The "Big Three" are no exception. Your success in performing the exercises in the following chapters depends upon your ability to perform these basic three.

Core Stiffening Exercise - Five important tips:

1. You must practice these exercises daily.
2. If you have a history of back pain, avoid performing these immediately after rising from bed. The optimal time would be mid-morning to dinnertime. Perform an additional round of the Big Three immediately before any gym training that day. Most people are not fresh enough to reap the benefits when performing these exercises right before bedtime either.
3. Choosing the dose of exercise within a single session is supremely important. Generally, start with three reps per side (10 second holds) and for three sets. Build to five sets of these 10 second reps as you develop and find them easier to perform.
4. Bracing the abdominal muscles, rather than "hollowing," or sucking them in, during exercise enhances power. To brace, tighten the entire core, "tuning" the effort to reduce pain. A good cue is to place the fingers on the lateral obliques and "image" pushing the muscles out laterally.
5. Try and maintain your spine in the neutral posture. Create motion about the shoulders and hips, not the spine.
6. Maintain controlled breathing to enhance stiffness, then add power breathing. Purse your lips making a small hole for the air to escape. Then force all of the air out of the lungs making a slow "hissing" sound." And I mean all of the air. This will enhance torso compression for more power on the platform. Read Pavel Tsatsouline's excellent book "Beyond Bodybuilding" for more cues and tips.

The Russian descending pyramid to design sets and reps:

This very clever system guides the number of sets and reps to build some stiffness without getting fatigued. It helps restore the oxygen and acid balance every 10-15 seconds, preserving strength by avoiding a dramatic challenge of the aerobic system. I learned it from Russian masters and honor them with the name.

Typically, there are 3 sets. The hold of each rep lasts about 10-15 seconds. The first set may be 6 holds with a brief rest of a few seconds between each hold. Now rest perhaps 10-20 seconds before the next set. For the second set the number of reps is less – usually 2 less than the previous, so the reps in this example will be 4. Rest again for 20 seconds. For the third set, subtract 2 more reps – in this example the reps will be 2. Now move on to the next exercise and use the same descending pyramid to structure your reps and sets for this as well.

THE BIG 3

1. THE CURL-UP

The setup: During the Curl-up there should be no movement through the lumbar spine. When lying down on the floor face-up, slide your hands under your low back stacked on top of one another to support the lumbar spine. This position will prevent the lower spine from flattening against the floor, minimize the stress on your back, and position it for stiffening. Keeping one leg extended, bring the other up into a bent position, with the foot planted on the floor in line with the knee of the extended leg.

Curl-up technique: Begin by stiffening the abdominal muscles with a conscious brace. Elevate your elbows off the floor so that they "float" at your sides, your hands still under your lumbar region. Maintain a neutral spine (including the neck) and slightly lift only the head and shoulders off the floor, avoiding a "curl" forward. The sensation should feel like a slight lift towards the ceiling as opposed to a sit-up motion. It is important to keep the neck (cervical spine) and lower torso (lumbar spine) as immobile as possible. It is also important to practice deep-belly breathing during the exercise. As this becomes comfortable, switch to Power Breathing. We will add compression breathing later.

The curl up. Setup requires the hands (palms down) under the lumbar region. The elbows are raised slightly to not touch the floor. The abdominal muscles are braced – the level of the brace is "tuned" by the individual to create the appropriate resistance challenge. The head/neck/shoulders are raised slightly – movement is minimal. Curl-up flaws include an over-flexing of the neck and placing the hands behind the neck instead of in the hollow of the lower back.

Progress to Stir-the-Pot.

2. THE SIDE BRIDGE OR SIDE PLANK

The side bridge family of exercises is unique in that they target the critical, but often neglected, frontal plane spine stabilizing muscles. It is one of the few exercises that works to integrate the quadratus lumborum muscle together with the abdominal wall. It does so in a very spine conserving manner by keeping one side of the lateral spine musculature relatively "quiet," while the other is active. It also integrates the important latissimus dorsi muscle. This exercise self-corrects any existing frontal plane strength imbalance.

The set-up: Begin by lying on your right side supported by the right elbow, hip and outer leg. Both feet are on the floor, top foot (left in this case) is in front of the right foot.

Side bridge technique: Using the support of your left elbow, press the hips up off the ground until you are supporting your body with your elbow and feet. The top hand can rest on the hip.

After 10-15 second, roll to a front plank, hold 5 seconds, then roll to the opposite side for a repeated 10-15 second hold. Movement flaws during the roll include initiating the movement with the pelvis, causing a twist in the spine. Master the roll and eliminate this flaw. Lock and stiffen the ribcage so that it remains constantly in the same plane as the pelvis and concentrate on creating the motion with the latissimus dorsi muscle.

Once the side plank is mastered and consistently executed with flawless form, different neuromuscular compartments of the abdominal wall can be activated and challenged in this advanced technique by subtly rolling the navel towards the floor then reversing to roll up towards the ceiling while facing sideways. This should occur without the need to place the second elbow on the floor. Ensure the motion occurs about the shoulders and pelvis and not with a spine twist. The torso should remain a block.

Add power breathing while performing the side plank.

3. THE BIRD-DOG

This exercise not only targets the lumbar and thoracic portions of multiple major back muscles (the longissimus, iliocostalis, and multifidus), with the right technique it increases essential stiffness and stability throughout the core and back as well.

The set-up: While on all fours, position the spine into neutral, its most resilient position, by moving with subtle flexion/extension manner, in order to find its "sweet spot." Remember that a neutral spine should have a slight hollow in the lower/lumbar region and a slight rounding in the upper/thoracic portion. With the spine in this neutral position, and the upper body running parallel to the floor, pay attention to the rest of the cues. The hips should be flexed with the knees contacting the floor directly under the hips. The hands are under the shoulders. Appropriately stiffen the abdominals to control the torso and to ensure that motion will be focused solely around the hips and shoulders.

Bird-dog technique: From this starting position, use core control to raise the opposite arm and leg simultaneously so that they are now outstretched, reaching away from the body and running parallel to the floor. Do not raise the arm higher than the shoulder nor the leg past height of the hips. The objective is to be able to hold the limbs in this position for about 10 to 15 seconds. The Bird-dog is improved by grazing the floor with the upraised hand and knee in between holds and immediately gliding back out into position. We refer to this motion as "sweeping the floor" and it should not involve bearing any weight on either the hand or the foot in motion. Remember that the spine is locked while only the shoulder and hip joints are moving.

Muscle contraction through the upper back can be enhanced during this exercise by clenching the upraised fist. To further target the low back, gluteal and hamstring muscles, try pushing the heel away while keeping the foot flexed (i.e. the opposite of pointing your toes.) This will also reduce the tendency for "hip hiking," a motion that twists the spine.

When you've mastered the basic "hold and sweep" pattern of repetitions, it's time to progress to "drawing squares." When in "hold" position, laterally draw the fist away from the midline of the torso and concentrate on arm extension. The foot follows the same pattern as the hand also moving away from the body's centre-line but in the opposite direction. Specifically, draw the hand/foot out and away, down, across to the midline, and up to the start position. The square should be no larger than a foot (30 cm) in size. The upper extensors, rhomboids, latissumus dorsi and lower trapezius will be greatly enhanced by this simple fist clinching movement.

Prescription: Create a set/rep program similar to the ones you personalized for the curl-up and side plank program in order to maintain core balance.

With the birddog, there is a tendency for some to lift the leg too high causing twist in the spine. Instead of focusing on raising the leg, "push the heel away." You will also notice that this cue stimulates more work in the back, buttock and leg muscles. It also adds torso compression.

Progressing the birddog continues by "drawing squares" with the hand and foot – square the hand/foot out away from the midline, down, across to the midline and up. All motion takes place about the shoulders and hips – none occurs in the spine.

BUILDING BALANCE AROUND THE TORSO WITH THE "BIG 3"

Our research on different groups has shown that those who maintain a balance between the big three exercises in terms of sets/reps, have a lower risk of future disorders and better athleticism in symmetric sports like lifting. For example, if you perform the curl-up with 6, 4, 2 reps, then you should perform the side bridge and bird dog with these same numbers on both sides. (For example: Set 1: 6 reps both sides; Set 2: 4 reps both sides; Set 3: 3 reps both sides). You should progress these numbers equally with each of the three exercises.

When beginning the program, some of you will notice an inherent deficit with just one exercise. Try and work towards restoring a balance where the difficulty is equal among the Big 3 when performing a balanced number of sets/reps.

BASIC MOVEMENT PATTERNS THAT BUILD THE FOUNDATION FOR STRENGTH

Here we make some suggestions for building a foundation for pain-free movement and beginning strength training in patterns. These patterns naturally balance the ability to create strength while skillfully steering forces through the body linkage for maximal effect.

PULLING:

These figures form an example of a pull exercise progression.

TRX pulls are very tolerable in early progressions of pull exercises. There is no shear load on the spine, and very modest compression. The body is stiffened, shoulders compressed down. The hands begin in a pronated position and rotate into hammer grip as the handles are pulled into the armpits.

Sled Work
Pushing through the knees, the torso is stiffened. Do not look down, but lift the neck and lock the eye gaze.

Bold Rope pulls
The essential hand-over-hand rope pulling exercise tests and trains grip strength.

Pulling from height with "wagon wheels" shifts stress in the body for those needing it. This mechanical advantage also increases the tolerable load. Choose how you wish to adjust these variables.

Similarly, pulling off blocks accomplishes the same thing.

PUSHING:

After the half bench pushes and remedial kettlebell presses have already been introduced, the athlete may add sled pushes.

Always take a high grip with pushes. Create a line of drive with the pushing force through the spine. Never plant the foot ahead of the hip (This slows people down and stresses the back). Keep neutral back curves.

Anterior chain pushes
Hinging only at the hips, the full anterior chain is challenged and stiffened. A good starting exercise for those who do not have spine shear triggered pain.

HIP HINGES:

Always begin this class of exercises with a hip assessment to determine the depth of the hip flexion and how this is influenced by adjusting hip width. Recall hip scour assessments and the pelvic rock test. Some athletes coming off injury will make tolerable headway starting with hip pull throughs. Although more discussion of the competitive squat for strength athletes is given in Sections 3 and 4, the recovering athlete may wish to progress to trap bar, yoke bar, front and back squats. Some will find the kettlebell swing to be of assistance, but only if they pass the prone instability test for pain provocation. *(see Low Back Disorders – This should be administered by a clinician trained in this test)*

Pull through is a good hip hinge drill.

Kneeling band hip pull-through drill where bands offer resistance.

The back squat loads the back and hips and unloads the knees. The front squat unloads the back and hips but loads the knees. The trap bar and yoke bar exaggerates these features. Tune the technique to your goals and tolerances.

The longer the horizontal distance of the joint to the vertical thrust line, the larger the joint load and the greater the strength demand at that joint.

What category of exercise is the swing? In fact, it trains elements of the squat with a hip hinge, grip strength, stop twist and torsion, core stiffness, and aerobic capacity. The ultimate combo platter! But, be sure you pass the prone instability test if you have had a history of pain.

BALANCING:

All of the following exercises enhance whole body balance. This is an essential skill to help make adjustments to joint position when stacking the body under the load: one leg standing (eyes open then closed), "big feet" (enhanced with toe and heel floor grip), leaning tower, dynamic marching (with stops red light /green light and nail down the static posture pose).

CARRYING:

You must carry for frontal plane strength. A typical progression begins with suitcase, then progresses to farmers, and bottoms up carry.

Sheri Whetham shows the Kettlebell carry progression from suitcase, to racked, to bottoms-up.

Other strongman implements assist in carry progressions for frontal plane core competency, and grip training.

STRENGTH ATHLETE MOBILITY:

There are certain mobility exercises that will enhance performance in some athletes. Here we compare two flaws involving the thoracic spine. Consider the person who is "chest proud." Every time they need to perform an exertion they lift their chest, extending through the thoracic spine. This excessive spine motion may be sufficient enough to cause discomfort or pain, or, even the best-case scenario, will decrease strength and performance. This motion may be the result of years of habit, or it may be simply poor form and poor coaching. The opposite motion, in which the chest seems to return to a default "concave" posture, may occur in others where the thoracic spine flexes into kyphosis. Thus, we have two flaws involving the thoracic spine: one that contains too much flexion, the other that contains too much extension. For the kyphotic spines, I would suggest the thoracic extension mobility drill demonstrated in chapter 9.

CORRECTIVES FOR CHEST LIFTERS:

Here, we introduce a supine drill that I named after Karel Lewit. It teaches torso compression, spine curve control and power breathing. The result is a load bearing posture that braces for strength without "chest poking."

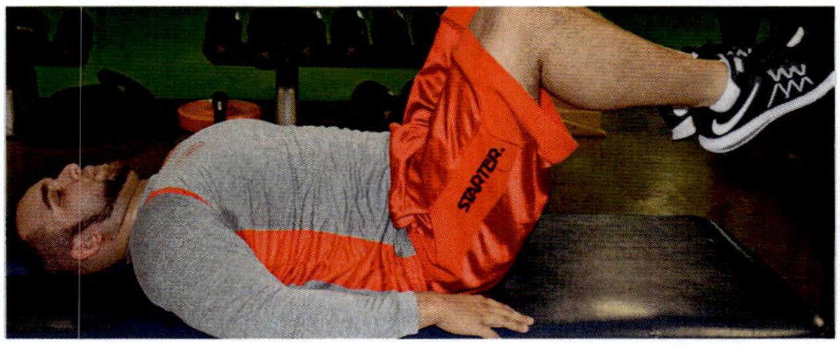

The Lewit drill starts with the athlete "crook lying." They teeter back and forth on the sacrum to achieve a neutral lumbar curve, which is maintained throughout the drill. Exhalation takes the breath to normal low tide. Now the drill begins. Purse the lips so there is only a very small hole for the remaining air to escape. Now, push every possible bit of air out of the lungs against the resistance of pursed lips. This pulls the chest down as the torso compresses. Repeat for a few breathing cycles.

The exercise is then repeated while standing. The strength losses of the "chest proud" lifter are cued with a technique of power breathing into torso compression. Here, the lips are pursed and all air is expelled from the lungs, pulling the rib cage down. Focus is also on abdominal, pec and lat muscles assisting compression and stiffness. Air refills the lungs, but the stiffened compression remains.

If you must do cardio...

Some strength athletes are compelled to do cardio training. If you must do cardio, skipping can be very helpful. Focus is placed on a stiff torso and creating a "tuned spring" within the body. Think of staying tight with a minimal, sharp wrist pulse with each rope turn. Boxers have found the great benefit of this style of skipping for years.

EXAMPLE PROGRAM:

Brian gives his program in the next section. However, here is a brief listing of a generic program that you could use as a start.

1) Reducing pain sensitivity:
- a. Practice spine sparing movements: Hip hinge squat
- b. Big 3: Descending pyramids of 10 second holds – 5 reps on the right then the left, 3 reps on the right then the left, 1 rep on the right, then the left
- c. Hip, shoulder, thoracic spine mobility
- d. Interval walking: walk 3 times per day, 15 minutes each. Progress to monster walks, backwards, uphill, then forward walks

2) Building a foundation for pain-free training:
- a. Warmup
- b. Push: Standing pushup on barbell rack
- c. Pull: TRX stiff back pulls
- d. Carry: Kettlebell suitcase carry, then bottoms up carry
- e. Lifts: Hip hinge pull-throughs

CHAPTER 10

SECTION THREE

BRIAN'S PROGRAM AND PROGRESS TIMELINE

This section provides the inside story of rebuilding a spine and the reprogramming of an athlete, complete with progressive sequences. Day to day and week to week progress is marked with personal messages and comments as Brian not only regained his strength, but exceeded his best lifts prior to injury. This personal story gives context to the "textbook" ideals of programming provided in the previous section.

CHAPTER 11
THE RE-INVENTING OF A STRENGTH ATHLETE

BRIAN:

In May of 2013, I hit the ground running with new life when I returned to Florida. My eyes were now opened to how badly I had treated my body for years. It was as if I learned a brand new subject in school. I got off the plane from Canada confident that I had found a start to a solution. But what I found was that my visit with Dr. McGill had provided much more than that.

I had a plan, a new sense of vigor and determination. I already felt more resilient within a couple of days of moving well and allowing my nerves to settle, and that small sense of relief provided me with a with a great deal of motivation and momentum to roll forward. This chapter is organized into blog posts, training logs, commentaries and a few breakout boxes. They follow the progression of time over the two years from being pain-free to regaining competitive strength.

BLOG POST: JULY 20, 2013

"I have been cleared to start lifting again, but proceed ahead with caution as the areas continue to callous and heal with adequate time between sessions. I will take my time with strength progressions, as I slowly make my way back to heavy poundage. I will know more about how I'm progressing in stage 3 in the next couple months, with plans to lift at the Arnold XPC finals in March of 2014."*

*Bone callous the fractured sacrum following McGill's protocol

COMMENTARY AUGUST 2013:
PROGRAM ADJUSTMENTS

My training split going forward was adjusted and looked this way as I made my way back to ultimate performance: I had this split divided up into 3 main days with 1 extra recovery day. I refer to this training split as "Combo day"- combination of squat and deadlift on one day. The traditional 3 day split with day 1 squat, day 2 bench, and day 3 deadlift, only leaves a few days between your squat and deadlift day. Having to turn around and squat again as your previous week ends with deadlift, can be hard on the body. This is especially true for those with a higher lifting age and years of damage to deal with. The weeks began to look like this:

Saturday: Day 1- Squat and deadlift
Sunday: Day off- 24hr to recover
Monday: Day 2- Bench press
Tuesday: Day Off- 24hr to recover
Wednesday: Day 3- Assistance for squat and deadlift
Thursday: Day off- 24hr to recover
Friday: Day 4 - Fluff & buff - this was a day where I would do extra core work and would button up some loose ends: Hip and thoracic spine mobility were a focus along with flushing blood around in my muscles (getting a pump), sled drags/pushes for extra work etc. Everything was extremely light and fast with more of a focus on recovery than anything else.

A note on phase 3 (returning to ultimate performance): I started completely over with ONLY the unloaded bar as directed – which was a mere 45-55lbs on each lift. Keep in mind, just 6 months earlier in March 2013, I squatted over 1100lbs in competition. There was no more room for ego and every lift was a gift, another chance, as I respected the unloaded bar as much as if it were my next All-Time World Record attempt. Even while in earlier stages of rehab, when I progressed with goblet squats, it was with the lightest kettlebell (12kg) in the gym. I reset completely as a novice lifter. As my training split evolved and my body allowed progressions, I returned to the competition lifts in their competition form (i.e. from block pulls to pulls from the floor).

At EliteFTS HQ on the comeback trail! Finally pulling over 400lbs off the blocks.

COMMENTARY SEPTEMBER 2013:
NEW GOALS

Moving forward as a powerlifter once again, I set my sights on the Arnold 2014 competition and I chose to push ahead and return to ultimate performance. This would be less than 1 year (only 10 months) after seeing Stu and getting my plan in place, then implementing it. I utilized the principles explained in earlier sections, but this time around, I set specific boundaries for my strength training and incorporated the wealth of knowledge obtained from Dr. McGill. In the past, these rules had been loosely followed at best during my less cerebral approach but now an athlete 24/7.

Then, adding in the stimuli of man-handling respectable bar-load once again, I catapulted in mass to over 295lbs, from a previous high of 285lbs! My size got away from me!

COMMENTARY OCTOBER 2013:
BACK TO WATERLOO

I went back to Waterloo at the end of October 2013 for a 6 month follow-up. The meeting went extremely well and Dr. McGill was very surprised that I had recovered as well as I did. He repeated his exams, testing, assessment and such to follow up and compare. Stu then showed me some "old-pro" tricks (picked up from the many greats) and shared technique cues on how to remain resilient as we discussed proceeding ahead with all cylinders firing.

As you can see, there was quite a difference in size and mass between the first 2 visits: April 2013 and October 2013. This was good and bad as you will read about soon.

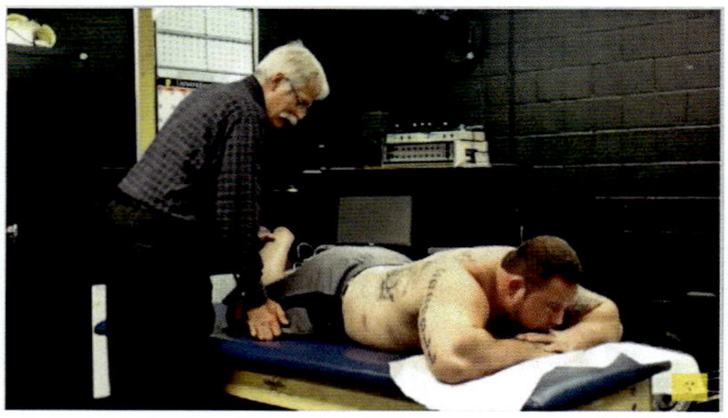

COMMENTARY NOVEMBER 2013:
THE NEXT 5 TRAINING WEEKS AFTER SECOND WATERLOO TRIP

I barreled ahead toward the lofty goal of winning the 2014 Arnold competition as my strength training kicked up. Strength and form progressed like clockwork, for the most part. My squat confidence and power returned almost immediately as my core foundation training was paying off big-time. I was more stable and locked-in than ever. My bench press came back quicker than expected with the added muscle and size, but something was missing. My deadlift didn't feel quite right. It felt slow, unathletic and slightly out of tune as I had a hard time getting into the perfect wedge position from the floor.

I wrapped up my offseason trial run with a confidence building and encouraging test day of a 750lbs squat, 500lbs bench and a 600lbs deadlift. I was in a good position to make the transition to a 10-week peaking cycle and I had a lot of positive momentum heading toward the "true" test.

COMMENTARY JANUARY 2014:
10 WEEK COUNTDOWN TO THE ARNOLD

Moving forward with my pre-contest training, it started off great. I smashed weights on the squat, even back over 1000lbs pretty damn quickly, certainly too quickly looking back. With the added mass, my bench press was better than ever and I was quickly handling in the 600's and 700's with extreme ease. But once again, the issue was the deadlift – the one lift that was the most impacted by my "career ending" injury. It was slow to respond which was frustrating.

COMMENTARY MARCH 2014:
ARNOLD 2014 MEET AND MAKING A SMART DECISION – NO MORE EGO AND ANOTHER LESSON LEARNED

A lot of eyes were on me leading into this meet as I had logged my whole comeback and put out a few videos with Stu and me pertaining to both our first and second evaluation. I had been vocal and an open book about my comeback process, with credit going to Dr. McGill, and I knew (I saw and heard) I had a lot of people wanting me to succeed as well as many wanting to see me fail.

I was indifferent and here is why: When people want me to fail, or doubt me it motivates me to an extreme point that I can't describe. But, in my experience, the wise man adheres to the following: You can let your naysayers fuel you and push you harder to motivate you going forward in YOUR goals, but do NOT let them determine your goals, nor change your approach, or direction.

When people are ONLY fueled by doubters, they end up like a dog rabidly chasing a car without a plan. They want to prove people wrong so badly that they let the "haters" determine their path, instead of properly channeling the motivation into helping achieve their goals.

They let it become their path and end up spinning their wheels and ultimately, letting their naysayers WIN. Don't be this guy, don't let others who don't have your best interests at heart influence you in this way. Use it as fuel for your tank, not your GPS navigation.

COMMENTARY MARCH 2014:
MEET DAY

As it was time to lift, I started my comprehensive warm-up and was on the ground birddogging. Giggles, questions, and a lot of distractions were surrounding me. But you know what – look around the strength world now. A lot of these "McGill movements" are now "common place" where prior, they were scoffed at and made fun of. Trust me, 4 years ago, nobody was doing this sort of stuff at a meet. They were too busy foam rolling, stretching, or simply not warming up at all!

People also took notice as I came into this meet HUGE, the biggest I'd ever been and weighed 295lbs on meet day, after cutting down making the 275lbs class. I was in "good shape" and felt confident. Most people hadn't seen me in a year, as I hadn't competed and had been more concerned about myself and my health.

COMMENTARY MARCH 2014:
THE YEAR AFTER LIMPING THROUGH AND FINISHING SECOND PLACE OVERALL

The meet started off pretty well – it was great to be back, but admittedly, I was quite nervous and conservative. I came out of the squat with an easy 1070lbs lift, which was a step in the right direction, although not a record, I was back on the board. Bench press went exceptionally - I benched my best ever with an 825lbs press. After the bench press, I was handily winning not just my return back to competition, but the meet as a whole. This was great!

An hour or two passed after the bench press and I started to notice my back tightening just a little bit, much like it would during the first and second stage of rehab when I would push it too much.

I figured it was just from the excessive extension during the bench press and the slight flexion and extension that takes place on the squat. I thought it would settle.

As minutes passed and eventually another hour, I started to feel worse. I still had to deadlift and the more I thought about it, the more it became clear to me that I needed to really think about what I was going to do next because it would really impact my next year of lifting, and in my case - my life! I needed to be very, very careful not to make any more emotional decisions as I had in the past.

COMMENTARY MARCH 2014:
PULLING OUT – WAS IT A MARK OF FAILURE OR PROFESSIONAL WISDOM?

As I got ready to deadlift, I could feel that it wasn't going to be wise to proceed ahead. I practiced my wedge, after doing my usual preparation work because I had cooled down a bit. I even used a few tricks that I'd learned from Dr. McGill and my experience in training when my back would be a little grumpy. Some light traction was at times useful- hanging from a bar between sets of deadlifts in a "pull-up" position, some pulsing birddogs to get good hip extension, etc. Unfortunately, nothing made it feel any better – actually worse. Nothing felt right and my back was not happy. I wrestled with this for a couple of minutes and then knew what the right choice was, even if just "one little" 700lbs deadlift attempt would sew up the win for me and I could quit for the day. I had to think about the rest of my life and how far I'd come in just 10 months. Was another win worth throwing away all the progress I'd made and lessons that I'd learned? What about the example I'd set to others by "listening and being good to your body" – as stated earlier, many were watching. This was an instance where time literally stood still. I had extreme tightness in my lumbar spine due to the nature of a powerlifting meet and reached down to pull 225lbs from the floor and stopped. I took off my lifting gear, told my coaches that I was out, and explained why. One thing about this, people noticed that I had changed. The old Brian, just like every year prior, would have proceeded ahead like a pitbull through the brick wall. This would have resulted in my own demise.

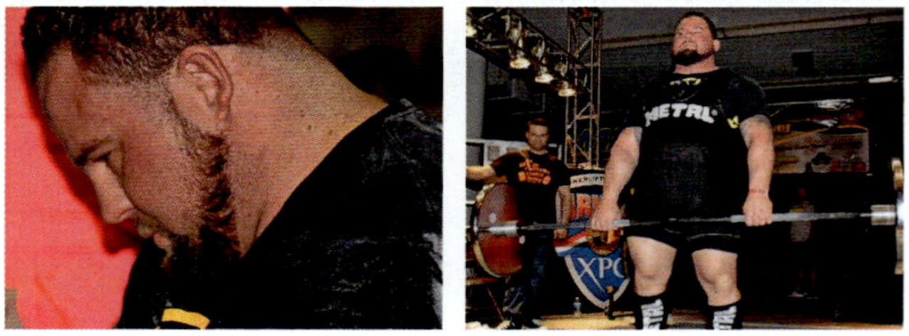

One of the most difficult deadlifts of my life

I still wanted to make my squat and bench count, so I took a "token" of 145lbs (deadlift), to make my squat and bench press "official" and finished the day on the sideline.

Actually, in many ways, it was the hardest thing I'd done since I'd come so far. Here I was at the big show not finishing the way I wanted to. I was not in good spirits and had a lot of contemplating to do. I'll never forget this day and having to explain to people why I didn't just pull one deadlift at 700lbs and win easily. It was a very tough day for me, but tough men are built by encountering tough days. Soft lives and easy circumstances make soft men.

Dave Tate and me (I was certainly not wanting to do an interview)

Time brings clarity – certainly in this case. With this in mind, I didn't make any decisions right away and just enjoyed the rest of the Arnold weekend as much as I could.

COMMENTARY MARCH 2014:
IT WAS TIME TO CONSULT MY MENTOR AND FRIEND ONCE AGAIN

"I'm happy for you Brian, of course I wished you could have deadlifted feeling resilient, but you did what the wise old pro's do- you made a leadership decision. Powerlifting preparation is about load tolerance and you have made your tolerance

Building strength, pushing your body and making adjustments along the way: An extremely important point to consider as you read this story is that nothing is linear. As established with the foundation of strength training with proper progressions and in some cases - regressions, one must take his or her time when coming back from injury during rehab and eventually to strength training. The difference between being "healthy" day to day and training for fun vs. ultimate world-class performance is obviously quite another hurdle to overcome. There will be setbacks, just as Dr. McGill told me there would be in May of 2013 and I now realized this, clearly. Looking back, it was not practical nor judicious for me to rush into a full strength training cycle to build strength, then right away go to peaking the strength less than 10 months after the start of rehab with a truly serious injury.

Following the disappointment at the 2014 Arnold, we tried another way and began to implement the "Jumbo Day."

much higher in the last 10 months, now we need to take it to the next step. Take a couple of weeks and then we will talk."
– Stu McGill March 2014

Before I emailed Stu, I was feeling much better and had an idea of a plan of attack (but not THE plan). I had already let the emotions run their course – up, down, mad, sad, then optimistic- BUT I didn't let it influence me one way or another. This was a turning point, since I was so close but I knew that there was more time and adjustments needed.

Going back to 2013, when I told him my plans and way before the meet was imminent, Stu was openly clear and concisely apprehensive about me 1. Returning to ultimate performance in general, but understood my mentality – hence the negotiation. 2. Doing a meet within 10 months and possibly pushing too hard and competing too soon after recovery.

Together, we formulated the "Jumbo day" plan - all 3 lifts - squat, bench and deadlift on one day to build the needed capacity to replicate meet day demands. We would start very moderately and light to build a baseline. As described earlier, you have to get into minimal flexion for the squat, extreme extension for bench and then a bit more flexion and extension for the pull. The key to this was not pushing too hard in each lift, easing into it and then the benefit of having a full week before loading the spine with the demanding day, comes around again. This would prove huge and as my work capacity increased, so did my tolerance for the different loading demands.

TRAINING LOG MARCH 2014:
IMPLEMENTING THE "JUMBO DAY" OFFSEASON

Week	**SATURDAY** Squat/bench/ deadlift	**MONDAY** Squat/bench/ deadlift Assistance	**WEDNESDAY** Fluff & Buff
10	**Squat:** 5x5 (1 top set of 5)	**Squat assistance:** b.3x12 c. 2-3 sets	*This day varied week to week
	Bench: 5x5 (1 top set of 5)	**Bench assistance:** b.3x12 c. 2-3 sets	
	Deadlift: 5x5 (1 top set of 5)	**Deadlift assistance:** b.3x12 c. 2-3 sets	

Sample template of "Jumbo day" split. *This day was dependent upon variables surrounding my current recovery and specific needs at the time.

"Jumbo day" would lay out like this:

- *Saturday:* Day 1 – Squat, bench and deadlift – no assistance work
- *Sunday:* Day off – 24hr to recover
- *Monday:* Day 2 – Squat, bench and deadlift assistance work
- *Tuesday:* Day off – 24hr to recover
- *Wednesday:* Day 3 – Fluff & buff
- *Thursday and Friday:* Day off from loading- 48hr to allow optimal recovery prior to Saturday's loading day.
- The 'off' days were spent doing the normal things that have long since become the everyday activities for me, such as walking, core work, etc.

This approach still needed some fine-tuning, but we were certainly onto something, I just knew it. After the 3-3week mini-cycles and 1 test week was up (10 weeks) total – I was pleased about my numbers, except the deadlift. There was no pain, but there was residual tightness/awkwardness, and it was lacking more explosiveness than I liked. There was something missing and I was about to discover it through a very tragic circumstance.

With our late friend Bob Ihlenfeldt, Stu, Brian, and Ben Lee (Dr. McGill's Master's student)

COMMENTARY MAY 2014: BOB'S PASSING AND DEEP REFLECTION

In May of 2014 – 2 months after the Arnold, following my first full offseason using the Jumbo approach, one of my very good friends, Bob, suddenly passed away. He was only 42 and seemingly in good health other than being a "bigger" guy (as most of us are in the strength game). This really rocked my world and, oddly enough in the weeks leading up to his death, I was joking to my training partners about how terrible weighing 295lbs felt walking across the parking lot compared to being lighter in the old days. I had a light bulb moment that very instant. I knew the missing piece: dialing in my bodyweight and my diet.

COMMENTARY MAY 2014: DROPPING A WEIGHT CLASS BACK TO THE FORMER 242LBS CLASS

Another call to Stu was made to discuss this weight reduction and he agreed that it would be better on my body as a whole and could certainly help my load tolerance. With that, I immediately decided to get healthier and drop about 30lbs. I felt that this will not only help me and my general health, I predicted that this would assist my deadlift and overall lifting repertoire because my positioning was suffering from being so big.

Louie Simmons, founder of Westside Barbell always had the protocol of "go up weight classes until your deadlift starts to suffer, then come back down one class."

I considered this wisdom from this very wise man and applied it.

Too heavy, unhealthy and asking too much of my body

COMMENTARY JULY 2014: MORE INVESTMENT IN DIET, MORE PAYOUT IN MY LIFTING

It should be no surprise, but as soon as I cleaned up my diet (got rid of the obvious, low-quality garbage like soda, dessert and snacks), the weight came off. I added more overall conditioning to my program and became more active. In turn, my body felt better, my deadlift went up and any sort of awkward tightness I had disappeared. My explosiveness on all lifts, especially the deadlift had returned. It was even better than prior to injury!

Stripping the fat and bloat off (most of it was bloat from a poor diet) took about 15 weeks with an efficient and balanced performance based diet while making more appropriate food choices. I had to be much more disciplined so I started to prepare food, instead of grazing on whatever was around. As an athlete who was in a very comfortable weight class, I had the luxury for a long time to eat whatever I wanted and could maintain my weight between 280-290lbs, depending on what phase I was in training. But, I realized that this too was not only part of my back's demise, it was also a stumbling block in my route to full recovery. There are so many moving parts that I was still learning how blinded I was by the medical field, in particular the surgeons who not ONE time suggested that 1. I move better overall, or 2. That I take better care of myself and as a medical doctor, it didn't occur to them to suggest losing some damn weight instead of worrying about my lifting! This should be a crime – operating on people without attacking and addressing the basics! They were too close-minded with their ignorant bias, lacked understanding of basic spine biomechanics, and the pathway to becoming healthy without medicine. Wasn't I going to have to lose weight, and move better anyway? I did, and hence the "virtual surgery" I performed and took away my day to day pain IMMEDIATELY.

COMMENTARY JULY 2014: A TEST/ TUNE-UP MEET IN THE FALL

After dropping down from the "fat" 290lbs range, to the leaner 260lbs range by utilizing a very balanced approach to dieting, I was finding that I felt so much better in day to day activities and my lifting was improving each week as I went into an offseason phase.

On the left at 260lbs vs. the right 290lbs

Admittedly, I felt much better under 270lbs, but my strength did climb fast once over 280lbs – though, at what cost? Availability supersedes ability, no matter how strong I could be, my body simply couldn't take the heavy weight day to day, as it becomes cumulative.

A new offseason with all of the pieces moving forward:
The offseason is the time where you take a step back and assess, make improvements, recover mentally and physically, attack weaknesses and conquer the sticking points. It's the time to introduce variables and experiment. Intensity of effort should be lower with volume effort higher. You can't maintain peaking strength year-round if you want to progress, build capacity and avoid injury.

I thought it would be prudent to pick a meet 4 months away with a completely dialed-in and adjusted plan. This provided 20 weeks (10 weeks offseason, 10 weeks peaking) from July until October 25 to put into practice not just what I absorbed in 2013, but the ever important lessons I obtained thus far in 2014 through trail and error.

TRAINING LOG JULY 2014: PLAN FOR OCTOBER MEET – MODIFIED "JUMBO DAY" OFFSEASON

WEEK	SATURDAY Squat/bench/ deadlift	MONDAY Squat/bench/ deadlift Assistance	WEDNESDAY Fluff & Buff
10.	**Squat:** 6x2 (1 top set of 2) **Bench:** 6x2 (1 top set of 2) **Deadlift:** 6x2 (1 top set of 2)	**Squat assistance:** b. Piston squat: 3x6 c. Single leg good morning: 3x12 **Bench assistance:** b. Incline DB press: 3x12 c. Skull crushers: 3x12 **Deadlift assistance:** b. Barbell row: 3x6 c. Sled drag: 300yds	*This day varied week to week

Explanation – same as before except: less repetitions per set but more sets total. Assistance work selection is custom and is explained in section 4.
*This day was dependent upon variables surrounding my current recovery and specific needs at the time.

This refined "Jumbo day" would lay out like this:

- *Saturday:* Day 1 – Squat, bench and deadlift – no assistance work
- *Sunday:* Day off – 24hr to recover
- *Monday:* Day 2 – Squat, bench and deadlift assistance work
- *Tuesday:* Day off – 24hr to recover
- *Wednesday:* Day 3 – Fluff & buff
- *Thursday and Friday*: Day off from loading. This allows 48 hours for optimal recovery prior to Saturday's big day.
- The "off' days were spent doing the normal things that have long since become the everyday activities for me, such as walking, core work, etc.

10-WEEK OFFSEASON "JUMBO DAY" FOR OCTOBER COMPETITION GOALS:

1. Continue to work on training all 3 lifts to build my training capacity and give myself adequate time, since had I rushed the Arnold 2014 comeback. This offseason was going to require far less tinkering to get the details right, especially with ALL I had already learned in 2013 and thus far in 2014.
2. The meet in October was simply another experiment with 2 very important-adjusted variables (Jumbo training split and my new bodyweight) and surely there would be more things I needed to dial-in for the big one in the coming months – March 2015.

Fast forward through offseason – nothing much to note other than it went to plan, 100%. I was able to make it through the ENTIRE training cycle with zero pain, or awkward tightness. This new "streamlined" physique not only had me feeling much more healthy, but I looked more aesthetically pleasing, which was just a bonus. The real benefit was that it contributed to my return to competitive resilience, once again!

PRE-CONTEST "COMBO DAY"

WEEK	SATURDAY Squat/ deadlift	MONDAY Bench	WEDNESDAY Squat/Deadlift assistance
10.	**Squat:** 70%x1x5 **Deadlift:** 70%x1x5 b. Pause Squat 3x3 b. Block Deadlift 3x3	**Bench:** 70x1x5 a. Incline press: 3x5 b. McGill one-arm bench: 3x10 c. Skull crushers, band flyes and farmers carry	McGill pull-up: 20 singles Barbell row: 3x5 Barbell shrug: 3x10 Piston squat: 3x5 One leg DL: 3x10 Suitcase carry Stir the pot

This is how my pre-contest training split for October 2014 meet was set-up:

- *Saturday:* Day 1 - Squat and deadlift
- *Sunday:* Day off - 24hr to recover
- *Monday:* Day 2 - Bench press
- *Tuesday:* Day off - 24hr to recover
- *Wednesday:* Day 3 - Assistance for squat and deadlift
- *Thursday:* Day off - 24hr to recover
- *Friday:* Day 4 - Fluff & buff day (as explained earlier with the same goals in mind)

10 week pre-contest peaking phase:
Peaking for competition is a whole different monster than the more relaxed offseason. You need the right amount of stimulation without pushing too hard, but hard enough to make it through the meet with enough conditioning. Resilience is a trade-off, like most other concepts laid out in this book. The volume is much lower during the pre-contest phase, but the intensity is much greater and more demanding on the body – and in particular the spine.

Going forward with pre-contest, I utilized the "Combo day" with squat and deadlift together, but every 4 weeks after the deload (so twice during the 10 week cycle) I would implement in a Jumbo pre-contest day that would simulate the meet like conditions with the accurate intensity since it's much higher than a normal offseason format. This was going to be a good indicator of how the meet would go. Going by the offseason, I was sure it was going to be successful. Things this time around, over 6 months later were shaping up much more naturally.

COMMENTARY AUGUST 2014: 3 GOALS GOING INTO THE MEET

1. Biggest goal: Finish the meet in one piece without pain, or tightness and be physically prepared to deadlift at the end of the meet, unlike the March attempt.
2. A lofty goal: Win the meet and accomplish a personal record total, as it had been a while since lifting in the 242lbs class, but I knew it was doable.
3. An even more lofty goal: Hit the current #1 total at 242lbs in the United States and World.

COMMENTARY OCTOBER 2014:

Before I knew it the meet was here and it went first-rate. Months of hard work paid off, and I was well on my road back to the Arnold 2015. My numbers were 1050lbs/780lbs/770lbs – my first ever 2600lbs total at 242lbs, beating my best ever total at 242lbs of 2570lbs, prior to any real back pain history in 2008.

No pain, big personal records and and a #1 ranking in the world at 242lbs. This was a colossal deal for me, but there was work to do yet. All 3 goals checked.

COMMENTARY DECEMBER 2014: SETTING SIGHTS ON THE ARNOLD 2015

October had given me the confidence in myself, my back, and my principles. November gave me some time to unload my spine, rest and give my body a bit of a reprieve for a few weeks.

My shortened offseason started in early December 2014, so I didn't have a full 10 weeks of offseason which is in most circumstances ideal, but choosing to take time to recover is in many cases the wiser choice instead of simply jumping right into training. This is especially true if you are dealing with an injury history. The goal here was to get in better shape overall and to continue to refine my form, not necessarily to be too greedy and push strength.

COMMENTARY JANUARY 2015: PEAK AND TAPER TO THE ARNOLD 2015 COMPETITION

The final 10 weeks is crucial for peaking strength and cannot be mixed up with an offseason approach. I'm going to provide a few thoughts on nutrition, supplementation, and training but keep in mind: these components must be COHESIVE and well-thought-out. Here, then are some basic guidelines for each 3-week mini-cycle (10 weeks peaking total), together with some details that applied directly to my comeback and preparation to peak for this meet:

- **Have a Baseline** – Something to start with and/or refer back to. It is extremely important to establish a baseline in your training (i.e. intensity, volume) supplementation (dosages and timing) and diet (sources of food- macros, micros and timing). A baseline is a starting point, your unique reference point, and can also be used as a reset button when needed. This is something that is established over time and will serve as your guide moving forward. Deviations from this point must be tracked and followed to fully understand what is truly working to yield results and what is not. By monitoring your progress in relation to your baseline you can easily track how changes to your training, nutrition and supplementation are working for you. If you don't keep track of the variables that are changing you will never know EXACTLY what worked and what did not. Don't throw the baby out with the bathwater! If you haven't established a baseline, do so immediately!

- **Deload every 3 weeks** – Every 3 weeks should be an assessment week, during which we back off on the load and intensity, dial-in pristine lifting form, do a real physical inventory of the body and let it heal. This is what I refer to as a deload (50% range of both weight and volume using single reps to grease the groove). This gives both the mind and body a break and prevents you from CNS overstimulation which can lead to a crash, potential injury and regression.

Demonstrating the lightened method (reverse band)

- **Utilize the Lightened method (also known as reverse bands)** – Used in this peaking phase to build positive physical & mental momentum, as well as confidence bearing heavier loads to prepare for the weeks to come. Bands are hung from the top of the rack, bench or ceiling to the end collar of the barbell to bear some of the load and lighten the weight of the barbell. As the weight is lifted, the elastic of the band returns closer to its original position and therefore provides less assistance as the lift progresses, making the top much heavier than the bottom. This builds speed in transition, confidence and gets you ready for the heavier weeks to come.

- **Sets and repetitions on the big 3 lifts and restrictions** – Personally, with my injury history, I cannot risk more than 1 rep, sometimes 2 reps at a time on the squat, bench and deadlift- especially using over 85% of my competition load. Each rep must be perfect, or I risk a re-injury, or worse. The risk of loading more volume into one set, is not worth the reward. So for my own training, I'll bump up my volume strictly for 'singles' (for example: instead of 3x3 at 70%, I'll do 5-6 singles at 70%). Ideally, if past injury isn't limiting your capacity, you would probably follow the higher rep/volume approach.

- **Volume and intensity** – Each person's body will have different requirements and respond differently to varied volume, intensity and stimuli. This is all personally dependent upon weak points, lifting experience, age, injury history, and level of preparation, as well as the many other factors discussed in this book. Again, use the baseline as your essential tool in establishing tolerance and optimal levels.

- **Assistance movements and warm-up exercises** – This should always be tailored to the individual and customized to your needs based on injury history, weak-points, etc. We give you specific guidelines in section 4.

- **Use percentages of your best lifts for the following pre-contest phase** – I suggest using your best competition lift. If you don't compete, use your best gym lift.

Peaking is an Art

There's an art to peaking strength for competition, as it's not easy programming to design. Get this wrong, and you're doomed to a weekend of CNS burnout, mental fatigue, injury, and defeat. It's no coincidence that you see many athletes peak in training five weeks out, then crash just before the meet and have a horrible day.

Any surfer will tell you that to be any good you need to be able to find the "sweet spot." The zone in which the board's balance and angle compliment the wave as it pushes you forward. Training as a strength athlete requires finding a similar kind of "sweet spot." If you try to stay on too long, you'll eventually crash by overtraining, getting injured, or regressing. I suggest always leaving something in the tank so you have enough juice to build momentum going forward.

You're simply trying to refine and peak strength with a proper taper going into a test, or competition day. Instead of the high volume of sets of 5's, 4's, 3's, your volume should much lower and this is where you go no more than 3's, and a lot of doubles and singles as you work toward your peak.

Going into my pre-contest phase in January of 2015, I was coming off of some really insightful learning experiences. This was a huge addition of positive momentum, so needless to say I was ready to attack the final 10 weeks with controlled tenacity and a great plan in hand.

In the coming pages I'm not only going to give the framework, but I'm going to outline the exact weights, percentages, sets, reps, and precisely how I felt each mini-wave. I will also detail my diet and weight cut protocol utilized to make the 242lbs class in preparation for the 2015 Arnold competition. For the sake of brevity, I will show you my training split, but only outline my day 1: "Combo day." This training day would take place on Saturday, which was my squat and deadlift day (in contrast to "Jumbo" day with all 3 big lifts on the same day). Saturday, I would only do minimal assistance, and save the lion's share of squat/deadlift assistance work for Wednesday. This allowed me to have adequate rest/recovery time between training sessions with a full week before I had to squat, or deadlift again.

January 2015 – week 10 with 735lbs on the squat

TRAINING LOG JANUARY 2015:
TAPER TO 2015 ARNOLD

My Custom Training "Combo split" for the Arnold 2015 started in early January for March 14 competition - 10 weeks out.

WEEK	SATURDAY Squat/Dead-lift	MONDAY Bench	WEDNESDAY Assistance
10.	**Squat:** 70%x1x5 **Deadlift:** 70%x1x5 b. Pause Squat 3x3 b. Block Deadlift 3x3	**Bench:** 70x1x5 a. Incline press: 3x5 b. McGill one-arm bench: 3x10 c. Skull crushers, band flye and farmers carry	McGill pull-up: 20 singles Barbell row: 3x5 Barbell shrug: 3x10 Piston squat: 3x5 One leg DL: 3x10 Suitcase carry Stir the pot

WEEK	SATURDAY Squat/Dead-lift	MONDAY Bench	WEDNESDAY Assistance
10.	**Squat:** 70%x3x3 **Deadlift:** 70%x3x3 b. Squat 3x10 b. Deadlift 3x10	**Bench: 70%x3x3** a. 2x3 b. 3x12 c. 2-3 sets	B: 2 squat B: 2 deadlift C: total of 3 combined

Here is how I would suggest an athlete start off when they can handle multiple reps under load. This may work for others – just not me post injury/recovery. Assistance work and selection is outlined in Section 4.

COMMENTARY JANUARY 2015: DIET AND SUPPLEMENTATION SPECIFICS LEADING INTO 2015 ARNOLD COMPETITION:

My diet and supplementation has evolved quite a bit over the years, but during this specific time, the following outline worked well for me. I was a VERY big 242lbs class lifter walking around at 265lbs and this diet kept my weight where I wanted it.

To give perspective on my size as a 242lbs lifter, here is another 242lbs lifter who I've competed against and a great champion – Matt Minuth.

Bodyweight 10 weeks out: 267lbs (wouldn't let it get higher than this).

Visual body indicators: maintaining visible abs, minimal bloating in face and overall, skin tone and hydration (under 270lbs was the magic number for my back – it didn't like being heavy).

Competition weight to make: 242.5lbs (had to stay within 25lbs for a safe cut).

My desirable weight range was already locked in during the first 3 weeks of training so I didn't need to change much of anything (only minor adjustments as you'll see) until the final week, when it was time to start cutting.

FINAL 10 WEEKS- EVERY DAY MENU LEADING ALL THE WAY TO 1 WEEK OUT FROM WEIGH-IN:

- *Upon awakening:* 2 cups coffee – heavy cream and coconut oil
- *Breakfast*: 5 eggs, 3 links of sausage, 1 cup cooked oatmeal
- *Lunch:* 8oz beef, 2 cups white rice, broccoli
- *Snack 1 :* 2 cups Greek yogurt with fruit, 4oz mixed nuts
- *Snack 2:* 2 scoops Magnum Quattro protein shake
- *Dinner:* 8oz chicken breast or beef, 2 cups white rice, broccoli
- *Snack 3 (optional):* 8-10 Oreos or 1 pint of ice cream or bowl of cereal- depending on my bodyweight

Variables & indicators – If, during this time, my bodyweight fell below 265lbs, I'd up my carb intake right away by about 100g at a time per day. If bodyweight went above 265lbs, or I noticed I was visibly softer in the mid-section or face first thing in the morning, I'd cut carbs back by 100g a day to start. These adjustments were usually directly applied to my nightly snack (#3).

Supplementation: Multi-vitamin to cover the bases: B3, B6, B12, D3, vitamin C, fish oil, magnesium & calcium, potassium (all 3 important going into a big cut), zinc and fiber. I'd typically split up half the total dose between lunch and dinner.

> Keep in mind strength athletes need to perform, not look a certain way. A performance diet should be a well-rounded approach to supply the athlete with food, vitamins, supplementation and rest/recovery to be as strong and as healthy as possible in a particular weight class, not achieve single digit bodyfat, or have a particular look. It should "fuel the machine." What may help a physique athlete could rob a strength athlete of performance, so keep this in mind while choosing your path, as you may see things as not a 'traditional' dieting approach. This isn't an open invitation to get as big as I did in my failed comeback, nor is it a cue to eat like a bodybuilder. This WILL vary person to person greatly. Keep track of your indicators and what your body is telling you.

TRAINING LOG JANUARY – FEBRUARY 2015

Wave 1/3: First 3 weeks of 10 (weeks 10, 9, 8) – Training wave 1– laying the foundation:

The first 3 weeks was a well-planned phase of "building momentum toward the peak" and looking towards the most important phase of training in the weeks that follow. The loads were not near max, around the 70 (on the lowest end) to 80% range (on the highest end at this point) with multiple sets and reps per day. In my unique case, I went with more singles instead of the higher rep-sets. This range is where the bulk of your gains are made (70-85% range), but to properly peak strength, you have to push the percentages higher to adjust and prime your body. Everything is a give and take. This will be apparent as you see how the waves work.

My percentages were based upon a 1050lbs squat and 770lbs deadlift from the last meet in October of 2014.

Training Weeks 10, 9, 8

- Week 10 Protocol: 70%x1x5
- Week 10 Weights lifted: Squat-735lbsx1x5, Deadlift-545lbsx1x5
- Week 9 Protocol: 75%x1x5, 80%x1x2 (lightened method)
- Week 9 Weights lifted: Squat-785lbsx1x5, 840lbsx1x2 (lightened method), Deadlift-580lbsx1x5, 615x1x2 (lightened method)
- Week 8 Protocol: 50%x1x5 (deload)
- Week 8 Weights lifted: Squat-525lbsx1x5, Deadlift-385lbsx1x5

Training log notes for this wave: "Finishing quite a bit of traveling during this time, and got in a training session in Michigan, which went great. Sleep sucks when I travel, but traveling is pretty much done until after the meet, as it should be. All the weights in this phase have felt light and the former Brian would have skipped the week 8 deload, but not this Brian. Diet and supplements are locked in, bodyweight is currently sitting at 265lbs (down from 267lbs), and everything feels super light and snappy so no changes needed. I started off this training cycle fresh and very prepared, and it's paying off. I'm looking forward to taking some big weights over the next few weeks. My deadlift feels better than it EVER has, even better than pre-injury."

Wave 2/3: Second 3 weeks of 10 (weeks 7,6,5) – Training wave 2 – starting to over-reach. This starts the apex of my training:

Things from here had to be near perfect leading into the competition- ritualistic. There was no room for distractions, or any changes of schedule – this should have shaken out in my first wave, if it were necessary. The following weeks were designed to push the envelope and set the tone for the final 3 weeks.

Weeks 7, 6, 5

- Week 7 Protocol: 85%x1x2, 90%x1x2 (lightened method)
- Week 7 Weights lifted: Squat-895lbsx1x2, 945lbsx1x2 (lightened method), Deadlift-655lbsx1x2, 690lbsx1x2 (lightened method)
- Week 6 Protocol: 90%x1x2, 95%x1, 99%x1 (lightened method)
- Week 6 Weights lifted: Squat-945lbsx1x2, 1000lbsx1, 1030lbsx1(lightened method), Deadlift 695lbsx1, 730lbsx1, 760lbsx1(lightened method)
- Week 5 Protocol: 50%x1x5 (deload)
- Week 5 Weights lifted: Squat-525lbsx1x5, Deadlift-385lbsx1x5

Training log notes for this wave: "I came into this wave totally fresh and it feels great to be handling big weights again. This phase is always very hard physically but I was primed for it. The first 3 weeks didn't take much out of me, but this second phase did and the deload was much needed week 5. Things feel great, and 1000lbs+ has never felt so manageable, especially at 262lbs which my weight has fallen to and been steady at. Diet and supplements are good, but I need to add a little bit more food (100g of carbs at a time) as my weight has dropped, which is not all that unusual in this phase with the physical and mental stressors. Sleep is better now and all of this core work over the last year plus has really paid off. Deadlift feels like it's my best lift right now, when it suffered the most from the injury. I don't think many are going to see this coming as I will pull close to 800lbs going by the way 730lbs and 760lbs felt. I will be hard to beat, no matter who shows up. Confidence is back. Time for the hard, final push."

Be patient: Don't overthink, worry, panic, or force yourself into trying to 'peak early,' or ahead of schedule by stuffing your face, taking heavier weights than scheduled, or slamming too much 'supplementation' too early. Have your indicators documented from former training cycles i.e. your weight, body composition, pictures and remember, what you do in the gym in terms of your numbers doesn't matter, especially not at 6-10 weeks out. All that matters is competition day. You're building most of your momentum in this phase, prior to the taper and peak in the next 3 weeks. Hold back! Don't let yourself follow the faults of the social media heroes who want likes and attention more than a good showing on the platform.

Wave 3/3 –my final 3-week (technically 4 - extra week for taper) wave – the most crucial time – taper down then peak for competition:

Things from here on out had to continue to be perfect leading into the competition and like the last wave, it had become a ritual. Time was running out, and the weights were heavy and volume was down with intensity peaking, like last wave but even heavier for the first 2 weeks- so very few mistakes could be made. In wave 3, the loads were all much closer to max, many around the 95-100% – This is where continuing my positive momentum built in wave 1 and 2 is key. After my deload week in wave 2, I felt pretty crappy, which was to be expected at that point in training.

Weeks 4, 3, 2, 1

- Week 4 Protocol: 90%x1, 97%x1, 101%x1 (lightened method)
- Week 4 Weights lifted: Squat-945lbsx1, 1020lbsx1, 1050lbsx1 (lightened method), Deadlift-695lbsx1, 750lbsx1, 780lbsx1 (lightened method)
- Week 3 Protocol: 90%x1, 95%x1, 101%x1- Keep in mind you will feel better and rejuvenated on meet day and have 21 days (at this point) to recover
- Week 3 Weights lifted: Squat-945lbsx1, 1020lbsx1, 1055lbsx1, Deadlift-695lbsx1, 720lbsx1,765lbsx1
- Week 2 Protocol: Deload 50%x1x5
- Week 2 Weights lifted: Squat-525lbsx1x5, Deadlift-385lbsx1x5
- Week 1 Protocol: (14 days out from the competition) – 85%x1– then done
- Week 1 Weights lifted: Squat-900lbsx1, Deadlift-655lbsx1 (as a rule of thumb, my attempts are always up to 85% in the backroom for my last warm-up, before my first official attempt).

Leading into competition: The rest of the work was super light and under 50% to keep fresh. I did "fluff & buff," stayed active, walked, did my warm-ups to flush blood around and did my core work.

Training log notes for this wave: "This was a tough last few weeks but expected – more mentally taxing than physically. At this point, I've grown tired of my routine day in and day out and I get tempted daily to take short cuts. The weights felt much heavier than the previous wave, even the lighter warm-up weights. I didn't miss any weights, but I was pretty close on a couple that made me work for them, especially in the heaviest week of the whole cycle, week 3. I'm pretty beat up at this point. Week 3 usually is and was by far the hardest week of the cycle, but I made it through it only because I knew I had a had a deload the following week. Week 1, the last training week- the 900lbs squat that I took felt slower than I'd like but I could already feel myself starting to recover and peak in contrast from the 2 weeks prior. The final 10 days, or so will be crucial for me to stay in my routine, and keep the path. I'm excited for the meet, but first this big weight cut. Weight is up and I'm sitting at 267lbs, so I'd like to clean up the diet a little bit more and make the cut to 242lbs as easy as possible. It's time for the Oreos to be eliminated in my diet."

242lbs on the left and 265lbs on the right

COMMENTARY MARCH 2015:
THE WEIGHT CUT GOING INTO THE ARNOLD

Objective: Take 25lbs of water off within a week, weighing 242lbs for about 2minutes, then working all day within the 24 hours I had between weigh-in and meet day to get as big as I was when I was training.

1 week out from weigh-in, 265lbs (7 days)- I cut out all carbs: No carbs (other than green veggies)

2 gallons of water starting Monday for Friday weigh-in: 2 gallons of water per day, to load the body with a deliberate surplus.

I did a glycogen flush on Monday, Tuesday and Wednesday with 5 exercises, 3 set of 20. This helped flatten me out and temporarily depleted me, and in turn I lost more weight. This also helped encourage the necessary rapid uptake of glycogen from carbs between weigh-in and competition. This was a "fluff & buff" style of training session.

Each day, I lost an average of 2lbs with the increased water load and lack of carbs. Fats and protein remained a large portion of the diet (carbs were less than 20g a day), but appetite suffered with the water load. This only helped the cutting process.

Cutting Diet outline: Saturday – Wed, low carb, moderate fat and protein

- *Breakfast:* 4 whole eggs, 4 slices bacon – half gallon of water
- *Lunch:* 8oz beef, cheddar cheese, broccoli – half gallon of water
- *Snack:* Mixed nuts, Greek yogurt – half gallon of water
- *Snack 2:* 4 hard-boiled eggs, 1 avocado
- *Dinner:* 8oz beef, cheddar cheese, broccoli – half gallon of water
- *Wednesday night before Friday weigh-in:* after my last meal has digested and right before bed – 2 bottles of magnesium citrate to clean out colon.
- *Thursday:* woke up at 253lbs – about 11lbs left to go

Only protein-based snacks to eat all day; an omelet was my choice this time around. Water was cut off at about 11am, only sips. This day was spent keeping calm and relaxed while inevitably, sweating and urinating all day and night until weight was made.

TRAINING LOG MARCH 2015:
FRIDAY REHYDRATE AND REFEED

One full week after the cut started, weigh-in 10am: 242.5lbs. This day was spent doing IV bags, eating copious amounts of carbs and sodium, along with drinking a lot of Pedialyte, Gatorade and water

Weight cut: The idea is not to "diet down" before a weigh-in, as this deprives your body of essential nutrients and actually weakens your performance. Rather, you must prep your body to shed your water weight naturally. We accomplish this by overloading the body with water beyond the levels it is usually accustomed to, and tricking it into expelling all excess water at once, cleaning out the excess waste in your colon along the way. This process is obviously very dehydrating, so we want to keep this period as brief as possible, enough to clock that perfect weigh-in before packing it back on as fast as possible in order to compete at your full potential. This unfortunately has been at times, the hardest part of having a good competition and is NOT for the weak minded, or faint-hearted. For the complete guide to cutting weight, make sure to check out *Cutting Weight – The ultimate guide to making weight in powerlifting and any weight class sport.*

Not to add any pressure to the day, but Stu happened to make it to the Arnold comeback meet

COMMENTARY MARCH 2015: MEET DAY WAS HERE – 2015 ARNOLD REDEMPTION

The day was buzzing. Intensity in the air would be an understatement. The crowd was large and there was literally standing room only. I was ready to make a statement that I was back and there was no doubt in my mind that it was going to happen. Once I started to prepare for my time to lift and got the nod from my coaches, I knew that I was going to open some people's eyes and close other people's mouths. It was time to flip the switch and "go there."

The pressure was on, but I had a great team of supporters, helpers, handlers and coaches with me, so I was up for the challenge. Of course, my wife Ria, was head front and center- my biggest asset and was there for me every step of the way.

I went through my rituals – my walk, my prayers and my focus that I do every meet with the following in mind, to lock into mentally and visualize it happening:

I had 3 goals, just like the October meet and they were all feasible:

1. Finish in one piece, and be able to deadlift. It was a reoccurring theme at this meet that the deadlift was always an issue since 2012.
2. Win my class and best lifter – this was most important.
3. Hit records.

It was game time. It was time to squat.

I went on to hit an easy first attempt of 1020lbs and a fast and smooth second attempt of 1065lbs, which was a PR for me in the 242lbs class. This was a great start so I tried to go big, with all the positive momentum I had and tried a massive 1100lbs on my third and last attempt, but I missed it. The silver lining was, I failed with 1100lbs and NOTHING even hurt, felt tight, or off. The amount of attention paid to conditioning, core stiffness and hard work we had done, was paying off in more ways than one.

An hour passed and I met with Stu, Ria, my coaches and did a physical, mental and overall inventory with what was going on, and and what was needed to ensure a victory. I was feeling great. It was time to bench press. This was going to be the real test – since it got my back wonky last year.

So close with 800lbs!

I didn't bench as well as I had hoped, but was still in a good spot in the standings and sitting in a solid second place overall. My biggest competition for the overall win benched and squatted very well- more than he had ever done. But, what I was focused on was my body. It felt great! I was ready and more fired up than ever to deadlift. This was going to be the true mental and physical test. The way I had learned to listen to my body and pick up on the specific indicators in the moment, I knew that I was going to pull what I needed to, to jump into first place. I was down by about 70lbs going into the deadlift.

The day was long, Stu and Kathryn had to leave, as they had to go visit their son Johnny for an event in Cincinnati. At this point, I said my goodbyes, but before, I pulled Stu to the side and said "I'll email you after I win." He smiled and said "OK - you will on both accounts."

The moment of truth, time to deadlift and turn on the mental furnace

Much like the finality of a football/hockey game in end of the 4th quarter or a baseball game in the 9th inning, a meet cannot be won until the deadlift is over. You can set yourself up for a nice win during the squat and the bench, but it's not official until the deadlift ends. Lots of crazy things happen in the deadlift when one is not prepared to do what is necessary for a well thought-out win. There is a lot of strategy that goes into attempts and this is better and more thoroughly discussed in my book *10/20/ Life - The Professional's guide to building strength.*

My good friend and coach reminding me what was at stake before my 780lbs pull

COMMENTARY MARCH 2015:
IT WAS TIME TO PULL... FINALLY

I flipped the switch, did my priming warm-up/preparation work, then got ready to pull. I took my first attempt of 720lbs and smashed it. It was now time to decide where to go next. We saw the other team put in their next attempt at 705lbs, and this was something that I could easily overcome, so we put in 780lbs for my second attempt to make up the 70lbs that I was down. I got a good talking to with my team, and was told some things that I cannot repeat other than – "you have worked too hard to go out there and not execute 'MFer' – go get what is yours." This got me right where I needed to be mentally, and I smashed it!

Now, I had retaken the lead- it was going to be a real crap-shoot for the final attempt of the day.

I needed my opponent to either miss his next and final pull, or I needed to make my final pull and I'd win either way – it was THAT close. My destiny was in my hands, completely. I watched with intensity as he started to pull his final deadlift, to put the pressure on me, but a MISS. To be honest, once I knew the meet was over and I had won, the edge came off for my final attempt, since I didn't need to pull it and with the pressure off, I went out and missed too. In hindsight, it's awful funny to know how the mind controls what the body does. If I had needed this pull for the win, there is no way I miss the lift, but since the meet was already over, I had little to gain.

2610lbs total – Arnold 2015 overall win- this was just another step in the right direction. The moment the dust settles and you achieve your goals and realize how it was all worth it.

And just like that, the chalk dust had settled- the day was over and I had achieved all 3 of my goals and more. I immediately emailed Stu, as I promised I would, the good news. We shared a few words, and I went on to be with my friends and family. It was a surreal moment.

For about 10 minutes, I went over in my mind and took in the last 2 years. It was all a blur: From April 2013 in a frenzy at Baptist Hospital, to meeting Stu and learning so much more about training, recovery, mental toughness and myself during this span. Coming so close just a year prior at this very same meet. It would have been easy to quit. Instead, adjusting, all while not giving up during very difficult times. Then finally, realizing at this very moment that it was all worth it. The goal, the impossible in many seasoned expert and professional's minds had been achieved. I won't ever forget this moment.

CHAPTER 11

SECTION FOUR

TECHNIQUE, COACHING, TRAINING, PROGRAMMING, AND THE ROAD BACK TO ULTIMATE PERFORMANCE

This section focuses on rebuilding strength and the skill of strength application. The section wraps up with some wisdom hard won from the journey Brian took.

IronDaw

SECTION FOUR

CHAPTER 12
RE-MASTERING THE POWERLIFTS FOR ALL

Having now addressed your general physicality and working to strike a balance among the many systems necessary to recover from injury, it's time to take things to the next level. The program you've created for yourself in Section 2 built a pain-free foundation. You are no longer fragile, but rather in colleague and friend Chris Duffin's words, you are training to become anti-fragile! Now, you must re-master your lifts from top to bottom to avoid repeating the mistakes that led to the original injury.

In the coming chapters, we'll give you Stuart and Brian's best insights into strength training at an elite level. You'll learn how to warm-up properly and efficiently, master the lifts and avoid the pitfalls that rob pain-free training capacity. This is the final component in the journey to reach ultimate performance.

It's important not to progress back into full lifts too quickly. Respecting the biological adaptation process within the history of injury implies that progressions must be patiently expected. It is equally important to remember that if, at any point, your pain resurfaces, or you experience a regression, go back to the basics established in Section 2. Failure to take the time to step back, address your basic movements to allow your body to reset and recover, will shorten your athleticism. You must work hard in an intelligent, optimal and efficient manner. In other words, become an athlete 24/7 if you wish to enhance your potential to make a return to the winner's podium possible.

Consider this perspective: Working towards ultimate performance, pushing the envelope for competition, or anything more than just basic health and fitness, is an absolute luxury and most certainly is NOT a right. Mistreating your body and ignoring concepts such as moving well outside of the gym and lifting platform, can strip away this luxury very quickly. Ultimate performance is a lifetime commitment, 24/7.

We begin this section with 5 basic training principles to maintain the integrity needed on your path back to ultimate performance. This is followed with much more information and insight that will help you succeed.

CHAPTER 12

THE 5 BASIC STRENGTH TRAINING PRINCIPLES

These principles were PARAMOUNT to my comeback and what I preach to others who attempt a comeback from back-pained, to being competitive again. For those who are currently pain-free, these principles will allow them to remain that way by avoiding the detrimental mistakes that I made. Admittedly, I broke all of these principles at one time, or another before and during the injury. Once pain-free and moving forward with this process, these principles were all kept in check and you should incorporate these principles when strength is the ultimate goal.

Here then, are the 5 principles of strength training for the cerebral strength athlete.

1. **Healthy Movement 24/7:** This principle is intended to grow the largest capacity to train as possible. Whether you are injured, pained, or not - being an athlete requires moving like one 24/7 – in and out of the gym. Employing proper form during menial daily tasks such as tying your shoes, taking out the garbage and walking the dog is just as essential as maintaining your technical cues under load with the powerlifts. There are 168 hours in a week and most of this time is spent outside of the gym.

By now, you know just how much of an impact this had on my day to day back pain, even within a few days of moving better after my first visit to Waterloo, when I was educated on it.

2. **Proper warm-up:** Warm-up potentiates the body to reduce the risk of damage while enhancing movement perfection. The process is non-negotiable each and every day and must be customized for your unique needs for that particular session. Never get under a bar before you are properly warm because it could be your last training day if you happen to get injured badly enough. I was a very incomplete lifter prior to my injury, and applying this wisdom was key to my return.

3. **Form:** Quite often, during my time as a coach, I've observed a lifter tweak and improve form on a movement and get an immediate 10% gain in weight lifted, just by utilizing their leverages better, getting into a better starting position, or simply being tighter overall.

Sadly, there are times I've witnessed an athlete CAUSING their injury/pain simply due to their improper lifting form. Stu and I are immense form advocates and realize the importance in performance, longevity, and safety. Every squat, every bench, and every deadlift should look the same day-to-day, week-to-week, and set-to-set.

4. **Training with a specific purpose:** Everything done in the gym should be seen as the means to achieving a specific goal. Assistance work, for example, is coordinated to bring up weak points – not for the sake of mindlessly doing more work after the main movement of the day. One must make careful selections of what is chosen both in and out of the gym. Following your favorite social media hero, or guru does not produce resilient performance. In the same vein, doing what you're naturally good at and what makes you look like a champ in the mirror unfortunately only makes your strengths even more dominant and further throws your body out of balance. Instead, do what you are poor at, bring up your weak points. We will guide you to identify, attack and eliminate these.

5. **Training in phases:** Your daily training and diet regimen should not look the same during your offseason as it does pre-contest, or during a tapering "wind-down." Strength athletes should not see their training as linear, rather, focus on the cycles involved in the competition lifestyle and adjust according to your imminent demands. Periods of maintenance and periods of growth are equally important and neither should be taken for granted. A strength athlete should incorporate a week of lighter load once every three to four weeks of their training, whether they feel they need it, or not. Lightening your loads in this way to about 50% keeps you honest. This deload, or "detox" week is a chance to refresh and recover mentally and physically as well as refine technique. Think of it as 'creating muscle memory' and good movement habits, so that when it's game-time, it's already engrained. While in offseason (not training for competition) intensity of sets and reps should be down, as the volume should go higher to build strength while working on established weak points. Akin to rehab and ultimate performance, one must NOT mix up phases of training. Always keep them specific to the goal at hand.

Here, Brian is shown taking Dan through a warm-up goblet squat to fine-tune his stiff hips prior to getting under the squat bar

YOUR WARM-UP GUIDE

Before we approach the powerlifts, lets focus on a very crucial aspect of training which often times is the most overlooked - the warm-up. Now, approaching 20 years of competing and coaching at top events, I've witnessed numerous top strength athletes put what appears to be little to no thought into getting properly warm prior to a big day of lifting. On the other hand, I've seen just as many athletes on the opposite side of the spectrum spend 30+ minutes foam rolling, stretching and unnecessarily fatiguing their body prior to the first event!

If you are an athlete serious about ultimate performance, consider a proper and efficient warm-up protocol to set the tone for the day. Ask yourself this question: What does my warmup look like and is it aligned with my particular goals? If it isn't, rethink and adjust.

CHAPTER 12

Although warming up is crucial for your preparation, health and performance, it shouldn't take longer than 15-20 minutes total (this will depend on lifting age, injury history, current ailments etc.). Your warm-up, contrary to popular belief, is not designed to condition you and it's not to make you 'supple' and loose – looseness is the enemy of power. The key to warming up (and everything) is to do just enough. If you don't do enough to be mentally and physically prepared, the risk of strain and injury possibility is real. If you do too much, you'll be going into your session fatigued, raising your risk.

"Do enough to be great, not as much as possible," quote by Buddy Morris.

Brian demonstrating some fine-tuned mobility

Ria demonstrating the McGill Big 3

UNDERSTAND YOUR PURPOSE

There are four areas to consider and understand as to why you need to warm up. Ever watch a room full of athletes before a big competition when the start time for the day is announced? You see some in a panic, a complete frenzy and end up warming up far too early, and some far too late. Others end up cold when it counts and some fatigued, or unprepared. Keep your warmup the same at all times and only change things when there is a need.

Chaos tends to emanate at the start of any competition – train for chaos, as my longtime friend Adam Driggers would say!

Always have a plan before it's too late

SECTION FOUR

The letters on this list correspond to the list of exercises in this section

A. **Break a sweat.** A good general warm-up will get your blood circulating, and it'll awaken your body and central nervous system (CNS).

B. **Stiffen your core.** The idea here is to develop both short-term and long-term core stiffness, strength, endurance, and resilience

C. **"Tuned mobility"** (when applicable) specific to your demands and/or needs. Assess and consider your chronic load and activity, ailments, weak points and injuries – this can change day to day. Choose these movements based on what you are training on this day, consistent with your daily plan. Also, think about what you're not good at. Is hip mobility an issue? Then do some goblet squats. Or, have you sat too long and need to undo the hip tightness? Then consider some lunge variations. Are your pecs tight? Warm them up with some push-ups, or band flyes. You may also add some light mobility work.

D. **Warm-up the movement – grease the groove.** This is why you need to get under an empty bar, and it's really that easy. Doing this gives you the chance to mentally prepare for your session, as well as dial in your set-up and form. Performing the movement unloaded/lightly loaded will help you dial in proper range of motion while avoiding the "silly stretches."

Some simply make the mistake of not being "warm," or prepared for the work to come, so they feel the need to do mobility work.

What I've found is they simply aren't properly prepared mentally, or physically. This is very common as they are "tight and stiff" and think they need 30 minutes of mobility work before getting under the bar. Not true – simply warming up efficiently and preparing for the work that is to come is key and usually the solution.

A. (PICK ONE): Five-minute walk, suitcase carries, farmer's walks, sled pulls, or sled pushes. 100-200 yards will be sufficient for any of the movements listed.

B. (DO ALL THREE): Bird dogs, rolling planks, and McGill curl-up (The "Big 3"). Follow the set/rep guidelines in Section 2 following the "Russian pyramid."

C. (PICK ONE OR TWO): This depends on what you need tuned – such as your ailments, weaknesses and what you're training on that particular day. Choose from some of the options below for 2-3 sets of 3-10 reps of whatever you do:

SQUAT: Goblet squat, thoracic stretch (see Section 2) bodyweight squat, hip airplane, and/or lunge.

BENCH: Glute bridge, DB press, band shoulder dislocation, push-up, and/or band flye.

DEADLIFT: Goblet squat, thoracic stretch, McGill pull-up, single-leg good morning, lifter's wedge with empty bar working your way down, dumbbell rows, or dumbbell shrugs.

D. (NON-NEGOTIABLE): 20-40 reps with an empty bar before you load it. Simply going through the motions with the bar before adding any plates can and will add years to your career.

COACHING THE POWERLIFTS

This section will make you a better coach, and a better strength athlete. First, you have to lift to suit the way your body was designed to lift. Going against your leverages, your build, and injury history in an effort to progress quickly might be a short fix for temporary success, but in the long run, it will not pay off.

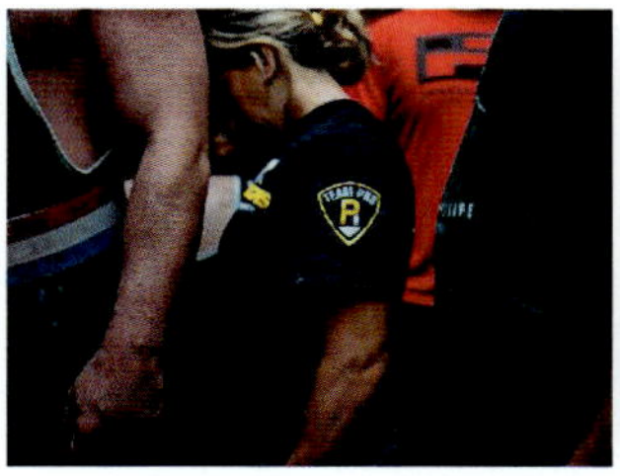

We are all built very differently - Lisa is barely 5ft tall, while Ken is well over 6ft tall - making Brian look more like Lisa's height! Form must be adjusted to many variables!

In this section we are going to completely break down the powerlifts as foundational strength exercises. Basic cues for the squat/bench/deadlift are provided that have proven useful for both maximizing strength and preventing injury.

Common to every lift:

1. Treat the lift as though it were a substantial challenge. You are creating perfect muscle memory and must not pollute the pattern with imperfection.
2. Consider the line of drive and thrust lines of the load through your body linkage. The more compact your joints are to this line, the more you lift.
3. The most powerful muscle is your mind – focus it.
4. Create cams in your body to allow the strongest joints to define performance.
5. Protect your back by minimizing buttwink and micro-movements as the lifts progress.
6. When lowering a load, or putting a load down, give it the same focus on good form as when lifting it up. Stay stiff and in control. Only relax the stiffness after the load is off and standing posture has been regained.
7. Make adjustments and adaptations recognizing and respecting your injury history. These will include considerations for range of motion such as squat depth, footwear with optimal heel heights, bar grips for symmetry, locking in stiffness to eliminate joint micro-movements, appropriate spine curves for leverage and resilience, and optimal preparation in a warmup to set the appropriate thoracic spine, hip mobility and posture, to name just a few.

We will review the preparation, the movement and strategies to address failure.

SQUAT:
TECHNIQUE AND COACHING CUES

Set-up and Preparation:

· Approach the bar preparing mentally and physically to brace joints that must not move and tune stiffness around those joints that must move.

· Take every approach and execution seriously, no matter the weight.

· Chalk your hands completely as well as the area of the traps you rest the bar upon.

· Always keep your body segments in alignment and under the bar when unracking, strive to be centered at all times. Project the force down through the body linkage with the joints as close to this line, recognizing your anatomical limitations.

· Make sure your feet are lined up as evenly as possible with the bar before you start the squat.

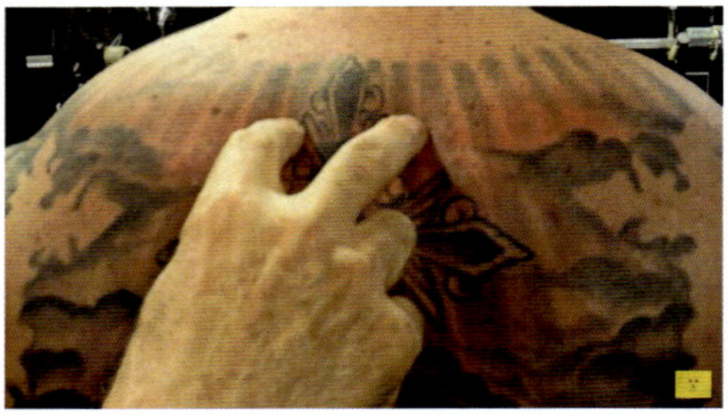

Stu pointing out where Brian's shelf is by the bar imprints, or marks

Position of the bar on back "shelf" will vary from person to person. Regardless of where it sits, it must be in a position that can be locked and sustained, using the traps as a secure shelf, for the duration of the lift. Ideally, the lower you can comfortably perch the bar, the better in terms of decreasing the lever of the bar working on your back. Start the bar in a place that feels like the middle of the road to you, not high, but not low – wherever feels natural to retain the best control. Find your spot and keep the bar there.

Lifter's wedge beautifully-solidified – Lisa is trying to pinch my fingers with her rhomboids

Set the lifter's wedge:

Stiffen into the wedge. Focus on two "twisting efforts." This first originates in the lower body. Grip the floor with your heels and toes like a monkey, and externally rotate with your hip muscles to create a sensation of spreading outwards through the feet. In the upper body, use a downward squeeze through the scapula to drive torque through the arms and create a sensation of "bending the bar," putting pressure on the outside of the hands. Imagine pushing the bar away in a "down and out" direction using your lats to add to the torso compression. When the time comes to begin the actual lift, initiate to motion using a pulse upwards by pulling your hips forward and through the space between your hands, all the while preventing the knee from travelling forward.

The lifter's wedge is the stiffened starting position that gives you the best possible leverage for your squat, bench and deadlift. The lifter's wedge is the foundation for solidifying not only a neutral spine, but complete core stiffness. It starts with the feet gripping the floor like a monkey and "rooting into the floor." Lats are pulled down, and elbows locked-in. Shoulders in an anti-shrug position and rhomboids squeezed together, while bending the bar, not just with your hands, but with your lats and rhomboids. This applies to any exercise, especially the squat, bench and deadlift. The head-neck is neutral for the squat and deadlift, with the neck packed. Your eyes are fixed somewhere between straight and where the wall hits the ceiling (not straight up or, straight forward and certainly not down). Chest is up, with minimal flexion of the spine. Once the back is locked into the wedge posture, there should be little change in this curve throughout the lift. Limit the depth to only what the hips will allow – you may choose appropriate footwear adjusting heel height and ankle flexion.

Grip:

· Bring your hands as close to your shoulders as possible. If you have shoulder mobility issues, try to increase your end range with each set, gradually moving them closer. Employ a proper shoulder warm-up before getting under any bar, even an empty one. A great movement for this is "band shoulder dislocation" drills. Recall the hand grip drill in Section 2, to enhance total body stiffness and strength.

Foot Position:

- Stand with the feet angled slightly outward, with your heels pointed in. Then make adjustments from there to allow proper technique, recalling the hips, knees and ankles to form a perfect aligned hinge. Modify foot width according to your findings from the self-assessment in Section 2.

- Out of this position, drive through your heels at the bottom of the lift.

Head Position:

- Start with the head and neck in a neutral posture. Use the cues in Section 2 to determine your best position. Then, this neck position should not change throughout the lift. Some lifters use neck extension to cue an extended lower back – this is poor coaching.

- Don't look straight up, or directly forward. Instead, allow the head and neck to follow in line with the torso as the squat is performed. This will likely mean that your point of visual focus will shift and change along with the motion. It is crucial that the head and neck remained locked to the spine. As Dr. McGill mentioned, those with a shorter neck like myself should "pack" it in place. Those with a longer neck may want to "lead the charge" with a small pulse starting from the neck that primes the traps without compromising its neutral position.

Band shoulder dislocation

Stance:

- Know your leverages. If you have short femurs and a long torso, you likely won't want a super wide stance (sumo). A good starting point is about shoulder width, maybe a touch wider. Conversely, if you have long legs and a shorter torso, you'll find squatting wider to be helpful in some cases. Know your physiology/mechanics – your body has a predisposed optimal lifting stance. Recall the science and assessment in Section 2.

- Wide stance squatting involves your glutes, hips, and hamstrings a lot more than squatting with a narrow stance. Keep this in mind when training muscle groups.

- If you have a strong posterior chain (i.e. glutes, hamstrings and calves), wide stance squatting helps take advantage of this strength.

The movement:

- The unrack – build tension in the core to reduce all buckling stress before the bar raises at all. The bar will actually come up easier.

Takeaway:

- Think "controlled, but strong and firm" – 10-20% effort into the bar when you unrack. But, keep in mind, the bar will want to come out with lighter weights, so adjust accordingly.

- Don't unrack the bar with one foot forward. Walk up, then insert yourself under it with a parallel, even stance.

- Walk the weight out by taking one step back with either foot – 2-3 steps total is ideal. Example – left, right and then one to center up. The walkout is a common element leading to back injury – all the weight on one leg tests the frontal plane strength foundation built by the athlete. It is crucial that your torso stiffness is maintained through this entire dismount.

Three step walkout is ideal

The hip hinge! This initiates the descent and is good on your back and your knees.

Sitting Back:

- Recall the short stop squat pattern introduced in Section 2. Begin with that basic form. Now, carry the bar on the shoulders, lock the lats down and form the lifter's wedge.

- Once you've walked the bar out, your first action should be to hip hinge. Do this before starting the motion of the squat at the knees.

- Unless you have extremely short legs, breaking your hips back first is a much more natural motion.

- Think of the movement pattern you have grooved into your body through your hip hinge training. Use it, and save your back.

Ensuring overall posture while maintaining the lifter's wedge:

- Take a mini-breath or "sip" in the form of a quick exhale/inhale – a hissing pulse – making sure your entire body is STIFF head to toe, starting with your toes gripping the floor, then inhale a larger breath and hold as you start your descent.

- Hold that breath the entire way down, maintaining that full body "Superstiffness" and pushing your stomach into your belt as if you're about to take a gut punch.

- To initiate the ascent, reinforce toe-grip to shorten the distance of the thrust line to the low back. Then as the drive starts, shift to a heel push strategy by driving your heels through the floor while keeping your lats locked and pulled down i.e. lifter's wedge. Stiffness through this entire sequence is key.

CORRECTING WEAKNESSES

Missing in the bottom of the squat:

Here, it's possibly time to address your hams, hips and glutes. If you can't perform a proper squat with minimal load, you shouldn't expect anything different to happen with near maximal. Start by addressing the most-simple and obvious problems that arise under light load, then move on to checking the more complicated aspects of your form and performance. The load may be simply too heavy.

Coaching keys:

Make sure you're staying as tight as possible throughout the entire lift. Review the floor grip and rooting. The idea here is to solidify your form from the ground up to lock everything in. Start with your toes, and you should feel a huge difference. Lats MUST be pulled down and locked in with the lifter's wedge. White knuckles are a must!

White knuckles personified

Only if appropriate for your injury history - Pause squats in the "hole," wide pause squats, wide box squats, low box squats, wide sumo deadlifts for reps, and wide-stance kettlebell swings. Also, use form and speed work for squats.

Comments on the box squat:

Some of the best athletes are simply not created to squat deep without going into severe flexion/buttwink, valgus and a host of other issues. Many of these athletes we work with, especially the "multi-million dollar ones," obviously are not trying to compete in powerlifting. You MUST treat these especially differently! These athletes are in many cases, better off squatting to a box set above parallel, depending on their hip depth, it could be 3-5" difference that could do the trick. This is done to shorten the ROM and lessen the risk of injury, while keeping their training sport-specific and NOT for powerlifting. Remember, "availability supersedes ability." Some athletes will be better off not back squatting at all and doing a version of a front squat, or another variation of the squat etc. Squat training for leg strength is biased towards front squats, while squats for hip and back strength are biased towards back squats. Choose the best form for the goal and injury resilience.

The athletes box squatting above are both maintaining a good, neutral spine. While the athlete squatting on the left is not achieving "legal depth," the one on the right is. An easy fix for an athlete not as gifted as the athlete on the right, would be to add more rubber "mats," or bumper plates to the box to limit ROM, and only squat to the point BEFORE a compromise in form. A legal squat is not needed for the non-competitive lifter. Our most recent data shows more leg power is created in a half squat rather than a full squat.

Missing in the middle:

This is where things get a little complicated, as there are several possible mechanisms, including bar position and leverage.

Coaching keys:

Check your bar position on your back. Are your elbows pulled down solidifying proper lat position? Are you properly wedged in an advantageous position to finish the lift?

Are your quads lacking power/drive throughout the lift? Ideally, the squat should be similar to a leg press in the middle of the movement, as you drive your heels through the floor. Is the core weak, or poorly controlled allowing small eccentric muscle lengthening? Are you out of control with small movement errors? Are you shaking like a leaf? Remember, killing your weak points won't make up for bad leverage, poor stability and control, or poor position/form.

A word on lifting belts: During the rehab stage, one should avoid using a lifting belt until proper core stability has been gained and pain completely eliminated. Once you are pain-free and looking to achieve ultimate performance, wearing a lifting belt will likely help you lift more weight by helping you create more intra-abdominal pressure, which leads to more Superstiffness. With a very long torso, and short legs, I prefer to wear my belt right across my navel during squats and deadlifts – right in the middle between my chest and my hips. Keep in mind, many variables including but not limited to torso length, lifting style and which exercise you are trying to maximize lifting potential in will determine where exactly your ideal belt placement will be. Belt tightness also differs between lifters. Some lifters prefer a very 'low' belt almost angled down where it 'catches' on the hips while in the hole, while others wear it much 'higher,' seemingly just under their chest. Start 'middle of the road,' with position and tightness, and experiment during your lighter sets to determine what works just right for you. But remember, it will not eliminate the risk of back injury, so don't think this allows for lack of proper approach and lifting form.

Movements that help:

Only if appropriate for your injury history - high box squats, piston squats (half squats), rack deadlifts, glute-ham raises, sled drags, half leg presses, front squats, and more core stiffening work.

If you go down too slowly, you'll lose your air, expend too much energy, and have no momentum, or stretch reflex. If you descend too quickly, you risk getting loose, falling out of your groove, and not having enough stopping power to turn the lift around by exploding on the rebound without leaking energy.

There's no substitute for being tight and locked in. Ask anyone who's ever lifted big weight: Looseness is the enemy of power and speed, and energy leakages will sap your power. Even the most subtle hint of sloppiness will sap your strength, or worse, stress a tissue.

Missing at lockout:

Many times, a lift is lost at the top due to a moment of arrogance, an unconscious decision that it's safe to ease off the gas pedal and coast. Stu discusses the great Jerzy Gregorek allowing the "internal smile," halfway through the lift and MISSED what should have been an easy lift. A simple slip in position at this stage can cost you the entire lift, as this is the last part of the squat and a lot can happen from the hole, through the middle, to the very top. You typically finish the way you start, so the set-up is always equally as crucial as what follows. It is here, the set-up, where you solidify your core and establish your base.

Another source for lockout failure is insufficient thoracic spine extension mobility and strength. Begin with the "Lewit" drill for extensor mobility. It helps a lot of very strong lifters with the lockout.

Coaching keys:

Make sure to drive the heels, and steer the load directly beneath you through the floor, all the while maintaining the lifter's wedge. The quads play a role here too. Continue to pull through with the hip extensors taking care to ensure the lumbar spine does not round, or change position.

Movements that help:

Only if appropriate for your injury history - Arched and locked back good mornings, bent over rows, split squats, lunge variations, heavy 100% eccentrics, reverse band squats (the lightened method) and heavy walkouts with stand and holds out of the rack.

Summary:

Many back injured athletes regain the ability to lift challenging load. They will need to respect their past injury history, understand the mechanism of their injury, and continually refine their technique and equipment to mitigate the risk of reoccurrence.

BENCH:
TECHNIQUE AND COACHING CUES

Stuart: It is so interesting when I ask a group of students if they know how to bench press, or better yet, coach the exercise. Nearly all say they know how to bench. Then they show me. They thought it was lying on their back, lowering, then pressing a bar. They had no idea about resilient strength. Then after about an hour coaching session, they started to appreciate the science and knowledge to master the lift!

Demonstrating the set-up with the rooted tripod of the feet and rigid back, with eyes under the bar.

Set-up and preparation:

- Sit on the bench and focus on what you're about to do – visualize each muscle group, activating and contracting in perfect sync before each set and rep. When you're ready, lay back onto the bench and get under the bar.

- Make sure your traps and hands are properly covered in chalk. If the surface is a little slick on the bench pad and/or floor, you may need stickum, or an adhesive spray to create and keep good contact for your back and shoes.

- Set your grip, then begin to set your feet. Use the same process every time.

· Once reclined, the eyes should be directly under the racked bar to prevent being too far back, or forward on the bench.

· Lock all parts of the body linkage in. Grip the floor beneath you with your feet. Work your upper back stiffening into the bench, while creating a slight arch in your lower spine. The arch is going to vary person to person. Here, more arch produces more push force, but can lead to back pain sensitization. You are seeking a middle ground. Make only small adjustments each time and a slight exaggeration of the spine curve.

· You should be rooted into a tripod, with your traps dug into the bench. Each foot rooted into the floor—as evenly as possible, forming the base. Imagine creating a second "bench" by stiffening your back – lay a bench on the bench.

· Unrack and hold the bar at arms-length while engaging your lats, (image a rhomboid squeeze) and driving your feet into the floor. You should feel that same sensation of "bending" the bar with a latissimus activation (lifter's wedge) that we established with the squat.

· Always remember that while the bench is obviously a pec dominant lift, it is a lift that should engage the full body and requires the same Superstiffness as our standing lifts. Think stiff as a statue. You should be driving your heels into the floor and your back into the bench, without collapsing into a flat torso, stay 'up.'

Grip:

· Set your hands to your ideal grip position to allow the type of bar-bending that will properly engage your lats. This will vary person to person. Start with a medium grip i.e. approximate natural push-up position, then experiment.

· Use the forearm muscles that connect with each finger to squeeze the bar and focus on keeping your upper body tight – think white knuckles. You should be anchored to the bench, with no rocking, or micro-movements.

· Always wrap your thumb completely around the bar at all times. NO false gripping.

Takeaway:

· Those with a bigger arch will usually touch a little bit lower (toward the feet), and those with a smaller arch will touch a bit higher toward their face.

Leverage:

· Know your leverages. If you have short arms, you'll usually start with a more-narrow grip on the bar.

· If you have long arms and a wide torso, you'll be able to use a wider grip in most cases.

· Wide-grip benching involves your pecs, delts, and lats a lot more than benching with a narrow grip.

· If you have a very strong chest, wide-grip benching helps exploit this and will work to your advantage.

· Most lifters will fall somewhere between the extremes of a narrow grip and a wide grip (medium).

A word on bench-press set-up: Tuning the setup to your body and injury history needs several considerations. Brian states, "Due to the help of my good friend and colleague Paul Key, a bench press legend, I currently teach the wide base (legs out, not tucked) – shown in example A. Many people prefer this method of benching as it's tried and true. This method is very easy to utilize and I feel the better of the two most popular set-ups. There is NOTHING wrong with example B but in my opinion, it's an inferior approach to the bench press, which should be a full body movement. I'll tell the attendees at my speaking engagements and lectures – the bench press is a FULL BODY movement and has been harder on my body, in ways, than the squat and deadlift. So bench press form, namely example B, in my experience did contribute to my back issues, as my back hurt in the set-up, even after starting my rehab process with Dr. McGill. Oddly enough, once I switched to the more-wide base example A, my issues with the pain and my subsequent healing overall was amplified. Also, my hips seemingly became healthier and functionally prepared and conditioned for the squat and the deadlift as if it got them ready for the work to come!"

Example A: Wide base set-up. This is how I prefer to teach bench set-up these days. Full-body recruitment is readily available.

Example A – Wide base set-up Pros	Example A – Wide Base set-up Cons
Better balance (wide base)	Smaller arch
Better/more leg drive	More advanced/difficult to get proper foot width due to hip positioning/mobility for some
More efficient bar path	Typically more stress/wear and tear on the hips
Utilization of full body for press	
Easier on the spine overall (less exaggerated extension)	

Example B: Tucked set-up. This is the most commonly used bench press set-up. As you can see, the 'arch' of the spine is significantly greater in comparison to Example A.

Example B - Tucked set-up Pros	Example B – Tucked set-up Cons
Larger arch of the spine, minimizing range of motion	More stress on the spine via extreme extension
Easy to learn – the most common bench press form	Far less leg drive due to leg positioning being behind vs. in front of the body, readily available
Not taxing on the hips if there are mobility issues, or an injury history	Difficult to get full body recruitment as the body should be pressing from top to bottom
	Balance often difficult which can cause micro-movements, or "rocking" back and forth under load - which sap power

Foot and Head Position:

- Foot position is usually a matter of preference. Some choose a hybrid approach (somewhere in the middle between A & B), but lose either performance, or injury resilience. Consistent set-ups are a key every time.

- Depending on your anatomy and flexibility, you may have problems setting up with a wide base – shown in example A. You may need some preparatory work in your warm-up.

- Experiment to converge on the best position from which you can drive from your heels at the bottom of the lift. Toes should be angled in slightly and heels angled out.

- Lock your head into the bench, and don't raise it. Find a focal point on the ceiling to stare at and maintain your gaze.

The movement

The Press:

- As you take the handoff (while maintaining 100% of your Superstiffness), lower the bar in a controlled fashion to your sternum and wait for the press command. This should be fast, but again, under control.

- Lower the bar down an imaginary ramp. Start with the bar over the shoulder joints then lower down to the sternum.

- With the bar now at the sternum, use that "bending" motion to activate your lats.

- As you descend, think of coiling up like a spring, or a snake that's getting ready to strike.

- Once you get the press command, drive your heels first, and then drive through your lats and pecs. As the bar moves, keep driving to lockout. You will add more focus to the elbow extensors (triceps) as you approach lockout.

- As you approach lockout, you can't allow any muscle linkage to loosen, or give, no matter how light the weight feels.

Any slippage in muscle engagement could allow the bar to sink, forcing you to press an additional few inches to achieve lockout.

Finished press held at lockout. Don't let your scapula loose, STOP – don't press the bar any further!

Many people underestimate the power of the shoulder blades. Keep them retracted throughout the whole movement – "stick" the lockout and hold. Allowing the shoulder blades to become loose (letting them become protracted) causes a loss of power, a lack of control, and a longer bar path. I've seen some bar paths shorten by 3" when properly harnessing the shoulder blades. Contrarily, gaining more travel distance can rob power and worse, can lead to an uneven, lop-sided lockout and injury as load is suddenly dumped on one side of the body i.e. triceps.

- With a narrower grip, you'll likely be faster off your chest, but you'll have to press the bar a longer distance.

- Descending quickly benefits some lifters with storage of elastic energy to recover during the ascent, but they mustn't sacrifice any of their control for speed.

- Take your preparative breath before you lower the bar (sip your air in).

- At the bottom, continue to hold your breath and push outward with your abdominals as you await the press command.

- Never fully release your breath, rather "grunt" on the way up.

CORRECTING WEAKNESSES

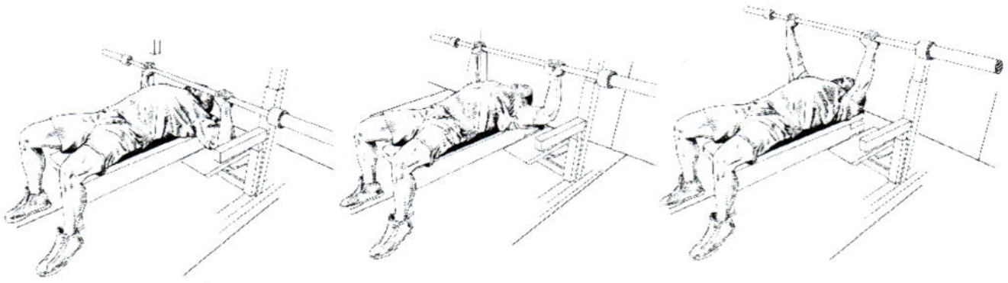

Poor technique illustrated by our friend, Jiří Hlaváček

Example bad pressing technique – this is an often used bodybuilding approach with a false grip on the bar (without thumbs wrapped). Never confuse creating hypertrophy with building strength while using heavy weight – focus on one or the other. More errors: Feet are floppy, legs are lazy, bar trajectory is high toward the clavicle, elbows are flared out. All of these rob power and increase risk for pec tears and shoulder problems.

Missing off the chest:

Here, it's possibly time to address pec major and pec minor. In other words, weakness in the chest could be a limiting factor, and the fix comes down to simply getting stronger in this region. Start by addressing the most-simple and obvious problems that arise under light load, then move on to checking the more complicated aspects of your form and performance.

Coaching keys:

Make sure you're treating the bench as a full body movement, dialing in your technique while making adjustments to find your optimal approach. Good form paves the way for those explosive lifts together with mindful training to ingrain the perfect motor patterns. The use of bands and chains may also be used to "educate" line of drive errors and recovery skills. Don't forget to white knuckle and bend the bar.

Movements that help:

Only if appropriate for your injury history - Wide-grip presses, weighted dips, and direct pec work i.e. dumbbell presses, pause presses, floor presses, and speed work i.e. bands and chains to create more force off the chest.

Consider pressing off boards (board presses), floor presses, or in the power rack with the pins set to add confidence and control.

Missing in the middle:

This is a weakness that is usually corrected by using strategies to eliminate the sticking point. This is typically at the transition point, where a shift occurs between a pec major strategy onto the triceps. Training with partial lifts working the transition point can be very beneficial.

Coaching keys:

Practice the mental shift in strategy at the sticking point. An additional coaching cue here is to squeeze your shoulder blades together and drive with your lats, then continuing through elbow extension to lockout.

Movements that help:

Only if appropriate for your injury history – 2 or 3 board presses and reverse band pressing. Depending on the load you can lift, the type of band used could vary from a mini-band to light, or average bands.

"Grinding" drills also add more neural efficiency. Densify the neural drive with mental thoughts to bend and spread the bar at the sticking point. This can enable a better shift from pec muscle dominance to triceps dominance in the upper phase of the lift.

Close-grip work is also very effective when your middle range of motion is lacking. Depending on what your normal bench grip is, switch it up so that you're training using both super-close and medium grips. You can do this with your board and reverse band pressing, too. These are more advanced assistance movements that are not recommended using until you've exhausted more basic methods listed above such as close grip bench and medium grip bench. Experiment with one component at a time and give it time to work. You want as few variables and moving parts at a time as possible.

Missing at lockout:

Lockout misses can be attributed to the triceps. Engaged and controlled triceps are only able to function at their maximum capacity when they are supported by a solid platform: a back that is stable and locked into position.

Coaching keys:

Do not underestimate the power of your back in regard to your bench press. Your chest is by no means the only leading player, and it's important to harness the power from your lats to help push you through this movement. That bar bend and shoulder-blade-squeeze that we keep mentioning is essential to activating this important muscle group.

Movements that help:

Only if appropriate for your injury history - Pin presses, higher board presses (4-5 board, depending on the length of your arms), bench dips, military presses, skull crushers, and basic triceps work such as press-downs and extensions. When it comes to back development, rows and pull-ups are important staples.

Missing due to stability issues:

Torso stability work applies to all exercises, and warm up.

Coaching keys:

Focus on core stability and the residual stiffness that lasts into your training session. This includes the torso together with muscles crossing the hips and shoulders: lats, glutes, back muscles (erectors, quadratus lumborum), and obliques.

In some lifters with thoracic kyphosis (rounded thoracic spine) it is difficult to lay their head back onto the bench. The thoracic extension PNF stretch introduced in Section 2 can reduce this stress and create a better contact and line of drive during the bench press.

Movements that help:

Thoratic Spine PNF Extension:
See Section 2.

Bird Dog:
Start off with five reps for each side, with 10-second holds, 3 sets.

Suitcase Carry:
One-arm dumbbell, or kettlebell holds for distance, while maintaining perfect upright torso posture. Focus on torso bracing.

One-Arm Kettleball Swing:
This isn't a squat. It's as its name implies—a swing, using your core. Utilize your hip hinge here to save your back.

Stir the Pot:
Another Dr. McGill emphasized movement that's excellent for developing core stability. This essentially entails planking on a Swiss ball while using the forearms to "stir" the ball in circles. Take a wide foot stance, lock the torso – all motion is about the shoulder joints.

McGill's One-arm Dumbbell press:
Another Dr. McGill movement that's excellent for creating balance from side to side. Press a dumbbell (or kettlebell), in one hand, while bracing and solidifying the side without weight to stabilize and balance the core.

Summary:

Know your pain mechanisms and tune the setup and movement to avoid them. Control of spine arch is a major consideration as is foot placement and the full linkage stiffness. Creating and facilitating strategic stability and mobility is the key to enabling best form. Then, execute best form!

DEADLIFT:
TECHNIQUE AND COACHING CUES
Set-up and preparation

Example 1 (left) shows too close to the bar, example 2 (right) shows correct starting position

Lining Up (Note these suggestions are for "average" body proportions):

· The distance between your shins and the bar will vary, so start somewhere just off the bar, but not against it, where your knees are out over it and you gouge your shins, or knee with the bar.

· Keep your hips low, as though you're on a power squat machine.

· Your head should be looking down through the bar to make sure your feet are lined up properly.

· Start with your feet slightly closer than shoulder width apart, with your toes angled out approximately two inches away from parallel.

Grip:

· Line up with your hands slightly outside your legs—at, or about a half-inch outside the bar's knurling.

- It is wise for most lifters with a back pain history to begin with symmetric overhand grips. This promotes better torso stiffness. Work on grip strength and athleticism to keep this grip as the weights increase (recall the grip coaching in Section 2). As the load reaches competitive levels, you may need to become proficient at using the over-under grip (switching over-under hands to avoid developmental issues in your back musculature is also wise). Set your "over" hand and lock it in, then set the "under" hand with a twisting motion, as though you're revving the engine of a motorcycle.

- Flex your triceps when you start your pull. The triceps are your antagonist muscle here, and this movement will help keep you from trying to curl the bar up at lockout, a mistake that causes energy leakages and tissue strain.

- Engage your lats, locking them in forming the wedge. This will get your chest up and keep your back in the proper position.

- Don't let your hands get wet. Keep a dry towel nearby to wipe your hands between sets, and reapply chalk often.

Foot and Head Position:

- The ratio between your tibia and fibula and your femur length should determine how far apart your legs should be. Most stances will be about shoulder width apart. This is usually a good starting point.

- Same head position as the squat no matter which way you pull– find a place where the wall meets the ceiling and keep your gaze fixed.

A longer necked lifter can create a shockwave to initiate the pull with a stiffened pulse from the neck in extension. A shorter neck should be packed and locked.

Setting your neck: Here we can readdress anatomical variation and advantage. A stiffened neck is essential to create the derrick from which the pulling musculature hangs. Some athletes have a shorter neck. As we mentioned earlier, for these athletes it is best to pack the neck and keep the head-neck position locked throughout the movement. Others have a longer neck. Remember that for these individuals, a small "pulse" into extension, while already in a stiffened position, can create a shockwave that leads the charge down the linkage initiating the pull.

An efficient wedge, ready to drive the heels through the floor

Leverage

- Be conscious of your lifter's wedge, with the common cues of gripping the floor, pulling your lats down, and bending the bar.

- Keep the bar as close into you as possible. The further the bar drifts away from your body, the more leverage it has on you, robbing power application and increasing the risk of collapsing into torso flexion.

The movement

The Pull:

- Stomp into the floor before you approach the bar to make sure your feet have traction and to wake up your CNS (Central Nervous System). A yell, bark, or a charging pulse is suggested.

- Keep your legs straight, as you set your grip. From here, drop your hips into the "power squat" position, putting 10-20% tension on the bar and pulling the "slack" out of your body and the bar itself. Lighter weights at 50%, or less will want to start to come off the floor when a proper wedge is utilized.
- You must take advantage of 'feeling' the weight before you

actually begin the lift. By engaging the body before the lift begins, you gain leverage and create a head to toe tightness that braces your body for the load.

· Once the wedge is set, you should initiate the pull by gripping the floor with your toes, then shifting to a heel push strategy through the floor. You don't yank on the bar, or snatch it up. Squeeze it up.

· Maintaining proper neutral head and neck position will raise your chest and put your weight on your heels. All of this will keep the path of the bar close to your body.

· You'll see blood from time to time up your shins. This happens. Continue to keep it close. Appropriate deadlift socks are a good idea here.

Quads flexed, heels driven through the floor and glute-squeeze at lockout all the while controlling the curves of the spine not to move.

Moving to Lockout:

· Try to feel as though you're firing your quads through the bar as it's coming up your shins.

· As the bar passes your knees, drive your chin up and head back, but not so far that you're looking directly up, keep packing your neck.

· At this point, as the bar begins to slow down, squeeze your glutes as hard as you can and push your hips through the bar. Conversely some lifters do better imaging "pulling" the hips through to the bar. Experiment with what works best for you.

· You're squeezing your glutes to get your hips into the best position to take advantage of your leg drive. Think of this as "humping the bar."

Take away:

· Be explosive, load and squeeze the bar up with your lifter's wedge and drive through the heels.

· Don't succumb to the weight and allow your back to round over just to pull the weight faster. Maintain the lifter's wedge. Here, form comes before speed.

· Be patient, the deadlift is a very technical lift.

· You see people routinely get stuck around their knees and end up 'hitching, or pumping the bar' up their legs (this means sacrificing the Superstiffness linkage and allowing a sloppy energy leak) instead of simply staying locked in and squeezing their glutes to pull the hips through and finish the lift strong and tight.

· If ever in doubt of lockout integrity, flex your quads even harder. This "imagery" as you finish the lift, can be aided by mentally reconnecting with the heel drive that initiated the pull in the first place.

SUMO DEADLIFT

Although in many ways the sumo is similar to the conventional method of deadlifting, this particular technique will give you slightly better leverage wedging under the bar if you have the proper mobility through the hips. The main differences in technique, lie in the grip and the stance. The sumo stance is more similar to that of a squat, as opposed to the conventional deadlift that demands a much closer, shoulder-width distance between the feet. In most cases, once in this position, the cues are the exact same as the conventional, except the grip is straight down in sumo and the stance is wider. The hips tend to be little lower – between 2-3" above parallel in most cases. The sumo style also usually involves engagement through the hips and legs versus the conventional, which places higher demands on the back. Remember like squatting, "spread the floor" through the hips.

Sumo pulling wisdom:

- You typically cannot count on merely "muscling up" a sumo deadlift. You have to stay in position and maintain proper form and even stiffness to "squeeze" the weight up.

- Your stance will depend on many factors, including your hips and femur length – set-up the width in your squat stance with toes positioned accordingly. Then adjust, making minor tweaks that will accommodate your unique dimensions and physiology.

- Lock in your arch/back with the lifter's wedge, play with how low you want your hips, push your knees out and squeeze the bar up by driving your heels through the floor.

- Your head and chest position will be about the same as it would be with a conventional pull.

- Play with your grip—which should be inside your legs—but remember that if it's too narrow, you won't be able to pull your chest through at the top, especially for wider/broader lifters.

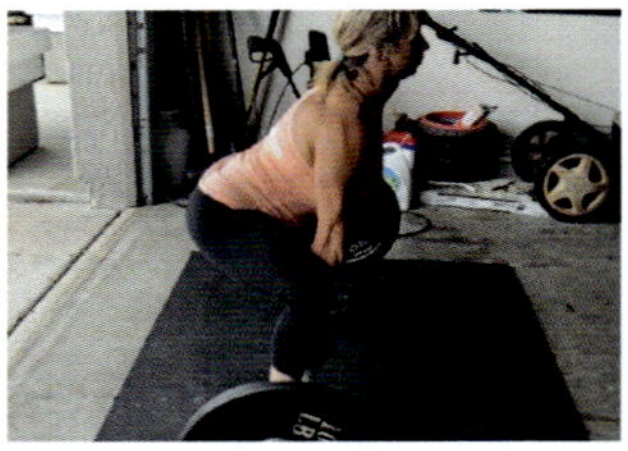

Sumo and conventional from the side look almost identical and should

DEADLIFTING:
CONVENTIONAL VS. SUMO

There's always debate about leverages in the deadlift with regard to the optimal pulling style, i.e., should you pull conventionally, or sumo?

Countless times I've seen those supposedly "built for sumo" pull extremely well using a conventional style, and vice-versa. Generally speaking, you'll see short, stout athletes with thick builds pull sumo, while tall, lanky athletes tend to pull conventionally. There's more to the picture here than just your build. Injury history and lifting age play a huge role in choosing a pulling style, along with your particular strengths and weaknesses as having athletic gifts. If you've experienced a significant amount of back trauma, I'd suggest pulling sumo for the sake of your back. In contrast, if your hips can't take the pounding they receive from squatting, setting up on the bench etc., you might want to consider a conventional pulling style.

Just keep in mind that it takes time to adjust to pulling in an opposite stance. If you're used to one, the other can be hard to master. Be patient and put your time in, while perfecting whichever you choose.

Pulling from blocks: when competition range is not required

CORRECTING WEAKNESSES

Missing off the floor:

Here, you need to figure out whether your hips and legs are strong and if they are in the correct position for maximum leverage. Do they succumb to heavy weight and immediately straighten out? Are you solely dependent upon your back power to complete lifts? Are you stiff-legging the movement? There are many possible reasons this lift could fall apart early.

Coaching keys:

Position is crucial here, and you have to make sure you're using your leverages optimally. Lock your arch/wedge in 100%, and squeeze the bar off the floor instead of jerking it. Your back should be tight and locked in, with your belly pushed out firmly into your belt.

Movements that help:

The mechanism of failure determines the best corrective. For example – if hip flexion is possible and spine flexion is not a past pain mechanism, then deficit deadlifts (standing on a block), opposite-stance deadlifts (for sumo, pulling conventional from time to time), leg presses, and box squats are suitable. Form pulls and explosive work: Find the fine line between babying a weight and jerking it off the floor. Find your optimum. Non-rounded back stiff-leg deadlifts, both sumo and conventional may assist.

Missing midway through the pull:

If this is a weak point for you, start by addressing your back: is it locked in its strongest possible position through the entire lift? A sense of fluidity is also required. Everything should be moving in harmony as you lift up in one continuous motion.

Coaching keys:

This concept of one smooth motion is crucial. Since this is a sticking point caused by a change in strategy from hips to leg, or vice versa, there is a tendency for some to rely instead on two herky-jerky ones, which is counterproductive. Your back should be locked in like a steel rod. Above all, patience is crucial during this part of the lift.

Movements that help:

Only if appropriate for your injury history – 4" block pulls, rack pulls at varying height, glute-ham raises, pull-throughs, barbell rows, bird dogs, and pull-ups.

Missing at the top of the deadlift:

The secret to finishing a big pull is that you must push your hips through at the top, no matter what style deadlifter you are. The idea here is to prevent yourself from hitching, or ramping the bar up your legs which is not only bad on your spine, it's also considered illegal in competition.

Coaching keys:

Squeeze your glutes. This is the motion that pulls your hips through to where they need to be in order to smoothly complete the lift. Be patient and let your back and hips do their job. The worst thing you can do at this point is to "scoot the bar" giving it an extra sloppy jolt to bring it up. There's nothing worse than failing to finish a big deadlift by hitching because you lost patience and panicked.

Movements that help:

Only if appropriate for your injury history - High rack pulls, 6" block pulls, good mornings, rows, shrugs, carries, bird dogs, and glute-ham raises.

Last word on the deadlift: Hook grip. This is a method of grip that hooks the thumb under the bar as the fingers wrap around the bar, then the thumb. Hook grip, when mastered, can be a deadly weapon to one's deadlift success. Not only does it provide better leverage off the floor vs. an over-under grip (one arm – the 'under' has to travel farther), but it can also save a biceps from tearing off due to this discrepancy in pulling distance. Hook gripper's also commonly boast about never dropping, or missing a deadlift due to grip. Once you get over the initial pain, discomfort and transition, it's now an "ironclad-vise." Stu often suggests one try hook grip to not only create better leverage, but to be better on the spine as well. Grip following the coaching in section 2, "bend the bar" to stiffen the core which means the hips pull through a stiffened mast of iron, sparing the spine. Under no circumstances do we SUGGEST using straps. We suggest building your grip with the exercises described in Section 2. During my rehab, I pulled every lift with a hook grip until the weights were limited by the pressure of my thumbs. Admittedly, I wasn't tough enough mentally, to endure the physical pain and pressure to master hook grip. Some strongman competitors, Olympic lifters, as well as powerlifters report such methods as holding the bar with hook grip for time to build capacity, pull for reps (which is very difficult) and some even report strategically hitting their thumb repeatedly with a blunt object (such as a hammer) to build pain tolerance over time, which we do not suggest. Once again, it is painful to pull hook grip, but once you 'make it' work mentally, you have a great tool to put in your tool box.

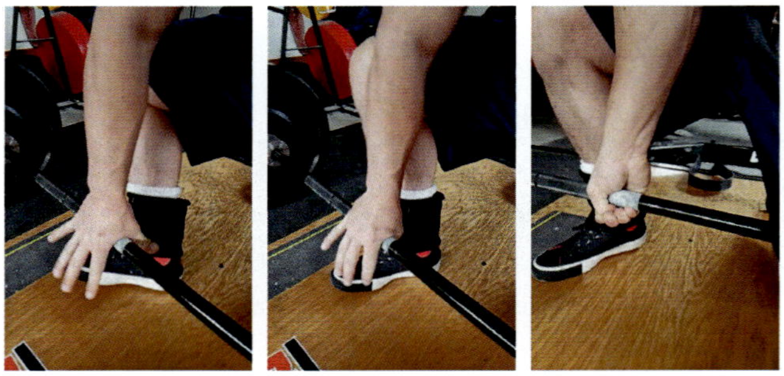

Summary:

The deadlift is a very technical lift. Top lifters will state they have spent years perfecting form and are still looking for the perfect lift. This speaks volumes. The deadlift is reported by too many patients as the task that injured their back. It is almost always due to poor form. This must not be you!

CHAPTER 12

PROGRAMMING ASSISTANCE WORK FOR THE BIG LIFTS

Appropriate assistance work enhances both performance and injury resilience. Proper programming builds capacity to train. We all have weak points. Beginners are usually just weaker in general, but accomplished strength athletes can address the weak link in the chain with targeted assistance work. Some believe that more work on the big lifts are all that is needed. This can be flawed thinking in that form will compromise resulting in tissue stresses that become problematic over time. The good news is even the smallest tweaks with a beginner make a significant difference.

Consider the various exercise drills shown in Section 2 to address weak links, tune strategic mobility, stiffness and stability, and enhance the skill of strength. Of course you do need to build minimal strength first – then enhance performance by creating a balance with these essential components.

A word on assistance work to build injury resilience from Stu:

Injured strength athletes often report a past training program consisting of higher repetitions and load for the main "big," or competition lifts i.e. squat/bench/deadlift. This may be problematic. It is interesting to compare the training of some very strong athletes. Many would see their reduced volume on these big lifts and think that they were undertrained! But, they work the big lifts with fewer repetitions and perform appropriate assistance work. What is going on?

Higher repetition with your big movement (not your assistance work) usually results in a compromise in form. Poor form pollutes "muscle memory" with compromised patterns. Your brain becomes unable to create best strength efforts. If you are a competitive strength athlete, limit the competition events in training. Instead, variations of the lift with less weight on a lighter scale can be acceptable.

I recall an athlete who came to see me with back pain. I had difficulty finding their pain during testing until I asked them to recreate their pain – they then demonstrated the dominant move of their sport. I asked how many reps do you train of this – they replied about 100 per day. Their mistake was in believing more reps of the competition movement would make them better. In reality it made them weaker and injured. They regained their pain-free resilience through assistance work.

SQUAT, BENCH AND DEADLIFT ASSISTANCE WORK INDEX AND GUIDELINES

SQUAT

Assistance A – first and most important assistance movement after your main lifts.
Pick one (2-4 sets for 2-6 reps):

- Pause Squats • Box Squats • Super-Wide Box Squats • Close-Stance Squats • Front Squats • Sumo Deadlift (dead stop OR touch-and-go for reps) • Piston Squats • Speed Squats • Form Squats • Front Pause Squats

Assistance B – secondary in importance for assistance work
Pick two (2-4 sets for 8-15 reps):

- Glute-Ham Raise • Arched-Back Good Mornings • Leg Press (with partial range of motion to keep pressure on quads...do these in a piston-fast but controlled manner) • Goblet Squats • Single leg Good Morning • Piston Squats (half squats) • Trap Bar deadlifts • Bulgarian split squats • Stationary lunge (bodyweight or kettlebell)

Assistance C – lower down list of importance, conditioning and finishers.
Pick one-two depending on needs (2-4 sets each):

- *Core work parameters are same as warm-up parameters for the "McGill big 3."*
- Leg Extensions (can be done with bands): 100 rep set to finish • Seated Leg Curls (can be done with bands): 100 rep set to finish • Rolling Planks • Kettlebell Bottoms-Up Carry • McGill Curl-Up • Stir the Pot • Bird Dog as a cool-down • Sled Drags (100 yards for 1-3 trips at a fast walking pace) • Prowler Sprints • Reverse Sled Drags (100 yards for 1-3 trips at a fast walking pace)

BENCH PRESS

Assistance A – first and most important assistance movement after your main lifts.
Pick one (2-4 sets for 2-6 reps):

- Floor Press • Board Press • Close-Grip Press • Reverse Band Board Press • Standing Barbell or Dumbbell Overhead Press Incline Barbell Press • Touch-and-Go Bench Press • Long Pause Presses (2 seconds or more) • Speed bench • Form bench

Assistance B - secondary in importance for assistance work.
Pick two (2-4 sets for 8-15 reps):

- Traditional Dips (weighted, or unweighted) • Bench Dips • Incline Dumbbell Press • Flat Dumbbell Press • JM Press • Skull crushers (dumbbell, or barbell)

Assistance C - lower down list of importance, conditioning and finishers.
Pick one-two depending on needs (2-4 sets each):

- Core work parameters are same as warm-up parameters as described in previous sections. You can do any of these moves to near-failure as conditioning finishers for your chest and triceps. For single-arm movements, the rep scheme is repeated per side.
- Band flyes (flush out your chest and finish it off): 100 reps Bird Dogs • McGill Curl-Up • Band Pushdowns: 100 reps as a finisher • Hammer Curls (to keep your biceps tendons fresh and healthy) • Reverse Barbell Curls (same rationale as hammer curl) • Push-ups for reps • Piston Pushdowns • McGill One-Arm Dumbbell Bench Press (stabilizing with tight core)

DEADLIFT

Assistance A - first and most important assistance movement after your main lifts.
Pick one (2-4 sets for 2-6 reps):

- Block Pulls (weight on block, 4 and 6-inch blocks) • Rack Pulls (both mid-shin and above the knee) • Deficit Pulls (standing on 2-inch block, or less) • Opposite Stance Deadlifts • Deadlift for reps • Pause Deadlifts (around mid-shin) Arched-Back Good Mornings • Non-Rounded Back Stiff-Leg Deadlift (sumo and conventional) • Speed Deadlifts • Form Deadlifts

Assistance B - secondary in importance for assistance work.
Pick two (2-4 sets for 8-15 reps):

- Barbell Rows (to the floor) • Rack barbell row with pause (super-strict form) • Pull-up • McGill pull-up (maximum contraction and effort for multiple sets of singles) • Kroc Rows (one-arm dumbbell row)
- Barbell, or Dumbbell Shrugs • Chest-Supported Rows • Wide-Stance Box Squats • Close-Stance Squats • Pause Squats • Glute-Ham Raise • Leg Press (piston-style with partial range of motion) • Front Pause Squats • Trap bar deadlifts

Assistance C - lower down list of importance, conditioning and finishers.
Pick one-two depending on needs (2-4 sets each):

- Core work parameters are same as warm-up parameters specified.
- Conditioning will be for distance in increments of 100-300 yards.
- Leg Extensions (can be done with bands): 100 rep set to finish • Seated Leg Curls (can be done with bands): 100 rep set to finish • Rolling Planks • Farmers Walk • Suitcase Carry • Kettlebell Bottoms-Up Carry • McGill Curl-Up • Stir the Pot Bird Dog as cool-down • Sled Drags (100 yards for 1-3 trips at a fast walking pace) Prowler Sprints • Reverse Sled Drags (100 yards for 1-3 trips at a fast walking pace)

With assistance work – leave some gas in the tank: For all sets of assistance work (especially on the more compound assistance movements A and B), consider leaving 2-3 repetitions "in the tank" at all times and avoiding failure. As a strength athlete, there is not much benefit in pushing to total exhaustion or failure – this does nothing positive mentally or physically. Your assistance work volume and intensity will typically peak in the middle of your training cycle then taper down toward the end, so program accordingly. For a further understanding of weak point/assistance work programming and application, please refer to the book 10/20/Life - *The Professional's Guide to Building Strength.*

Putting it all together: Here is an example of a three week deadlift mini-cycle for a lifter with a sticking point near lockout. Your intensity and volume for the main lift will be contingent upon phase of training and ultimate goal. Assistance work is carefully selected from the "exercise index." Remember to choose your A, B and C assistance work according to the coaching suggestions provided in the "correcting weaknesses" portion of this section.

WEEK ONE:

All work - *70% effort: Conventional Deadlift: 5x5. Work up to 1 top set of 5

A. 6" Block Pull: Work up to 1 top set of 3

B. McGill Pull-up: 10 singles

B. Barbell Shrug: 3x12

C. Sled drag: 100yd x2

C. Farmers walk: 100yd x2

WEEK TWO:

All work - *75% effort: Conventional Deadlift: 4x4. Work up to 1 top set of 4

A. 6" Block Pull: Work up to 1 top set of 3

B. McGill Pull-up: 12 singles

B. Barbell Shrug: 3x15

C. Sled Drag: 100yd x3

C. Farmers walk: 100yd x3

WEEK THREE: DELOAD – this is a light week

Maintain and dial in form.

Moderate intensity with everything else.

All work – 50% effort: Sumo * Deadlift: 5 singles, focusing on tightness and form with short rest periods

A. 6" Block Pull: Work up to 1 top set of 3

B. McGill Pull-up: 8 singles

B. Barbell Shrug: 3x10

C. Sled drag: 100yd x2

C. Farmers walk: 100yd x2

CHAPTER 13
TRAINING WISDOM – LESSONS EARNED THE HARD WAY

Casual cannot coexist with ultimate performance

TRAINING MINDSET AND APPROACH

When I came to Stu's lab in May of 2013, one of the first things we did after the initial evaluation, was pull from the blocks, giving him an opportunity to analyze my form. Right away, he noticed how casually I was treating the empty bar on the deadlift. Not just with my form, but with my mentality and approach. This lax attitude was the FIRST thing he nipped in the bud with my rehab process. I challenge you to step up your attitude as well. You are not "above" any weight, no matter how light, and failure to respect that weight will cost you. Remember, even a world champion strength athlete can herniate a disk or send their muscles into spasm if they don't employ proper approach and technique while hoisting the family Basset Hound into the back of the car. Nothing can be casual at any time, no matter the situation, no matter the weight, no matter the place. You must be of the mindset of an athlete 24/7.

BIG WEIGHTS REQUIRE BIG MINDSET

When it comes to heavier weights, there is truly no room for error – mental, or physical. I used to build my sets with increasing load from moderate to heavy, all the while adjusting my internal power box accordingly: from mild, to medium hot, to what I perceived to be raging hot. As it turns out, this slow ramp-up was a huge mistake. There is no room to be self-conscious, or worry about how others in the gym may perceive you. Since overcoming my injury, and adjusting my way of thinking, I crank the internal furnace so that I start at inferno hot, and end up totally consumed by the fire by the time my body notices that a weight is heavy. If you start at this level, your body will continue to stoke the fire naturally as you progress through your sets and increase the weight. Step up to that barbell ready to fight to the death, from your first lift of the day to your last. It is here that you have to trust the foundation you've laid through perfecting form, and believe that your body has now been conditioned to sustain the battlefield without compromising technique and exposing yourself to injury.

VISUALIZATION

Before every lift, I visualize what I'm about to do, from what it's going to look like from the outside, to how it's going to feel, reassuring myself how flawlessly all the elements will converge into a smooth, easy lift. Lifting with friends, colleagues, or clients adds the unique pressure of having to set a good example and it is in these times that I have to double down and focus even harder, in an effort to block out the microscope I'm under. Each set, I practice exerting my body as if driving towards my maximum capacity, harnessing all available body tightness, ferocity and intensity. I deliberately create an extreme scenario in my mind that triggers my primal fight, or flight instinct.

At times, I play mind games with myself to initiate that motivation– I'll call myself a coward if I don't step up and crush this weight. I'll think about having been overlooked at some point, or being disrespected, the people who have counted me out, or the ones that wait for me to fail again– something that has gotten under my skin and channel it into anger. There is no room for happiness during a lift. NONE. This is not fun and games. It's sometimes life, or death and one should remember this. Sometimes I'm terrified, not that I will get hurt, but that I will underachieve and miss a weight that I should never miss. I work myself up to get angry – pissed off at the thought of sucking, or embarrassing myself. Little things like this always keep me sharp when the bar is loaded and waiting for me.

When it comes to being just a fraction of a percentage better, there are little things that should be considered to become just a bit sharper, better, or more ready. To some, this will sound silly and that's fine, but there are a lot of parallels in lifting related to life. We have all prepared for speeches, toasts, lectures, or even conflict and practiced this beforehand, right? So, to me, there really isn't a difference. To be successful, you have to believe that you can achieve your goal and what better way to build this confidence than to actually visualize yourself doing it? This is just another way we practice to succeed.

This self-talk is something that very few people will actually understand. They won't always get it and that's OK, but when you're under over half a ton (my best is 1185lbs) you've been to a place the majority of the population would never have reason to go and therefore will not ever be able to relate to. If you ever doubt the power of the mind to flood the body with an increase of natural stimulants and hormones, think of the powerful chemical reaction that happens any time your mouth floods with saliva at the mere thought of your favorite food. You have the power to 'up your game' with visualization; it's just as much a scientific practice as it is a mental and spiritual one.

Allow me to walk you through how visualization and self-talk affect my mental game as I prep for a meet:

THE NIGHT BEFORE

The night before a big squat or deadlift session, I begin some of my pre-visualization. I play everything out in my head for the next morning – what I'll be wearing, how I'll feel going to gym, what I want to weigh. I think about the music I'll choose for the car ride to the gym, what my warm-up will consist of, the sweat I'm going to have built up before I even step up to the bar. I see in my mind's eye each plate being added and the feeling that although the weight is increasing, each progression seems lighter and easier to me. I imagine my team watching me crush the lift with perfect form, seeing them run over with a slap across the neck and some encouragement yelled in my ear. This is a rehearsal for me mentally. Then, I go and do it for real the next day. In my mind, I've already had one perfect run-through, it's time to just do it again!

GAME DAY

The night before an actual competition, my mental routine is very similar. I go to bed a little earlier to make sure I'm well rested (although this goes against my usual night-owl tendencies). Before I go to sleep, I lie in bed and think about what's at stake the next day. I acknowledge that each meet could be my last, but feel grateful and humbled that I am even competing again after my injury. After all the work I've dedicated to rehab and training, I owe it to myself to give every fiber of my body and soul on competition day. This feeling of anticipation, anxiety and absolute readiness has become addictive. My mind starts to hook into the circuitry that stimulates my fight or flight instincts. I feel assured that my body will know what to do in the crucial moments of the lift in about 13 to 14 hours. I acknowledge this excitement, then I let it settle and bring my mind back to a more neutral peaceful state as I drift off. No need to burn up adrenaline.

In the days leading up to competition, unless I'm cutting weight, I make sure to eat what I normally eat each weekend prior to training, so that no new variables are introduced and my body feels like its routine has been maintained. On game day, I get to the meet very early and hook back into my visualization of what the day is going to entail, what the crowd will look like, what they'll see and be thinking as I'm lifting, and how effortless it will all appear. Then, I always go for a walk outside and take a moment to pray.

I pray for protection. I pray to execute the lifts to the best of my ability and I pray to handle myself like a professional.

After I'm done praying, I'll walk a little more, and think about how far I have come and where I would be if I didn't take the right steps to reclaim my health and I'm grateful. I'm content for that one second, and realize that it can be taken away from me again and that I must seize the moment.

THE FINAL COUNTDOWN

Once back inside the competition venue, I continue pacing and maintain my self-talk. I take an inventory of my body and assess how I'm feeling. It's important that I take this moment to see beyond the adrenaline and give myself an honest once-over. Does anything feel off? Does anything hurt? Do I feel like I should on a normal day? What adjustments might I need to make? At this point, if something needs to be done, I go and take care of it. This could mean taking more caffeine, applying some heat on my hips, re-centering my focus, or a number of other things. Depending on how much longer I have at this point until showtime, I'll either go start my warm-up, or I'll eat, or drink some more, go over to my handlers/coaches to reiterate my game plan, then sit and get off my feet for a bit and maintain the focus. I don't start really stoking the inner fire we discussed earlier until I approach my first squat set in warm-up. That's when I stop talking altogether and get that inner engine revving, allowing my fight or flight instincts to consume me. Then before I know it, the moment arrives and I'm stepping up to the bar: Go Time.

A PHYSICAL CUE

Stu taught me to grunt/HUUUAHHHHHH and stomp the floor before approaching the bar, regardless of its weight to 'wake up my body and mind' (CNS stimulation) and it really works. A sharp bark also works well. I have found this cue slipping into my psyche as I've caught myself many times since this adjustment tightening my muscles, gripping something very hard and grunting when nobody is around, as if I was approaching a loaded bar while in the kitchen, or at my desk. That may sound a little crazy, but this quirk happened to be one of the byproducts of my "24/7 Athlete" mentality. They say practice makes perfect, and I've found that the more I groove this pattern into my brain, the more readily accessible it is when I need it in the gym.

TRAP SLAP AND ADRENALINE

Some athletes respond to being yelled at, or enjoy words of encouragement (or other) while mentally preparing for the task at hand. Some love to be left alone and not bothered. I, on the other hand, really respond well to being slapped, as do others – especially strongmen and powerlifters before a big lift, due to the adrenaline charge this brings with the flight or fight. For me personally, this takes away the over-thinking aspect of the situation and makes it fight time. Some athletes have been trying to 'get up' for so long, they need this edge to ensure not overthinking the situation and to gain an edge. Caution: There are 2 potential side-effects: 1. Hitting someone too hard near their head can scramble their brain and give them a flash knock-out (I've seen it) – this will ruin the lift and maybe their day. 2. Some have not ingrained the specific motor patterns to be automatic under the bar and go brain dead and screw up the lift because they are too wound up and full of adrenaline (this is more common).

I suggest practicing in the gym (practice the way you play), but this is something that has been key for me. Again, this is a slap across the meat of the trap and not a punch to the neck, or back (especially the head). Even as silly as it sounds, establish your baseline with your motivation – find the middle of the road and only turn it up when necessary, don't abuse your, or your partner's adrenal glands and body for that matter, until the appropriate time.

Remember, everyone is wired differently. Want a good example of the different mental "game day" approaches? Pay attention to the athletes in the UFC as they come out of their locker room, approach and enter the octagon. Some are completely wired and wound up, jumping up and down while coming out to hard music like DMX, hitting themselves in the face and clinching their fists. The internal intensity clearly manifesting on the outside.

On the flip side, other athletes walk out slow and seemingly tuned-down, as cool as a cucumber, calm and collected – almost monk-like (like a traditional martial artist). Sometimes walking out to easy-listening-music, and unassumingly wait for their time. They have their own way of going there or "turning it on" without the external show.

Brian pictured receiving a nice trap-slap!

CONSISTENCY AND THAT AUTOMATIC FEELING

Your approach and physicality shouldn't suffer a huge adjustment when you increase weight, or are in a competition scenario. This is why we drill proper approach, form and intensity during training, so that proper technique becomes second nature to you. This being said, the body will naturally make some adjustments to compensate for higher load levels. As long as these tweaks are minimal and do not cause lapses in form, or stiffness, they are fine. For instance, I have very tight hips and lack hypermobility in this area of my body that some other lifters possess. I have a hard time sinking my hips low on the squat with super light-weight, but have no issue getting down to legal depth with heavy weight. My point is this – although I do work on my hip mobility and health, I consciously do not push and extend them beyond my existing genetic range of motion – I use fine tuning mobility when needed. Although I find it harder to get low with a lighter weight, I will never sacrifice form for squat depth. I go deeper with each set until I'm legal and then I stay there. NO compromises, no matter the weight.

INDICATORS

I always ask my coaches and training partners for feedback on how I'm looking each training day and certainly between each lift at the meet. I record my lifts and watch them over and over, then ask their opinion again as they observe the video with me. I'm looking for brutally honest feedback –not "yes man" stuff. Another set of eyes often helps me determine if anything is off. Is my form locked in and normal? Why did I pitch forward during that squat? What can I do better next set to adjust? I get irritated when they point out my flaws, more at myself than at my coach, but I know I need to hear it and I adjust accordingly. There is nothing wrong with a little bit of anger – it's better than being happy, or content during training. Contentment breeds mediocrity and is the enemy of excellence. This verbal and video feedback, coupled with my own judgments of how my body is feeling, provide indicators of areas that could be addressed immediately, or in the training days that follow.

Indicator example: When I returned from injury, my hips were often very stiff and far too tight. Now, when I feel that my hips are a little too stiff, I'll first check to make sure that I have been warming up properly, then, if so, I'll choose to incorporate a little bit of fine tuning mobility work into my training that week to get it just right. Identifying the exercise that will properly strengthen your indicated weakness is crucial. For my hips, Stu taught me to use a kettlebell in a goblet squat and while in the hole, hold my posture and add small side-to-side rocks, slowly opening up each side of my hip sockets.

MUSIC

Stu and I have differing opinions on this one and this is due to my background – powerlifting meets and powerlifting gyms are always full of hard music and all sorts of distractions, so I'm used to tuning them out whenever necessary. In contrast, Stu chooses quiet with a mental focus on the body without distractions which is paramount when meeting an athlete and working carefully to get them healthy. He won't allow gum. He does not allow hats so he can follow the eye movement of the athlete. I have found certain types of music to increase my adrenaline and encourage focus and maximum drive. When I'm locked in "the zone," most of the time, I'm not even conscious of the noise that may be around me. In the gym, it's possible to see music as just another variable out of your control that you can use your inner monologue to fight against. On the other hand, we all have "pump up" music that we know creates a certain sense of urgency, and in some instances, can immediately create a sense of higher stakes when lifting. This type of music can be helpful and can be used to your advantage as an energy boost. In my opinion, as long as you're not jamming out under the bar and worried about what song is playing when you're walking up to prep a lift, there's no harm in it. If given a choice, I would pick Pantera, or Tool in the background while focusing on the task at hand, similar to what would be playing at an event. I'm not 'listening to the music,' rather hearing it as background noise that sets the tone of my lifting environment so I can take care of business under the bar. To me, music reinforces my focus, but if I ever find that it becomes more of a diversion, it goes off immediately.

Some others don't seem to treat music this way. I don't think anything makes me more-mad than seeing some of these so-called athletes walk up to a loaded bar, dancing and singing along to whatever's blasting through their earbuds, casual as ever, thinking they're going to magically summon their game face at the last second. This lack of intensity and commitment to the sport is disheartening, especially when I see younger lifters following this poor example, thinking it's OK.

You cannot allow distractions to sidetrack you even for a moment when approaching a loaded bar. If you find something drawing your focus away from the lift at hand, eliminate it, no matter what it is. In certain cases, it may be a training partner that won't shut up when you're under the bar. If they don't take lifting seriously, nor have goals of pushing the limits as you do and staying healthy while doing so, then you need to run them off by any means necessary. This is just another form of unnecessary chatter that muddles your energy instead of stoking your fire. In my 15 years of training with Team Samson, a small private powerlifting gym in Jacksonville, Florida, we have had all types come out and subsequently quit, or get run off due to them not getting the intensity and what we are working toward accomplishing. Nasty things happen to people who wander into the lion's den unprepared.

SECTION FOUR

CHAPTER 14
RETIREMENT: KNOWING WHEN TO STEP AWAY

2017 Arnold Classic overall winner – my final meet

There is a time for everything. Age brings wisdom, and as I've progressed through my career I've gained invaluable insights on training to be a champion and a leader. I've also come to accept the truth: being an elite athlete is not healthy. The statistics paint a stark picture. For pro footballers, every year spent in the NFL takes, on average, three years off an individual's overall life expectancy. Powerlifters haven't been formally studied for longevity, but to find similar statistics would not be unexpected.

Many strength athletes die prematurely from heart failure due to the demands an elevated blood pressures places on the valves. The hypertrophy-focused training programs also hypertrophy the heart. A stiff and strong heart often robs this vital organ of its efficiency as a pump.

Carrying large muscle mass, and the eating requirements necessary (outlined and more) to sustain this mass creates a blood chemistry that pushes the limits of what is usually asked of a healthy body.

Although I continued to do well, rank #1 each year at 242, dominate in meets and establish new world records after my recovery, my body was showing signs of inevitable wear and tear along with the aging that comes along with such physical stress on the body. I knew my day of reckoning would eventually come and I would have to face the reality that every great athlete's career has a life expectancy of its own and that nothing lasts forever.

Over time, year in, year out, my business and the demands pulling me away from my lifting grew. My once thought-of "hobby," evolved into one giant meshed-together life revolving around lifting – yet lifting competitively was the one thing that had to go, ironic as that is. Such is evolution.

I could see the writing on the wall, the indicators - not the physical, but the mental aspect of it all wearing me DOWN. Granted, my body could probably (too many variables to speak absolutes) have taken many more years of beating, record setting and huge lifts - but for what? What did I have left to prove? This is what I had to ask myself and what you need to ask yourself: is the juice worth the squeeze? *It was time to retire, shed the weight and dedicate a good life to Ria.*

CHAPTER 14

Before finishing, I even got my wife to do a lifting competition with me!

242lbs vs 275lbs – and MUCH healthier! On the left, 2017 – Arnold winner with a 2615lbs total in the 242lbs class. On the Right 2012, Arnold winner with a 2600lbs total at 275lbs, but in agonizing pain. I did what I came back to do and more since the injury. I had nothing left to prove to anyone.

I look back often to the day in Stu's lab in May of 2013. I told him that I wanted to buy just a few more years in the sport and use the time to hit a few numbers that I had been chasing. After that, I would be satisfied and done with my lifting career. Remember that Stu cautioned me at this point that although he felt we could eliminate my pain, he was hesitant about encouraging me to get back under the bar. He acknowledged that not only did I have a severe injury, but that I was approaching that age that many strength athletes retire. Although it was more than four years ago, this realization is still as vivid in my mind as if it were yesterday. I am so proud and grateful that I beat the odds and returned to compete stronger than ever pursuing my greatest passion. This "second coming" doesn't change the fact that before long, the undefeated best fighter in history, also known as "Father Time," will come back to remind me that my hourglass has been close to empty for a while and that it's time to walk away.

The professor and the athlete – It has been a wonderful journey!

The potential regret of not accomplishing a couple of things that I wanted to, pales in comparison to the decades of regret awaiting me if I pushed it too hard out of desperation and had to live out my years with a broken body. I'm not dumb. Even though my movement and training overhaul eliminated my day-to-day pain, there was a great chance that the cumulative trauma to my bones, muscles, tendons and ligaments over the years would start to give me some aches and pains of a different nature. What I've been told by retired athletes is that these tend to sneak up on you and present themselves when you finally choose to slow down.

In my retirement, I plan to continue lifting, walking and eating well, this time without the sense of urgency that comes with a looming competition. I will still do the McGill Big 3, as well as different variations of my squat, bench and dead. I will also continue to train with my team in Jacksonville –but of course all the loads will be much lighter- hell, maybe I'll be a PowerBuilder! I'll be writing a book on PowerBuilding with colleagues Danny Vega and Tucker Loken. I plan on bringing my bodyweight down to 220lbs, then eventually closer to 200 and work toward the next goal. There is no need to walk around at 265lbs if you're not bracing for an impending lifting season. It will be a process to get back down to a healthier weight, but it's something that needs to be done for my overall health and longevity.

Coaching will keep me young!

As I'm winding down and finding myself at the end of my lifting career, there's a large part of me that's looking forward to moving into phase two of my life as I gravitate away from competition, and slowly focus my efforts more toward speaking, writing and coaching.

Such a cliché thing to say, I know, but I really wish that I knew 20 years ago, what I know now.

I have so much more knowledge now than I had even five years ago that I would have loved to implement on my younger body. I feel that it's my duty to help others whenever possible, and guide them to avoid the bone-headed mistakes I made myself as an overly-aggressive testosterone-filled male. I understand that not everyone will listen. I can only hope to share the lessons I've learned with those who take their craft seriously and are open to growth and improvement. The hard science and many, many years of experience and knowledge in and outside of the lab that is contained in this book may be laughed at and ignored by those that are closed-minded and stubborn. The types who are set-in their ways and know it all. These types that always have a "better" (although usually less-informed) method are the same ones who will argue with you on the Internet, happy to try and contradict any blogs, or articles written based on truth and fact.

I have learned that there is no such thing as a one-size-fits-all approach to strength training. This book and the information contained in it is a GREAT start toward success. I hope the message came through loud and clear: my journey was one of failure and success, but I did learn that if strength athletes listen to their bodies and use the tools outlined in these chapters, they will build their own approach to recovery, and to their ultimate performance.

My journey is far from over, and I plan on continuing my study into what makes good strength athletes great, eager for the potential discoveries waiting to be made. We are all capable of greatness, if only we remain equally humble, driven and curious.

CHAPTER 14

SECTION FOUR

CHAPTER 15
CONCLUSION & EPILOGUE

In every mutually beneficial relationship, be it the clownfish and the anemone, the zebra and the oxpecker, or the athlete and professor, there is a sense of give and take that is necessary for each party to thrive. Working together to rehabilitate Brian's injury, restore him to his lifting glory, and subsequently write this book has been an incredible learning experience for the both of us. Whereas initially, Stu was the teacher and Brian was the student in the traditional sense, there were times when the roles were reversed and Brian helped Stu deepen his understanding of the various components that go into training to compete as a strength athlete. The result has been a fusion of our two areas of expertise, presented here as a companion for those injured strength athletes who aren't ready to give up just because they've fallen on hard times, as well as for the lifters in their prime who want to avoid injury in the first place and continue to "up their game."

What started as somewhat of an unlikely pairing in a university lab, turned into a great friendship and ultimately a triumphant success story. The final key player in this relationship is you, the reader. We are confident that you are now equipped with the basic knowledge required to resurrect yourself from the black hole of back pain and get back to lifting at your best.

Your movements, postures and loads, both inside and outside the gym will forever be key players in this. The time for casual and mindless bending over to reach the floor is over. You now have no excuse not to maintain less stressed postures as you train and carry about your daily business. The attention that you direct to your form and technique during competitive lifts must also be directed towards seemingly mundane activities. Be kind to your body. Remember, you are an athlete 24/7 and you must commit to this mindset if you plan on summoning your best on competition day.

No matter what, always move well

CHAPTER 15

Just as crucial as the movements you eliminate, are the ones you replace them with. Incorporating the McGill 3 into your daily regimen is a must in your quest to build an internal "girdle" that will strengthen your core control and protect you from injury. Any additional rehabilitative exercises you adopt must address your individual weak points and aid in meeting the unique requirements of your chosen sport.

Thank you for joining us on this journey and for opening yourself to the vast amount of information we have been excited to share for years now. If you find yourself seeking additional material and information on any of the specifics we outlined in this book, the pair of us have a number of other titles available regarding our respective specializations. Never forget, however, that the greatest well of information available to you is the volumes your own body could write on what triggers its pain, builds its structures, and fuels its fire. Always listen first, and respond second.

Our mutual friend, strength coach Pavel Tsatsouline, has said "Strength is not a data point; it's not a number. It's an attitude." We couldn't agree more. The fact that you've chosen to pursue strength and are taking it seriously enough to seek out additional resources, such as this book, already speaks volumes about your ambition and tenacity. In this industry, there will inevitably be setbacks and frustrations, but it's how you deal with these that determines your longevity in the field. It was in his darkest moments that Brian tapped back into his undeniable passion for training and competition as a strength athlete. With Dr. McGill's insight and guidance, he had to reassess certain components of his labor of love, and his will to succeed and openness to new information allowed him to rise back to the top and shatter his previous records. You too, now armed with the right knowledge can enhance your strength and resilience for life.

We hope you enjoyed the journey with us.

EPILOGUE:

OCTOBER 3, 2020 NEWS HEADLINE:

POWERLIFTER BRIAN CARROLL SETS WORLD RECORD WITH 1306LBS SQUAT!

You, the reader, have taken this journey with me. Beginning from the darkest place disabled and in pain back in 2013, discovering the science and techniques from Professor McGill, and creating the adaptations over the next 7 years needed to heal and build my body and mind to do something never done before. The story needed completion.

Both Stu and myself have loved to hear about your success too, following the wisdom in *Gift of Injury* and regaining your pain-free strength. Even though the book was finished 3 years ago, the story was not quite finished. I fought with what was next, even though I knew that it was necessary for me to move-on from powerlifting and start the next phase – to have children and work on coaching other lifters not knowing if my training approaches would sustain further extreme challenges. It ate at me – I felt I could do more and was leaving something in the tank – a little too much for my comfort. I wanted to do something BIG before I left the sport for good. My life had changed a great deal in 2020 - we gave birth to twin girls, and they were approaching 6months old. They need their daddy around, healthy and strong. But I had no pain day-to-day, my strength increased with wisdom fusing more science and experience. But......If I was to do something, it needed to be sooner than later.

One day I called up Stu and told him this wild thought that I had ran by Ria: I wanted to hit the biggest lift in the history of the world. Regardless of weight class, federation, chosen sport i.e. Olympic lifting, Powerlifting, Strongman, etc. – I wanted to lift the biggest lift of all-time in my best lift – the squat. Stu's response was "OK, let's get it done then. Do you need help?"

Stu's science and techniques speak for themselves - he has helped many return to record performance in so many different sports. But there is no silver bullet, no quick cure for back pain much to the chagrin of some. Rebuilding the body requires precise loading – this is the language that your body's cells respond to. It's about managing capacity, respecting biology, and Stu interpreting the science for me – I took this and applied it along with what we already know works for the best strength athletes in the world. Some scoff at training deloads, rest periods (and time completely off from load) and some foundational training that appears simple but it feeds what biology demands. The approach is vindicated when these same people have come to Stu and me for help years later. The knowledge and practical advice in *Gift of Injury* remains solid.

With a laser focus training cycles and a dialed in taper down, Ria and I loaded up the girls for a 10hr road trip to Tennessee, for the meet where my plan was to finish the story. At that time, the biggest squat in history was completed by a man weighing 450lbs and set it at 1278 pounds. My plan was to better this squat and be the first lifter, regardless of bodyweight (mine was 303lbs), to break the 1300 pound squat barrier.

Willing the body to get under this amount of load is the ultimate test of preparation and mental control. You must follow the little details we have given you here. Many have wondered if I'm truly retired this time from competition, and the truth is YES. I'm very thankful that I've been able to do what I have, but the way things went at the meet will not be possible to replicate. It was just too perfect to revisit; and with all I've gone through getting back to the platform you know when you know.

I will not miss the incredible levels of stress that goes into preparation before a world-record-setting lift. The things that go through my head are a mix of fear, terror, anger, mixed with rational thoughts like "you could die from this." You have to override every sense of self-preservation, followed by an overwhelming sense of relief and accomplishment when it's over. I love it, but I have too much to lose at this point. I have a beautiful wife Ria, and two amazing 6month old daughters, Reagan Leigh and Rylee Chennel that I do not wish to rob more time from. It's truly time to dedicate a good life to Ria and my two daughters. You are empowered with the knowledge in *Gift of Injury,* I wish you the same success!

SECTION FIVE

LOGS AND NOTES

TRAINING NOTES

LOGS + NOTES

SECTION FIVE

FORM CUES CHEAT SHEET

Squat cues:

- Approach - Head to toe stiffness on the unrack, bending the bar with your hands firmly "white-knuckling" the bar
- Walk-out with as few steps as possible, 2-3 is optimal – focus the eyes on where the wall meets the ceiling
- Deep breath, hip hinge to start the squat while gripping the floor like a monkey
- Maintain the lifter's wedge on the descent (lats down, chest and head up) and knees out (spread the floor)
- To come up, drive heels through the floor while pulling lats down and chest up

Bench cues:

- Eyes directly under the bar while in the rack
- Set-up like a tripod: both feet gripping the floor and traps dug into the bench
- Bend the bar with your lats, and retract your scapula while lowering the bar (with your elbows tucked) to your sternum
- To initiate the press, start by driving your heels through the floor and pushing the bar back toward the rack
- Don't press the bar so far that your back disengages and your scapula release

Deadlift cues:

- Set-up with the shins just off the bar an inch or two, stance shoulder width apart and hands directly outside the legs (this will vary slightly person to person depending on leg to torso ratio, lower leg to quad length ratio, flexibility and experience)
- Wedge down into position (lifter's wedge) so that your back is flat, weight is on your heels, lats are pulled down and you are stiff
- Pull the "slack" out of the bar to gain tightness and leverage (bend the bar)
- To initiate the pull, simply drive your heels through the floor while keeping the bar close
- As the bar crosses the knees drive your head back and squeeze your glutes at lockout

HELPFUL TOOLS

Assessment:

List the demands the sport requires of the athlete in order to be successful. Next, assess your current capability for the specific demand. Then, choose the best exercise, or training tool and address the deficit to enhance performance.

Essential demands of the sport	Capabilities of the person	Training tool
Legal squat depth	Sufficient	N/A
Hip hinge power	Hips lag behind leg	Back squats at speed
Grip strength	Insufficient	Suitcase Carry and squeeze 2-10 kg plates

Training Logs:

Create 2-week training cycles and re-assess.

Always make notes on your objectives, priorities, maintenance items, efficacy of the tools, amount of volume, and your rest and restoration capacity.

GYM BAG ESSENTIALS AND STRENGTH PERFORMANCE AIDS

Below you'll find my recommendations and guidance on what you should have readily accessible, dependent upon goals. We'll cover the basics and essentials for you below.

Bands: It's great to have a full set of bands for a variety of purposes, but the two essentials are the light and average bands. They're great for adding tension to the bar as well as the lightened method, but they're also ideal for warming up and enhancing your assistance exercises.

Chalk: This is obviously a must for lifters, but some gyms don't allow it. If you train at a gym that has an issue with chalk use, keep it in a Tupperware container in your gym bag, along with a wet washcloth. Keeping chalk in the container will keep your mess to a minimum, and it'll also hide it. Bringing in a wet washcloth is good gym etiquette. Wipe as you go and cover your tracks. If you show management you're willing to clean up after yourself and not leave a mess, they may even let you use your chalk.

Liquid chalk: If chalk is completely banned in your gym (which is often the case), this stuff is worth a try. It doesn't leave residue and make a mess, and it seems to work very well for a lot of lifters.

Stickum: Some gym floors will be extremely slick. No matter what you do, you'll slip and slide all over the place, especially when you're benching—and it makes no difference what type of shoes you're wearing. When this happens, sit on the bench, lift one shoe up at a time, and spray a healthy coating of stickum all over the bottom of your shoe. Let this "tack" for a minute before putting your foot on the floor, then do the other shoe. This will make a huge difference, and you won't slide anymore. You can also stickum your upper back if you're sliding as you bench, or set-up to bench. Some advanced lifters even use stickum to help their knee wraps adhere better.

Tripod: No excuses not to get video of your movements. Make sure to record yourself with your smart phone, so you can be your own coach and your worst critic. Don't depend on anyone else to do your recording for you. Most people don't want to be bothered in the gym.

Good fuel: I suggest keeping good fluids, fats, proteins and carbs in your gym bag just for the time that happens that you never think will happen. Whether being rushed to, or from the gym and having to skip a meal, a sudden onset of hypoglycemia during a training session, or simply having to leave the gym in a hurry to attend a meeting without a time window to stop to fuel your body. A "cliff bar," a shaker of protein powder or two, Gatorades and the like are always a welcomed surprise when you need it most.

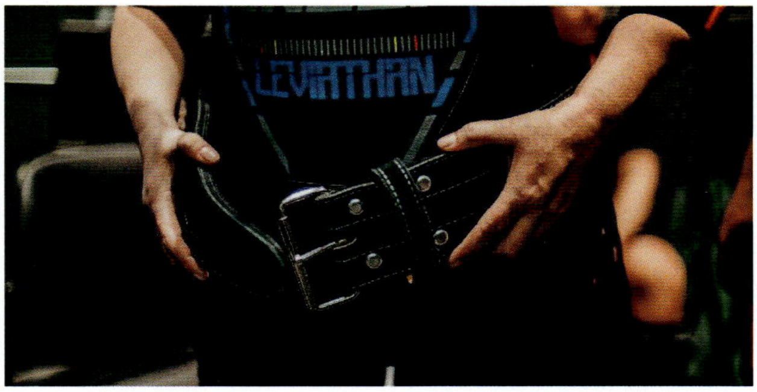

Belt: When you're handling heavy loads, you need a thick belt, and it needs to be very durable. The Inzer forever belt is an excellent choice, and it's available in a single, or double-prong, as well as a lever buckle. I'd suggest the 10mm model for women, and 13mm for men.

Remember – belts won't magically prevent injuries from occurring. Their primary purpose is to bolster your core and help you lift greater loads. If you really want to protect yourself, the best thing you can do is strengthen your "internal belt" by using stabilizing movements like Dr. McGill's Big 3.

Shoes: If you want to keep things totally simple, and save yourself some money, you can just buy a pair of Chuck Taylors and use them for all three lifts. I used to rely solely on my Adidas

Superstars, but have come to embrace the tried and true Chuck. They may not be the most comfortable shoes you can buy, but once you get used to them, it's hard to argue with the durability they'll give you without a huge price tag. These are the shoes I go with now on all three lifts as well as what I recommend to many of my clients and friends. For those who feel they may need an elevated heel, see Section 2 for more information.

Knee and wrist wraps: Go for what I'd call a "middle of the road" wrap here. You don't want wraps that are too tight and thick, but you also don't want them to be too thin and stretchy, either. The Inzer grippers somehow provide rebound while still offering the cast-like benefits. They are arguably the easiest wraps to use, as the fabric grips to itself and locks each revolution in place. You can also find these at www.inzernet.com.

Elbow and knee sleeves: Those that want to ensure that their elbows and knees are protected should consider these simple additions. Inzer makes some great black and red elbow and knee sleeves that are adjustable and provide a lot of warmth and support during the lifts.

When bench pressing, deadlifting, and even squatting, you could consider wearing elbow sleeves to reduce the stress on the joint, as well as to keep it warm.

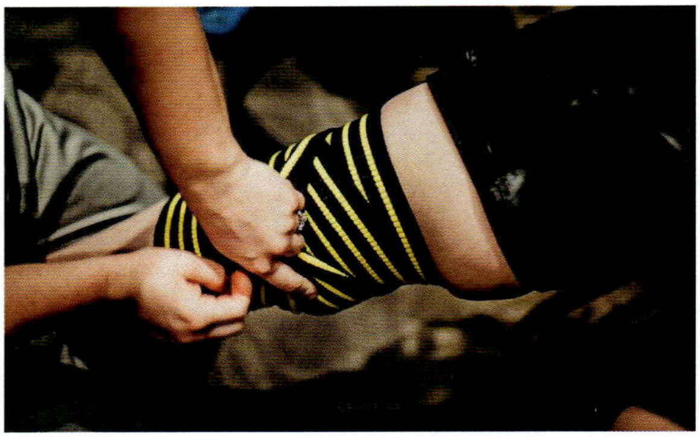

How to Wrap Your Knees:

Begin each turn of the wrap moving outward, then around as hard as you can, keeping the bulk of the fabric as close to your knee as possible with an added crank on each turn. Once your knee is completely covered in either an X, or scissor pattern, use the remaining part of the wrap to go back down over the meat of your knee, and finish X'ing it out until all the wrap is gone.

Calculate your turns and be ready to close it off as you run out of wrap. To finish, simply loop your finger under the material to create a pocket. Save some space. Then, on your final turn, slide the remaining wrap into the pocket, pull it through, and cinch it down.

This should feel like you're wearing a cast, and it should hurt. Don't waste time in getting to the bar at this point. You should be mentally preparing for your lift as you wrap. Find your belt, go through your mental checklist, get tight, and go squat with pristine form.

How to Wrap Your Wrists:

Loop the thumbhole over the tip of your thumb, but not so deep that it will be hard to pull off after you finish wrapping. This just works to keep things in place.

Start at the back of your hand, make a strong loop, and crank the slack as you make a turn back around. With the next turn, go up your arm, behind your lateral wrist bone, and then crisscross back down. Follow this with an X pattern as you make your way back down to the back of your hand. Continue making the X patterns until you run out of wrap.

Prepare to start loosening the thumbhole as you near the end, and be ready to pull it off before you make your final turn. Lifting during competition with the thumb loop still attached is against the rules, so get used to taking it off. Again, once complete, the wrap should not be painful, or particularly uncomfortable, but it should be quite snug: your hand should not be able to move backward if you apply pressure to it.

SECTION FIVE

LOGS + NOTES